# MOUNTAIN WALKING IN
# MALLORCA

## About the Author

Paddy Dillon is a prolific walker and guide-book writer, with over 90 guidebooks to his name and contributions to 40 other titles. He has written for several outdoor magazines and other publications, and has appeared on radio and television.

Paddy uses a tablet computer to write as he walks. His descriptions are therefore precise, having been written at the very point at which the reader uses them.

He is an indefatigable long-distance walker who has walked all of Britain's National Trails and several European trails. He has also walked in Nepal, Tibet, Korea and the Rocky Mountains of Canada and the US. Paddy is a member of the Outdoor Writers and Photographers Guild.

### Other Cicerone guides by the author

Glyndŵr's Way
The Cleveland Way and the
   Yorkshire Wolds Way
The GR5 Trail
The GR20 Corsica
The Great Glen Way
The Irish Coast to Coast Walk
The Mountains of Ireland
The National Trails
The North York Moors
The Pennine Way
The Reivers Way
The South West Coast Path
The Teesdale Way
The Wales Coast Path
Trekking in Greenland
Trekking in Mallorca
Trekking in the Alps
Walking and Trekking in Iceland

Walking in County Durham
Walking in Madeira
Walking in Menorca
Walking in Sardinia
Walking in the Isles of Scilly
Walking in the North Pennines
Walking on Arran
Walking on Gran Canaria
Walking on Guernsey
Walking on Jersey
Walking on La Gomera and El
   Hierro
Walking on Lanzarote and
   Fuerteventura
Walking on La Palma
Walking on Malta
Walking on Tenerife
Walking the Galloway Hills

# MOUNTAIN WALKING IN MALLORCA

## 50 ROUTES IN MALLORCA'S TRAMUNTANA

### by Paddy Dillon

CICERONE

JUNIPER HOUSE, MURLEY MOSS,
OXENHOLME ROAD, KENDAL, CUMBRIA LA9 7RL
www.cicerone.co.uk

# DOWNLOAD THE ROUTES IN GPX FORMAT

All the routes in this guide are available for download from:

**www.cicerone.co.uk/949/GPX**

as GPX files. You should be able to load them into most formats of mobile device, whether GPS or smartphone.

When you go to this link, you will be asked for your email address and where you purchased the guide, and have the option to subscribe to the Cicerone e-newsletter.

www.cicerone.co.uk

# Mountain Walking in Mallorca

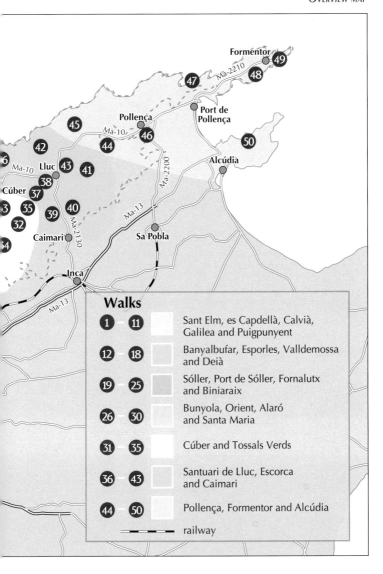

Formentor

Ma-2210

47  48  49

Port de
Pollença

Pollença

45  Ma-10  46  50

42  44  Alcúdia

6  Ma-10  Lluc  43  41

Cúber  38

3  37

35  39  40

32

34  Caimari  Ma-2130  Sa Pobla

Inca

Ma-13

**Walks**

| 1 – 11 | | Sant Elm, es Capdellà, Calvià, Galilea and Puigpunyent |
| 12 – 18 | | Banyalbufar, Esporles, Valldemossa and Deià |
| 19 – 25 | | Sóller, Port de Sóller, Fornalutx and Biniaraix |
| 26 – 30 | | Bunyola, Orient, Alaró and Santa Maria |
| 31 – 35 | | Cúber and Tossals Verds |
| 36 – 43 | | Santuari de Lluc, Escorca and Caimari |
| 44 – 50 | | Pollença, Formentor and Alcúdia |
| ——— | | railway |

# Map Key

| | | | |
|---|---|---|---|
| ~~ | main route | ★ ☒ | lighthouse/telecoms mast |
| ~~ | alternative route | ♠ ☖ ✝ | church or hermitage/cemetery/cross |
| (人)(人) | start point/finish point | ∴ | archaeological site |
| (人) | start/finish point | ⚇ ▮ | ruined castle/watchtower |
| (人) | alternative start/ finish point | ✳ ● | bunker/stone cattle pen |
| ▬▬▬ | dual carriageway | ○ | snowpit |
| ▬▬▬ | main road | ⌣ | stream/gorge |
| ═══ | local road | ◌ | lake |
| ═══ | paved track | ☁ | marshland |
| ──── | dirt track | ρ ○ | water source/well or drinking trough |
| ----- | footpath | ⌂ | cave |
| ── - - - | high-tension line | Ⓗ | hotel |
| +--+--+ | town boundary | ☒ | restaurant |
| ▬▬▬ | limit of protected area | Ⓜ | museum |
| Ⓟ | parking area | ◉ | information centre |
| ▰ | village centre | ⓘ | tourist office |
| • ▫ | building/ruin | ✚ | hospital |
| | | ⚘ | viewpoint |
| ▭ | forest | ✳ | point of interest |
| ▭ | brushwood and meadow | ▣ | bus stop |
| ▭ | farmland/rock | ♣ | picnic site |

N

0        0.5
▬▬▬▬▬▬▬
          km

# Mountain safety

Every mountain walk has its dangers, and those described in this guidebook are no exception. All who walk or climb in the mountains should recognise this and take responsibility for themselves and their companions along the way. The author and publisher have made every effort to ensure that the information contained in this guide was correct when it went to press, but, except for any liability that cannot be excluded by law, they cannot accept responsibility for any loss, injury or inconvenience sustained by any person using this book.

**International Distress Signal** *(emergency only)*
Six blasts on a whistle (and flashes with a torch after dark) spaced evenly for one minute, followed by a minute's pause. Repeat until an answer is received. The response is three signals per minute followed by a minute's pause.

**Helicopter Rescue**
The following signals are used to communicate with a helicopter:

Help needed:
raise both arms
above head to
form a 'Y'

Help not needed:
raise one arm
above head, extend
other arm downward

**Emergency telephone numbers**
The standard European emergency number 112 can be used to call the police, ambulance, fire service or mountain rescue.

There are two professional mountain rescue teams: one from the fire service, or Bomberos (tel 080 or 112), and the other from the *Guardia Civil* (tel 062 or 112).

**Weather reports**
TV stations and Mallorcan newspapers carry daily weather reports. For hourly forecasts, check www.eltiempo.es/baleares

# ROUTE SUMMARY TABLE

## Sant Elm, es Capdellà, Calvià, Galilea and Puigpunyent

| | Start/Finish | Distance | Time | Ascent | Descent | Page |
|---|---|---|---|---|---|---|
| Walk 1 | Cala Lladó | 20.5km (12¾ miles) | 6hrs | 620m (2035ft) | 620m (2035ft) | 41 |
| Walk 2 | Port d'Andratx/Sant Elm | 9km (5½ miles) | 3hrs | 370m (1215ft) | 370m (1215ft) | 44 |
| Walk 3 | Sant Elm/s'Arracó | 13km (8 miles) | 5hrs | 570m (1870ft) | 500m (1640ft) | 48 |
| Walk 4 | Ses Fontanelles | 9km (5½ miles) | 4hrs | 770m (2525ft) | 770m (2525ft) | 54 |
| Walk 5 | es Capdellà | 19km (12 miles) | 6hrs | 810m (2660ft) | 810m (2660ft) | 57 |
| Walk 6 | Km97 on the Ma-10 road | 9.5km (5¾ miles) | 3hrs 30mins | 630m (2065ft) | 630m (2065ft) | 61 |
| Walk 7 | Km97 on the Ma-10 road | 10.5km (6½ miles) | 4hrs 30mins | 850m (2790ft) | 850m (2790ft) | 64 |
| Walk 8 | Font des Pi or Galilea | 4km (2½ miles) or 10km (6¼ miles) | 2hrs or 4hrs | 500m (1640ft) or 880m (2890ft) | 500m (1640ft) or 880m (2890ft) | 67 |
| Walk 9 | es Capdellà | 23km (14¼ miles) | 8hrs | 1030m (3380ft) | 1030m (3380ft) | 71 |
| Walk 10 | Calvià/Galilea or Puigpunyent | 8.5km (5¼ miles) or 9.5km (6 miles) or 12km (7½ miles) | 3hrs or 3hrs 30mins or 4hrs | 400m (1310ft) | 310m (1015ft) | 75 |
| Walk 11 | Puigpunyent | 11km (6¾ miles) | 4hrs | 520m (1705ft) | 520m (1705ft) | 80 |

| | Start/Finish | Distance | Time | Ascent | Descent | Page |
|---|---|---|---|---|---|---|
| **Banyalbufar, Esporles, Valldemossa and Deià** | | | | | | |
| Walk 12 | Banyalbufar | 13.5km (8½ miles) or 17.5km (11 miles) | 5hrs or 6hrs 30mins | 860m (2820ft) or 1020m (3345ft) | 860m (2820ft) or 1020m (3345ft) | 85 |
| Walk 13 | Banyalbufar | 24km (15 miles) | 8hrs | 920m (3020ft) | 920m (3020ft) | 89 |
| Walk 14 | Esporles/Valldemossa | 9.5km (6 miles) | 3hrs 30mins | 650m (2130ft) | 440m (1445ft) | 96 |
| Walk 15 | Valldemossa | 8km (5 miles) or 9.5km (6 miles) | 3hrs or 3hrs 30mins | 370m (1215ft) or 420m (1380ft) | 370m (1215ft) or 420m (1380ft) | 101 |
| Walk 16 | Valldemossa | 13km (8 miles) or 15km (9¼ miles) | 5hrs or 5hrs 45mins | 635m (2085ft) or 820m (2690ft) | 635m (2085ft) or 820m (2690ft) | 104 |
| Walk 17 | Valldemossa/Deià | 10.5km (6½ miles) | 4hrs | 610m (2000ft) | 870m (2855ft) | 109 |
| Walk 18 | Deià | 13.5km (8¼ miles) | 5hrs | 500m (1640ft) | 500m (1640ft) | 114 |
| **Sóller, Port de Sóller, Fornalutx and Biniaraix** | | | | | | |
| Walk 19 | Sóller | 6km (3¾ miles) or 7.5km (4¾ miles) | 2hrs or 2hrs 30mins | 280m (920ft) or 300m (985ft) | 280m (920ft) or 300m (985ft) | 121 |
| Walk 20 | Sóller | 8km (5 miles) or 10km (6¼ miles) | 3hrs or 3hrs 30mins | 300m (985ft) or 400m (1310ft) | 300m (985ft) or 400m (1310ft) | 124 |
| Walk 21 | Mirador de ses Barques/ Cala Tuent | 10km (6¼ miles) or 11km (6¾ miles) | 3hrs or 3hrs 30mins | 330m (1080ft) or 480m (1570ft) | 730m (2395ft) or 880m (2885ft) | 128 |
| Walk 22 | Port de Sóller | 15km (9¼ miles) | 6hrs | 750m (2460ft) | 750m (2460ft) | 132 |
| Walk 23 | Sóller | 16.5km (10¼ miles) | 7hrs | 1200m (3935ft) | 1200m (3935ft) | 137 |
| Walk 24 | Fornalutx | 13.5km (8¼ miles) | 5hrs | 800m (2625ft) | 800m (2625ft) | 141 |
| Walk 25 | Km37.6 on the Ma-10 road | 6km (3¾ miles) | 4hrs | 610m (2000ft) | 610m (2000ft) | 145 |

| | Start/Finish | Distance | Time | Ascent | Descent | Page |
|---|---|---|---|---|---|---|
| **Bunyola, Orient, Alaró and Santa Maria** | | | | | | |
| Walk 26 | Bunyola | 12.5km (7¾ miles) | 4hrs | 470m (1540ft) | 470m (1540ft) | 151 |
| Walk 27 | Bunyola | 14.5km (9 miles) or 8.5km (5¼ miles) | 4hrs or 2hrs 30mins | 750m (2460ft) or 640m (2100ft) | 750m (2460ft) or 640m (2100ft) | 154 |
| Walk 28 | Orient/Santa Maria | 13km (8 miles) or 14km (8½ miles) | 3hrs 30mins or 4hrs | 100m (330ft) or 200m (660ft) | 420m (1380ft) or 520m (1705ft) | 158 |
| Walk 29 | Alaró | 15.5km (9¾ miles) or 14km (8¾ miles) | 4hrs 30mins or 4hrs | 700m (2295ft) | 700m (2295ft) | 162 |
| Walk 30 | Orient | 16km (10 miles) | 7hrs | 800m (2625ft) | 800m (2625ft) | 166 |
| **Cúber and Tossals Verds** | | | | | | |
| Walk 31 | Font des Noguer | 11km (7 miles) or 9.5km (6 miles) | 4hrs 30mins or 4hrs | 600m (1970ft) or 470m (1545ft) | 600m (1970ft) or 470m (1545ft) | 173 |
| Walk 32 | Font des Noguer | 11.5km (7 miles) | 4hrs 30mins | 500m (1640ft) | 500m (1640ft) | 177 |
| Walk 33 | Font des Noguer | 8km (5 miles) | 5hrs | 600m (1970ft) | 600m (1970ft) | 181 |
| Walk 34 | Font des Noguer/Alaró | 14.5km (9 miles) | 5hrs | 350m (1150ft) | 880m (2890ft) | 184 |
| Walk 35 | Font des Noguer/Lluc | 16km (10 miles) | 6hrs | 660m (2165ft) | 830m (2725ft) | 191 |

| | Start/Finish | Distance | Time | Ascent | Descent | Page |
|---|---|---|---|---|---|---|
| **Santuari de Lluc, Escorca and Caimari** | | | | | | |
| Walk 36 | Escorca/Sa Calobra | 7km (4½ miles) | 5hrs | 50m (165ft) | 640m (2100ft) | 199 |
| Walk 37 | Coll de sa Batalla | 13km (8 miles) | 5hrs | 820m (2690ft) | 820m (2690ft) | 204 |
| Walk 38 | Lluc | 10.5km (6½ miles) | 5hrs | 750m (2460ft) | 750m (2460ft) | 207 |
| Walk 39 | Caimari | 12km (7½ miles) | 5hrs | 900m (2950ft) | 900m (2950ft) | 212 |
| Walk 40 | Caimari | 16.5km (10¼ miles) | 5hrs 30mins | 630m (2065ft) | 630m (2065ft) | 217 |
| Walk 41 | Lluc | 19km (12 miles) | 8hrs | 950m (3115ft) | 950m (3115ft) | 222 |
| Walk 42 | Mossa gate/Lluc | 17.5km (10¾ miles) | 5hrs or 5hrs 30mins | 420m (1380ft) | 450m (1475ft) | 228 |
| Walk 43 | Lluc | 9.5km (6 miles) | 3hrs | 250m (820ft) | 250m (820ft) | 233 |
| **Pollença, Formentor and Alcúdia** | | | | | | |
| Walk 44 | Lluc/Pollença | 19.5km (12 miles) | 6hrs | 330m (1080ft) | 760m (2495ft) | 239 |
| Walk 45 | Mortitx gate | 7.5km (4¾ miles) or 10km (6¼ miles) | 4hrs or 3hrs | 300m (985ft) | 300m (985ft) | 246 |
| Walk 46 | Pollença | 5.5km (3½ miles) | 2hrs | 275m (900ft) | 275m (900ft) | 250 |
| Walk 47 | Port de Pollença | 9.5km (6 miles) | 5hrs | 450m (1475ft) | 450m (1475ft) | 253 |
| Walk 48 | Formentor car park | 8km (5 miles) | 3hrs | 350m (1150ft) | 350m (1150ft) | 258 |
| Walk 49 | Cala Figuera car park | 10km (6¼ miles) | 3hrs 30mins | 400m (1310ft) | 400m (1310ft) | 261 |
| Walk 50 | Bar s'Illot, La Victòria | 13km (8 miles) | 5hrs | 700m (2295ft) | 700m (2295ft) | 264 |

15

*There are splendid bird's-eye views of Pollença on Walk 46*

# INTRODUCTION

Walkers descend carefully to the top of Cingles de Son Rul.lan (Walk 17)

Mallorca is the largest of the Balearic Islands, basking in sunny splendour in the Mediterranean between Spain and Algeria. It has been a favourite destination for sun-starved northern Europeans for many decades. While beach holidays remain popular, more and more visitors seek the quieter pleasures of rural Mallorca, especially taking opportunities to explore the island's most rugged mountain range, the Serra de Tramuntana.

In the high mountains there is more shade among the evergreen oak and pines, with cooling breezes to temper the heat of the sun. Away from the bustling resorts the pace of life in the mountain villages is more sedate and relaxing. Almond and orange trees burst into blossom and vineyards yield heavy bunches of grapes. Kid goats bleat plaintively, often unseen among the undergrowth, while bongling bells alert shepherds to the location of their free-range sheep and cattle. Every so often, emerging from the forests, walkers discover the sun-scorched façades of palatial country mansions, wayside *ermitas* (hermitages) and little *casetas* (huts). In a sense, the visitor who is prepared to walk can forget everything they've ever heard about Mallorca, and start afresh by making new discoveries every day, around every corner.

As walking became more and more popular over the years and guidebooks proliferated in many

17

languages, the island authorities began to purchase some extensive rural estates, protecting them from development and marking paths and tracks for walkers. In due course they turned their attention to the creation of long-distance walking routes, which are still gradually being pieced together.

## SERRA DE TRAMUNTANA

Serra de Tramuntana translates as 'Mountains of the North', and they form an incredibly rugged range stretching all the way along the northern flank of Mallorca. The Paratge Natural de la Serra de Tramuntana, or Nature Area of the Serra de Tramuntana, was designated in 2007, covering an area of approximately 625 square kilometres (240 square miles). In 2011 it became a World Heritage Site, due to its importance as a cultural landscape. Although the mountains are predominantly limestone, the coastline often features a complex mix of rock types. Pine forests and extensive holm oak woodlands abound, with cultivated areas featuring olive groves, citrus groves and nut groves. Terraced slopes near the towns and villages produce abundant crops, while bare, rocky mountainsides are colonised by tough plants that form dense maquis, or patchy garigue formations. These rugged mountains form the backdrop for walking in Mallorca.

Around 90% of the Serra de Tramuntana is private property, and many regular walkers can tell tales about access problems. On the other hand, every few years extensive

*Looking towards Mallorca's highest mountains from Puig d'Alaró (Walk 29)*

mountain estates come onto the market and some of these have been purchased and opened to the public. Some of the most notable acquisitions and recreational areas, from west to east, include: Finca Galatzó, Sa Coma d'en Vidal, Son Fortuny, Planícia, Son Moragues, Cúber, Binifaldó and Menut. There are plenty of places where walkers are welcome, or at least tolerated.

The provision of the long-distance GR221 allows walkers to trek all the way through the Serra de Tramuntana. Although many stretches of the GR221 are included in this book, they do not run consecutively, nor always in the same direction. For full details of the GR221, described in its entirety as a long-distance route, see *Trekking in Mallorca* by Paddy Dillon, published by Cicerone.

Pine trees are common in the mountains of Mallorca

## BRIEF HISTORY OF MALLORCA

Mallorca has been inhabited for more than 6000 years, when the earliest settlers lived in caves, hunted and kept animals, made stone tools and employed certain rituals when burying their dead. Around 4000 years ago, stone buildings and large towers, or *talaiots*, were constructed, suggesting highly organised societies working together for the common good, while clearly engaging in serious disputes with their neighbours.

The Carthaginians established trading posts and often recruited local people to defend them. Most of the

ports on the island had their origins around this time. The Romans invaded Mallorca in 123BC, but much of their work was later destroyed by Vandals from North Africa. After the breakup of the Roman Empire, the Byzantine general Belisarius dealt with the Vandals, and the Balearic islands were linked with what is now Tunisia. As part of the Byzantine Empire, Mallorca again became a trading post protected by military might.

Arab raids commenced in AD707. Arab settlers profoundly influenced the development of agriculture. The legacy of these times is recalled in placenames – *bini* means 'house of', as in Binibassi and Biniaraix. In the city of Palma the Moorish arches of the Almudaina palace and the Arab baths can still be seen.

In 1229 Jaume I of Aragon, 'The Conqueror', led a fleet of 150 ships and an army of 16,000 men to Mallorca. Their intention was to land at Port de Pollença, but they were prevented by storms so they sheltered in the lee of sa Dragonera and later landed at Santa Ponça. The re-conquest was completed in 1230, but this didn't lead to peaceful times. Disputes between Jaume's sons, passed on to their sons and heirs, led to successive invasions, but the royal line continued through Jaume II and Jaume III, the latter being killed in battle in 1349. The reign of independent kings ended, and Aragon took direct control of the island.

Mallorca's chequered history continued with invasions, rebellions and natural disasters such as earthquakes, floods, and outbreaks of cholera and bubonic plague. Watchtowers, or *talaies*, were built between 1550 and 1650 on high vantage points, so that invaders and pirates could be spotted in good time. In 1716 Mallorca finally lost the title of kingdom and became a province of Spain. Neighbouring islands had similarly convoluted histories, with Menorca spending the best part of the 18th century as a British possession. In the 20th century, the Catalan language was suppressed under Franco's dictatorship, but has since flourished and is now very evident throughout Mallorca.

## MOUNTAIN HERITAGE

Most of the mountainous terrain in Mallorca is made of limestone. The built heritage of the mountains often uses nothing more basic than roughly hewn lumps of limestone. On the lower cultivated slopes, terraces are held in place by massive drystone buttresses (*marges*) and watered by stone-lined channels (*canaletes*). Water may be stored in tanks (*cisternes*) or small underground reservoirs (*aljubs*), all built of stone.

On the lower wooded slopes, where fuel was readily available, are large stone-lined pits which are former limekilns (*forns de calç*). On the highest mountainsides, larger and deeper stone-lined snow-pits (*cases de neu*) were used for storing snow and ice. In dense holm oak woodland there are dark, flat, circular, moss-grown remains of charcoal-burning platforms (*sitges*). Trekkers sometimes use these as wild-camp sites, but it is very difficult to get pegs into the hard-baked ground. Somewhere nearby will be the low remains of the circular huts of the charcoal burner (*barraca de carboner*). Stone-built outdoor bread ovens (*forns de pa*) are also likely to be spotted nearby. Drystone walls and cairns abound almost everywhere.

### Snow collecting

The highest paths on Mallorca were built by snow collectors (*nevaters*). Snow was collected to make ice for use in the summer and conserved in snow-pits. These are found

*Snow used to be collected and stored in pits on the mountains*

scattered around Puig Major, Puig de Massanella, Puig Tomir, Puig des Teix and Serra d'Alfàbia, mostly above 900m (2950ft). The pits were usually circular, oval, or occasionally rectangular, partly or wholly below ground level. When the mountains were covered with snow, groups of men went up to gather it into baskets. Flat platforms were made and cleared of vegetation, where the snow was arranged in layers and trampled down hard to pack it into ice.

The packed snow was put into the pit and each layer was covered with *càrritx*, a tall pampas-like grass, to make it easier to split the blocks later. When the pit was full it was covered with ashes, branches and more *càrritx*, then carefully guarded. On summer nights blocks of ice were taken down on mules to the villages and towns. It was not only used for ice creams and cooling drinks, but also for medicinal preparations. The local authority controlled the price and a tax was fixed on it. Sometimes ice had to be imported from the mainland, but in glut years it was exported to neighbouring Menorca. The last time a snow-pit was used was in 1925 on Puig de Massanella. The industry was killed stone-dead by the advent of modern refrigeration techniques.

### Charcoal burning

Complex networks of paths were made by charcoal burners (*carboners*). Almost every evergreen oakwood was once used for the production of charcoal. Charcoal-burning hearths are flat circular areas, often ringed by stones and now covered with bright green moss. They often serve as

21

landmarks in the route descriptions in this guidebook. They are referred to as 'sitges' (singular sitja). Charcoal burning lasted until butane gas became popular in the 1920s, although in some areas production lasted a while longer. Charcoal was used specifically for cooking, being preferred over wood because it was cleaner and gave a steadier heat.

Carboners started work in April, living and working all summer in the woods with their families. They had to watch their hearths carefully, as charcoal burning was a delicate operation and everything could be ruined in a moment of neglect. The idea was to carbonise the wood, not burn it to ash. Carboners lived in simple, circular stone huts, roofed with branches and grass. The remains of huts, as well as modern reconstructions, are often seen in the woods, along with beehive-like stone bread ovens nearby.

Axes and enormous two-handed saws were used to fell large oaks, of a diameter stipulated by the landowner. Each carboner had his own area, or ranxo. A circular site was prepared, with stones carefully arranged so that the air intake was limited, causing the wood to carbonise without igniting it. Logs and branches were arranged in a dome, leaving a narrow central chimney. Gravel and clay were heaped over it, and a ladder was used to reach the chimney, so that the carboner could start the firing process.

The weight of the wood was reduced by 75–80% and each firing

lasted up to 12 days. Sieved earth was used for quenching and the covering was then removed. The hot charcoal was extracted with a shovel and rake, and an average burn could produce around 2800 kilos (2¾ tons) of produce. Once cool, the charcoal pieces were graded, loaded onto mules and taken to towns and villages for sale. Bark from the oak trees was also collected and used for tanning.

## Lime burning

Limekilns are seen throughout the woodlands in the mountains. They are quite different from those seen in Britain, as they lack a draw-hole at the bottom, and are simply deep, stone-lined pits. Great heat was needed to split the calcium carbonate ($CaCO_3$) into calcium oxide ($CaO$) and carbon dioxide ($CO_2$), so a plentiful supply of wood was necessary. Although a vast amount of limestone is available, the stones used to produce lime were always chosen very carefully, and were referred to as pedra viva or 'living stones'.

At the base of the pit, a dome was built of large stones with gaps left between them for aeration. Above the dome, more stones were built up, and the spaces around the sides of the kiln were filled with the actual stones that were to be converted into lime. The interior was filled with wood and the top of the kiln was covered with earth. The fire was lit and kept burning for up to two weeks, with more wood added continually. Huge quantities of wood

*A simple, restored hut used by a carboner, or charcoal-burner (above); a sitja is a circular stone structure once used for burning charcoal*

were needed – up to 155,000 kilos (150 tons) – leading to devastation of the forests and producing as little as 10,000 kilos (10 tons) of lime. It was very hard work and it brought little financial reward. According to an old proverb, *'qui fa calç, va descalç'*, or 'he who makes lime goes barefoot'. Lime was used for the annual whitewashing of houses and also for making mortar.

23

## WILDLIFE

### Trees, shrubs and flowers

Trees on Mallorca come in four main types – pines, oaks, olives and palms – but there are also several minor types. Overall, the forests and woodlands are green and leafy throughout the year owing to the predominance of evergreen species. Abundant Aleppo pines can grow almost anywhere from sea level to 1000m (3280ft). They usually grow tall and straight, but can be twisted in exposed locations. Holm oaks are the commonest of the evergreen oaks. They grow in dense woodlands and were exploited for the production of charcoal. Olives may have grown wild on Mallorca before being cultivated. Some of the thickest and most gnarled specimens are over

*Asphodels flourish on many sunny and stony slopes*

1000 years old. Dwarf fan palms grow mostly at lower elevations, but some thrive in the mountains.

Other common trees include the strawberry tree, with its strange edible fruit, and the carob which produces distinctive pods that are high in sugar but contain tooth-breaking seeds. Citrus fruits, oranges and lemons, are picked around January and are most abundant around Sóller. Almond trees blossom pink and white around February, and were first planted on a large scale in 1765.

Woody shrubs include various species of broom, including some that bristle with thorns, blazing with yellow flowers in March and April. The resin-scented lentisk grows almost anywhere, and aromatic rosemary is also common. Heather tends to form

*Carob trees bear distinctive seed pods*

A rock rose looks like crumpled tissue paper

feathery clumps and some species are like small trees.

Plants such as asphodels thrive in rocky, barren places, but many other flowering plants manage to eke out an existence. There are Mallorcan varieties of St John's Wort, for example, and several species of cistus. Two species of spiny plants, despite being quite separate, are both referred to as *coixinets de monja* or 'nuns' sewing cushions'. Another spiny plant is smilax, known locally as *aritja*, giving rise to the place-name *aritges*. Shrubby euphorbias, or spurges, contain a milky, latex sap, and some bushy species are referred to as tree spurges. Delightful little flowers include tiny crocuses and cyclamens, sometimes appearing to grow from bare rock but actually rooted in tiny crevices.

Most open mountainsides, as well as sunny spots inside woods and forests, may be covered with the tall pampas-like grass, *Ampelodesmus mauritanica*, which is best referred to by its common name of *càrritx*. It looks innocuous from a distance, but can prove troublesome on closer acquaintance. Avoid stepping on its long fronds with one foot as they can form a loop, tripping walkers as they bring their next foot forward. Get into the habit of high-stepping past *càrritx* to avoid tripping.

## Animals

Whatever large mammals once roamed Mallorca, only feral goats remain, along with domesticated sheep, a few cattle and fewer pigs. Bells draw attention to farm stock foraging on the mountainsides. Signs reading 'Big Game Hunting' might seem alarming, but they refer to the hunting of feral goats, which is permitted on Tuesdays, Thursdays, Saturdays and Sundays from October to February. Hunters are unlikely to shoot across popular paths, but walkers should be aware of their presence. In the unlikely event that you find yourself close to a shooting party, yell loudly in any language!

Most of the mammals native to the island are small, including pine martens, weasels, hedgehogs, bats, hares, rabbits and rodents, and many of them are hunted by birds of prey. South American coatis are causing concern since being released into

Goats are seen in the mountains and hunted as 'big game'

the wild, as they prey on native animals. Snakes are only rarely spotted and should cause no concern to walkers. Geckos are unlikely to be seen, except by those keeping a keen watch. Frogs and toads may be common in well-watered areas, and they are notable near the large reservoirs at Cúber and Gorg Blau (Walks 31–35). Snails can be easy to spot because of their distinctive shells. Insect life includes abundant butterflies in spring and summer, and even more species of moths. In the hot summer months cicadas and grasshoppers chirp and whir in the vegetation.

A notable 'pest' insect is the pine processionary moth. The female lays up to 200 eggs, which hatch into voracious caterpillars that can cause great damage to trees. They live in dense, spherical webs and move to new foraging areas by marching nose-to-tail, thus giving rise to their name. Avoid handling them, as they are covered in hairs that can irritate the skin. Other 'pest' insects include the red palm weevil, which destroys palms.

## Birdwatching

Serious birdwatchers should get in touch with the local experts, the Grup Ornitològic Balear (GOB), www.gob-mallorca.com. GOB has long been involved in renovating an old building as a refugi (refuge) at La Trapa, above Sant Elm (Walk 3). Unfortunately, construction has stalled and its future is in doubt. Other Mallorcans have a passion for hunting birds, especially thrushes, which cause a lot of damage to olive groves. Shooting and netting take place from the end of August to the end of January, but this should not inconvenience walkers as it usually occurs in the evening and at dawn. Most species of birds are protected.

The black vulture is unmistakeable when seen above remote mountains. Numbers dropped alarmingly in the last century and a programme was set up to assist their recovery. This involves minimising disturbance, leaving carrion out for them, setting up breeding programmes and introducing black vultures from other areas. The breeding season is exceptionally long, extending from January through to July. Black vultures are usually seen over the mountains between Sóller and Pollença.

Raptors include red kites, peregrines, kestrels and booted eagles. Harriers are occasional visitors, while ospreys may be seen at the large reservoirs at Cúber and Gorg Blau. Eleonora's falcon breeds along the northern coastal cliffs.

Hoopoes are eagerly spotted in many places, while large flocks of crag martins are notable in the mountains in winter. Alpine accentors also frequent the highest mountains in winter. The blue rock thrush keeps itself out of sight, while swifts breed safely on cliffs. During the winter there is a big influx of birds from northern Europe, including starlings, thrushes, finches, waders and wildfowl. Woodlands support blackcaps, black redstarts, crossbills and goldfinches. Look out for white wagtail, meadow pipits, serins and greenfinches. Linnets and great tits are common and robins and chaffinches are abundant. Firecrests are found fairly high in the mountains.

## TRAVEL TO MALLORCA

### By air

Most visitors fly to Mallorca from airports as far apart as Iceland and Israel, from all over Europe, including over two dozen British airports. The choice of routes and airlines is bewildering, but there are plenty of budget operators and deals for those willing to search online. It is worth accessing the Palma de Mallorca airport website to discover just how many routes and operators are available, www.aena.es (English-language option available; select 'choose airport').

### By road or rail

Few travellers consider an overland journey to Mallorca, but the Mediterranean ports of Barcelona, Valencia and Dènia are served by trains and buses. For coach travel

*A juvenile gull displays typical mottled plumage*

check Eurolines, www.eurolines.com, or for trains check www.renfe.com. Driving overland is a very time-consuming approach, but may suit expatriates living in southern Spain.

### Ferries

Ferries sail from Barcelona, Valencia and Dènia to Palma, including Trasmediterranea, www.trasmediterranea.es, and Balearia, www.balearia.com. Ferries berth so close to Palma that it is possible to walk straight through the historic city centre for onward bus or rail connections, or use EMT bus 1 to get from the port to the Estació Intermodal on Plaça d'Espanya. Some buses heading west can be caught near the ferryport, without the need to go into the city. These include bus 102 to Port d'Andratx and bus 111 to Calvià and es Capdellà.

*Passing beneath an overhang on the way to es Horts (Walk 39)*

### Taking or hiring a car

Car hire can be arranged in advance, on arrival at the airport or through most hotels. Before considering this approach, bear in mind that using a car to access a walk means returning to it afterwards. There are plenty of excellent linear walks that link with public transport, for which a car is a liability.

### TRAVEL AROUND MALLORCA

### By train

There are only two railway lines leaving the centre of Palma. An expensive, rickety, vintage train called the Ferrocarril de Sóller runs northwards to Bunyola. It then passes through 13 tunnels beneath the Serra d'Alfàbia and spirals down to Sóller, where it links with an electric tram to Port de Sóller. For timetables, tel 971 752051 or 971 752028, www.trendesoller.com.

Serveis Ferroviaris de Mallorca (SFM) trains only serve the end of one route (Walk 28), but they link with buses that serve a few more walking routes. For instance, bus 320 links the Consell-Alaró station with Alaró, and bus 330 links the Inca station with Caimari and Lluc. For train timetables, tel 971 177777, www.tib.org.

### By bus

Bus timetables are published to cover the summer (April to September) and winter (October to March) seasons.

*A colourful bus crosses a vintage railway line in Bunyola*

The combined bus/rail station, the Estació Intermodal in Palma, provides photocopies for a few cents, and they are posted on brightly coloured bus stops around Mallorca, but otherwise printed copies are difficult to obtain. Most buses, but by no means all of them, are red and yellow. Buses run from early until late, but some remote villages have few buses. A list of useful bus services is given in Appendix B; for more details, tel 971 177777, www.tib.org.

**By taxi**

Taxis are available in all towns and most villages throughout Mallorca, usually close to the main squares or near popular hotels. Cars are generally white, with a stripe bearing the crest of the local municipality. The green sign *Lliure/Libre* means 'free' and any taxi displaying this can be used. In case of difficulty ask your hotel, or a roadside bar, to call one for you. Offer a couple of Euros if they seem reluctant to phone. A general rule of thumb is that a long taxi journey will cost five times more than the bus fare. If three or four walkers share a taxi, the individual cost is close to the bus fare for the same journey. You can ask to see a scale of charges approved by the local municipality, but if you want to go on a long journey you may have to pay the fare both ways even if you're not returning. Bear in mind that when asking for a taxi pick-up in a remote place, at short notice, it could be an hour or more before it arrives.

## WHEN TO GO

In theory it is possible to walk in Mallorca at any time of the year, but the peak summer period is very hot

Rampant flowers on the way from es Capdella to the Finca Galatzó (Walk 9)

and any strenuous activity is quite exhausting. Spring and autumn are usually warm and clear, with a chance of rain, and most walkers would be happy with conditions at these times. The winter months can be clear and warm, but there is a greater risk of rain and the possibility of cold winds and snow on higher ground. Roughly every 20 years the whole of Mallorca is covered in snow, all the way down to the beaches, making transport to the mountains and walks along paths difficult.

Note the large number of religious or cultural holidays, or *festes*, on the island. Many businesses close on these days and public transport operates a reduced level of service.

The main dates are 1 and 6 January, 1 March, Easter (Thursday to Monday), 1 May, 25 July, 15 August, 12 October, 1 November and 6, 8, 25 and 26 December. Some towns and villages have local festes, but these usually only affect local businesses and not public transport.

## MOUNTAIN WEATHER

Mallorca has a typical Mediterranean climate with mild, damp winters and hot, dry summers. The relative humidity is around 70% throughout the year. This, together with sea breezes, makes the hot summer days bearable, providing you are not walking uphill too much. There are nearly 300 sunny days in the year and even the winter months see an average of five hours of sunshine a day.

Rain usually falls in heavy showers that soon clear up, although there are occasional days of torrential rain in the late autumn and early spring. The rainfall is greatest over the high mountains and least on the south coast. Snow is common on the mountain tops in winter but very rare at sea level, with falls there recorded in 1956, 1985 and 2005. When snow falls deeply on the mountain paths, they can be quite difficult to follow.

Take nothing for granted with the weather, and obtain a forecast whenever possible. TV stations and Mallorcan newspapers carry daily weather reports. For hourly forecasts, check www.eltiempo.es/baleares.

## ACCOMMODATION

The main tourism website for Mallorca is www.infomallorca.net. Tourist information offices are located in all the main resorts, but some of them operate only during the summer. Staff at these offices usually speak English and can assist with information about accommodation, transport and visitor attractions. There is a tourist information office at the airport and others in the city of Palma.

Accommodation varies widely, from dirt-cheap independent hostels to incredibly expensive hotels. While the bulk of tourists book package holidays, walkers may wish to stay in quiet rural locations or mountain villages. When choosing accommodation, think carefully about how far you are willing to travel in order to complete walking routes, as the island is big and travelling along winding mountain roads can be slow.

If a car is being used, then accommodation could be located anywhere, but if bus services are being used, then accommodation needs to be chosen somewhere close to a bus station or bus stop, preferably in a place offering services in many directions. Staying close to the Estació Intermodal in Palma makes it possible to commute to and from every walking route in Mallorca, for those willing to start early and finish late.

Some of the walks pass *refugis*, part of a small network established by the Consell de Mallorca and administered either by the Consell or independently. Often in restored buildings, they are equipped to a high standard and offer dormitory accommodation at very good prices. However, the refuges are more likely to be of interest to trekkers on the GR221 and are not really suited to use as a walking base – although hungry and thirsty passers-by may be grateful of the refreshments on offer. If you do wish to stay in a *refugi*, be aware that Mallorcans are very quick to take advantage of such economic yet quality accommodation, so weekends tend to be busy with family groups.

## LANGUAGE

There are two official languages in Mallorca: Catalan and Castilian Spanish. Catalan is spoken from Andorra to València, as well as on the Balearic Islands. Mallorquí is a dialect of Catalan and includes words of French and Arabic origin. No-one expects visitors to learn Catalan, let alone Mallorquí, and any Spanish you learn will be readily understood. Many people in the main resorts and large hotels speak English, German and other languages but this may not be the case in small villages and in the countryside.

Catalan in its written form may be understood by anyone with a knowledge of Spanish, but the spoken language is another matter. Between themselves, most islanders speak Mallorquí, so conversations on buses and in bars and shops may be incomprehensible to visitors. However, if you speak a little Spanish you will find that people are delighted and will help you all they can, and even more so if you attempt to converse in Catalan. It is well worth taking the trouble to learn a few words and phrases so as to be able to pass the time of day with local people.

**Placenames**

Most places in Mallorca had two names in the past, Spanish and Mallorquí. Since Mallorquí was given equal status with Spanish, almost all Spanish placenames have vanished from signposts and street signs. In fact, only in a few tourist resorts are there any Spanish signs to be seen, and Mallorquí may be the only language in evidence in rural areas.

Confusion is likely to arise if you use old maps and guidebooks, which generally show only Spanish place-names. The popular Editorial Alpina maps use authentic Mallorquí place-names. As a rule, many placenames look similar, regardless of whether they are in Spanish or Mallorquí, but some hotels and businesses insist on using Spanish forms for their addresses. For visitors, this could be confusing if your hotel is listed as being in Puerto Sóller or Pollensa, but the only road signs you see are for Port de Sóller or Pollença!

See Appendix A for basic phrases and useful words in English, Spanish and Catalan, along with a topographical glossary for use when interpreting placenames on maps.

## MONEY

The Euro is the currency of Mallorca. Large-denomination Euro notes are difficult to use for small purchases, so avoid the €500 and €200 notes altogether, and avoid the €100 notes if you can. The rest are fine: €50, €20, €10 and €5. Coins come in €2 and €1. Small denomination coins come in values of 50c, 20c, 10c, 5c, 2c and 1c. Bus drivers will appreciate the correct change and will frown on large notes. Many accommodation providers will accept major credit and debit cards, as will large supermarkets, but small bars, shops and cafés deal only in cash.

## FOOD AND DRINK

All the towns and villages offer the opportunity to buy food and drink. In some places there may only be one or two shops selling food, but there will always be a bar-restaurant, and there are often opportunities to sample local fare. There are occasional roadside bar-restaurants, and refreshment options are mentioned in walk descriptions where relevant. (Note that refreshments are not available on all walks.) Shops generally open from 9am–1pm and 4pm–8pm. Long lunch hours are common, but some shops open all day, while some close on Saturday afternoons, and some may not open at all on Sundays.

Mallorquín cuisine, or *cuina Mallorquina*, can differ from that of Catalonia on the mainland. Fish

A popular path is followed from l'Ofre into the Barranc de Biniaraix (Walk 23)

dishes are a speciality and so are *tapas*, served with drinks in many bars. They are usually behind glass on the counter, so you can point to the ones you want. Small or large helpings are offered and a large one can make a substantial meal. See Appendix A for translations of many types of local specialities that may appear on menus.

## KIT CHECK

Think carefully about the gear you plan to wear and carry. Ground conditions are often hard and stony, but there are plenty of easier tracks and roads. Wear boots or shoes according to your personal preference over such terrain. Bear in mind that hot feet might be more of a problem than wet feet, so think carefully when choosing footwear and socks.

Clothing should be lightweight and light coloured, offering good protection from the sun, while being able to offer good ventilation for sweat. It could be cold on the high mountains, especially in the winter. Waterproofs and windproofs might only be used rarely, so lightweight items will usually be fine. On sunny days, use sunscreen on exposed skin and wear a good sun hat. Bare limestone is very bright in the full sun, so consider taking sunglasses. Ample water must be carried on hot days – a minimum of two litres. Guard against sunburn and heat exhaustion at all times, but be prepared for colder and wetter days too.

## MOUNTAIN MAPS

Many of the walking routes in this guidebook are signposted or

through solid rock and often built laboriously by hand. Some of the paths were engineered as zigzagging mule tracks from village to village, and these are often quite plain and obvious to follow. Others were made to exploit woodlands for charcoal, so they tend to fan out among dense woodlands, with many spurs reaching dead-ends. On these tracks it is necessary to pay careful attention to maps and route descriptions, confirming your location at every junction before making the next move. Even when the signposting and waymarking is good, remember that markers can go missing.

Conditions underfoot range from bare rock to stone-paved paths. However, there are also some uncomfortably stony stretches, and some waymarked, but many of them aren't, and may require careful route-finding. This guidebook contains extracts from the excellent Editorial Alpina 1:25,000-scale maps, which cover the entire Serra de Tramuntana. The Editorial Alpina maps are far and away the best and most popular maps for exploring the mountains, and are widely available around Mallorca. For details see www.editorialalpina.com.

Maps can be ordered in advance from British suppliers such as Stanfords (www.stanfords.co.uk) or The Map Shop (www.themapshop.co.uk).

## PATH CONDITIONS

For the most part, clear paths and tracks are followed, sometimes cut

*Many routes in the mountains – including Walk 32 – involve exposed rocky scrambles*

*The route could be in the Torrent de la Vall d'en Marc after rain (Walk 44)*

paths are deeply eroded. Leaf-mould can obscure uneven surfaces, so tread carefully. Some mountainsides are covered in huge grassy tussocks of *càrritx*. Walkers quickly learn to high-step through *càrritx*, because stepping onto the tough fronds can cause the other foot to be caught as it is swung forward!

## GUIDED WALKING

Various companies and individuals offer guided walks in Mallorca. While this guidebook gives all the information you need to complete a variety of walks, some readers might be discouraged by some of the tougher routes involving intricate or exposed scrambling on rock (see route descriptions to get an idea of the potential challenges involved; Walks 36 and 47 may be prime candidates). For these routes it could be worth seeking an experienced local guide who specialises in individuals or small groups. Some hotels will put guests in touch with walking guides and companies that they have dealt with in the past and tourist offices will have some useful contacts. There are opportunities to join guided walking groups, and these may be advertised in tourist resorts. Tramuntana Tours, tel 971 632423, www.tramuntanatours.com, offers a variety of walks that anyone can join. Jaume Tort, www.camins-mallorca. info, guides individuals and groups, and having done all the research for the Editorial Alpina maps of Mallorca, his knowledge of the mountains is extensive.

### EMERGENCIES

Until 1995 there was only a voluntary mountain rescue service on Mallorca, but now there are two professional teams: one from the fire service or *Bomberos* (tel 080 or 112) and the other from the *Guardia Civil* (tel 062 or 112). There are three police forces: the *Policía Local* wear blue uniforms and are attached to local municipalities; the *Policía Nacional* wear brown uniforms; and the Guardia Civil wear green uniforms and are often seen in rural areas. All three police forces may be called upon in an emergency, tel 112.

Mountain rescue is free of charge and unfortunately has been kept very busy. However, getting a message out in an emergency is not always easy. Mobile phones and GPS units may not get a good signal in some places, and time lost trying to get a signal can be crucial.

Carry a first aid kit to deal with the usual cuts, scrapes and blisters. For other health issues there are pharmacies in the towns and most villages. If any regular medication is needed, include it in your pack. If a doctor or a trip to a hospital is required, an insurance policy might help to offset the cost of certain treatments. Some insurance policies may class walking in the mountains of Mallorca as a hazardous pursuit, in which case you might not be covered. Others, such as the BMC (www.thebmc.co.uk/insurance), are more likely to class it as ordinary walking.

Best of all, walk safely and avoid suffering any injuries.

*The rugged coast from Torre de Lluc to Morro de sa Vaca (Walk 42)*

*The overhanging peak of el Fumat towers above Cala Figuera (Walk 49)*

## USING THIS GUIDE

This guidebook offers all the information you need to organise a successful walk in the mountains, whether the route is waymarked or not. The routes may be adapted and amended, bearing in mind any alternatives that are suggested. Many of the routes link with, or run concurrent with other routes, allowing for significant variation.

If using public transport to reach a route and depart afterwards, be sure to check current bus and train timetables online, or obtain them from the Estació Intermodal in Palma. If you have timetables to hand, then you can refer to them easily. If you don't have them, then you risk missing a bus by

a matter of minutes and might discover that the next one will not arrive for several hours, or even a couple of days! If a taxi is likely to be needed, be sure to get a local taxi number in advance. At the last minute, bars and restaurants usually have the numbers for local taxis.

Read the walk descriptions in advance to see where refreshments are located, and be sure to buy provisions to cover for long walks that lack refreshment options.

An information box at the beginning of each route provides the essentials for the day's walk: start and finish points, distance covered, total ascent and descent, the length of time it's likely to take to complete the route, the title of the sheet map you should carry with you, refreshment options, and details of public transport. The nature of the terrain is always described, so that you know which routes involve open mountainside, which are in dense forest, which are on rugged paths and which run along gentle tracks. Some routes involve hands-on scrambling, agility and a head for heights; any potential difficulties or challenges are highlighted in the walk information boxes.

In the route description, significant places or features along the way that also appear on the map extracts are highlighted in **bold** to aid navigation. As well as the route being described in detail, information about local places is provided in brief.

Many things are likely to influence the time it takes to complete a day's walk. The timings given in this guidebook are walking times, and do not account for breaks along the way. If you keep beating the stated times,

you probably always will, and you can plan ahead on that basis. If you fall behind the stated times, then work out by how much, and apply that to future routes.

If stuck for words, needing a handy phrase, wondering what an item of food is on a menu, or just idly curious about the meaning of some of the placenames on maps, check the glossary in Appendix A – which includes a topgraphical glossary containing terms used within route descriptions. Detailed information about public transport, including which buses can be used for which walks, is given in Appendix B. Useful contacts are listed in Appendix C.

## GPX tracks

GPX tracks for the routes in this guidebook are available to download free at www.cicerone.co.uk/949/GPX. A GPS device is an excellent aid to navigation, but you should also carry a map and compass and know how to use them.

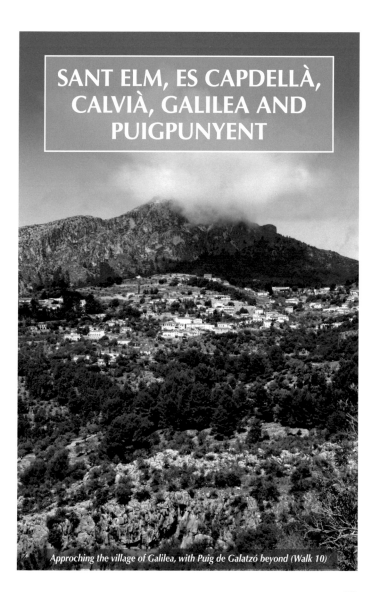

# SANT ELM, ES CAPDELLÀ, CALVIÀ, GALILEA AND PUIGPUNYENT

*Approching the village of Galilea, with Puig de Galatzó beyond (Walk 10)*

High on na Pòpia, looking towards the lighthouse on Cap de Llebeig (Walk 1)

The western extremity of Mallorca contains the sizeable town of Andratx, the lovely village of s'Arracó, the bustling resort of Port d'Andratx and the quiet little seaside village of Sant Elm. The mountains are small and never reach as high as 500m (1640ft), and while they are quite rugged, they are also criss-crossed with paths and tracks that allow most parts to be explored. A ruined Trappist monastery occupies a remote valley in the mountains, proving to be a popular attraction for walkers (Walk 3). The cliff coastline is formidable, although there are beaches and rocky coves that are fairly easy to access. Sant Elm offers a ferry connection with the splendid island of sa Dragonera (Walk 1), which looks like a miniature mountain range.

Higher and more remote mountains rise further inland, with Mola de s'Esclop (Walks 4–6) and Puig de Galatzó (Walks 7–9) being particularly prominent; the latter rising to 1027m (3369ft). In recent years, the extensive estate of Finca Galatzó was made public, allowing both mountains to be climbed from a beautiful valley. In earlier years, they were usually climbed from another public estate, Son Fortuny above Estellencs. Motorists who climb these mountains often have to retrace steps to their cars, but walkers who use buses can traverse both mountains and finish far from where they started.

Other fine walks include one from the town of Calvià to the hilltop village of Galilea (Walk 10), with an option to continue to Puigpunyent. (There is a route from Galilea to Puig de Galatzó.) Another route from Puigpunyent climbs the old mountain road of Camí Vell d'Estellencs, descending along the old Camí de Superna to return to Puigpunyent (Walk 11).

# WALK 1
## sa Dragonera

| | |
|---|---|
| **Start/Finish** | Calo Lladó, sa Dragonera |
| **Distance** | 20.5km (12¾ miles) |
| **Total ascent/descent** | 620m (2035ft) |
| **Time** | 6hrs |
| **Terrain** | Mostly old roads and tracks, with easy paths, despite the steep slopes |
| **Map** | Alpina Tramuntana Sud |
| **Refreshment** | Plenty of choice at Sant Elm, drinks available on the Margarita ferry |
| **Transport** | Buses serve Sant Elm from Andratx and Port d'Andratx. For the Margarita ferry, tel 629 606 614 or 639 617 545. For the WaterTaxi, tel 638 779 001. The Bergantin and Jumbo II offer day-trips only. |

The island of sa Dragonera can only be seen from the western parts of Mallorca. It appears as a dragon-back ridge with a sharp edge and rocky peaks. It has been protected as a natural park since 1995 and is currently equipped with four trails that allow a thorough exploration – although walking all of them in a day is a big undertaking. Countless numbers of lizards will dash out of your way all day!

Buses serving Sant Elm stop on the Plaça de na Caragola, where a very short walk leads down to the ferry landing. The landing on sa Dragonera is at Cala Lladó. Walk up to the information centre and spare a few moments to learn about the natural history of the island, and to study maps showing the layout of the trails. These are numbered from 1 to 4 and are signposted at crucial junctions. This walk takes in all four trails, but it can be shortened, making a good excuse to return for another trip.

- Itinerari 1 – na Miranda – 1.2km circular
- Itinerari 2 – Far de Tramuntana – 1.7km one-way
- Itinerari 3 – Far de Llebeig – 4.5km one-way
- Itinerari 4 – Far Vell – 3.8km one-way

Leave the information centre to reach a point where tracks intersect and signposts list all the trails and destinations. Turn left to follow *itineraris* 3 and 4 along an old tarmac road, later passing a gate, turning a sharp bend, then reaching a junction and another signpost. Turn right for *itinerari* 4 to Far Vell,

walking up a stony track and passing through a gateway at **es Tancat**. The winding track climbs, passing a little house and eventually reaching the gap of **Coll Roig**; a viewpoint at 98m (322ft).

Keep climbing and an amazing, tightly zigzagging path rises at a gentle gradient, despite the steepness of the bushy slope. It reaches the crumbling lighthouse of **Far Vell**, on the summit of **na Pòpia**, at 349m (1145ft).

A **watchtower** was constructed on na Pòpia in 1581, and then demolished in 1850 to make way for the lighthouse of Far Vell, which was in a poor position as it was sometimes obscured by mist. In 1910 two more lighthouses, Far de Llebeig and Far de Tramuntana (see below), were built and Far Vell was allowed to fall into ruins.

Admire the length of the island and the cliff coast of western Mallorca, then retrace

*Cala Lladó is the start and finish of the walk on sa Dragonera*

steps all the way down to the old tarmac road. If time is limited, turn left to return to Calo Lladó.

Turn right along the road, as signposted for *itinerari* 3 to Far de Llebeig. Simply follow the road as it rises gently, passing a small reservoir. Later, when a signpost indicates a path on the right, it is worth a very short diversion along it to see a ruined limekiln. The road later has a wall alongside, where a cliff drops to the sea, and a lighthouse can be seen ahead.

The road is very bendy as it approaches the lighthouse, which is **Far de Llebeig** (the light is operational but the buildings are derelict), and there is also the option of taking a short path down to the left to look at a watchtower, **Torre des Llebeig**, which can be entered by those with the nerve to climb a 16-rung ladder.

Retrace steps all the way back to **Cala Lladó** and consider if there is enough time to walk further. Turn left to follow *itinerari* 2 for Far de Tramuntana, passing toilets and rising along a stony track through woods. Pass a signpost, and note its position for the return. The track leaves the woods and descends to yet another lighthouse; **Far de Tramuntana**. This is also the closest of the three lighthouses to Mallorca.

Once again, retrace steps, but when the signpost is reached that was noted on the outward journey, turn left down a path with steps on a wooded slope. A track continues, passing a crenellated tower. Reach a **viewpoint** and picnic area at **na Miranda**, then follow the track down past cultivated terraces to return to **Calo Lladó**. Any remaining time can be spent admiring a tiny botanic garden.

# WALK 2
*Port d'Andratx and Pintal Vermell*

| | |
|---|---|
| **Start** | Footbridge, Port d'Andratx |
| **Finish** | Bus stop, Sant Elm |
| **Distance** | 9km (5½ miles) |
| **Total ascent/descent** | 370m (1215ft) |
| **Time** | 3hrs |
| **Terrain** | Fairly easy roads, tracks and paths, but one path needs care to locate |
| **Map** | Alpina Tramuntana Sud |
| **Refreshment** | Plenty of choice at Port d'Andratx and Sant Elm |
| **Transport** | Buses serve Port d'Andratx and Sant Elm from Andratx |

The forested hills between Port d'Andratx and Sant Elm are popular with walkers. The following route is not signposted or waymarked, but it has long been considered the first stage of the long-distance GR221 trail. It is an easy linear walk, with the summit of Pintal Vermell offering fine views in the middle, and there are bus services at either end.

Leave the head of the bay at **Port d'Andratx** by crossing a humped footbridge over a river at **s'Aulet**. Follow a broad palm-fringed promenade past the Club de Vela boatyard and a marina. Turn right as signposted for Mon Port, up Carretera Aldea Blanca. Turn left at a crossroads along Carrer de Cala d'Egos, again signposted for Mon Port. Keep right when the road forks, as left is for the **Mon Port Hotel** and a striking windpump.

Pass old olive terraces and avoid a road climbing steeply on the right, rising gently into pine forest instead. Watch for a steep and stony path on the right, often worn to bedrock. (The road could be followed uphill, but it is very convoluted.) The path climbs straight uphill, clipping three bends on the road. Take care at weekends, when mountain bikers tend to hurtle down the path, making the road a safer option. It is possible to switch between the road and the path at all three bends, as well as one more time where the path and road cross each other.

The path finally reaches a track junction on the gap of **Coll des Vent**, at 163m (535ft). There are a couple of ruined limekilns nearby and views back to Port d'Andratx. Turn left to follow a track away from the gap, keeping right at two junctions that appear soon afterwards. The track runs gradually downhill on a forested slope, reaching another junction around 110m (360ft). Keep right again, but note that a left turn leads down to a rugged little beach at Cala d'Egos.

*Pas Vermell offers an easy route past a sheer cliff face*

Follow the track uphill, climbing steeply at times, and keep left at a junction where there is a *sitja*. When a higher junction is reached below **Puig d'en Ric**, turn left to climb further, passing back and forth beneath a pylon line. Cross a high crest where there is a view north-east to Mola de s'Esclop; the mountain rising beyond the village of s'Arracó.

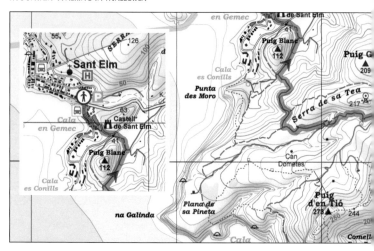

Follow the track towards a prominent red and white mast, but pass below it, rather than climbing to it. Watch carefully for a series of vague paths on the right, mostly marked with little cairns. All of these lead up to a rocky crest touching 300m. However, stay on the track for the time being, descending gently then climbing steeply a short way. It ends just below a trig point on **Pintal Vermell**, at 312m (1024ft). There are splendid views to the island of sa Dragonera, Sant Elm and the mountains beyond.

Double back along the track and turn left up one of the cairned paths to cross the rocky crest. Scout around to find a splendid mountain path which cuts across the natural breach of **Pas Vermell**, easily avoiding fearsome overhanging cliffs. The path then drops through a well-worn groove, passing pines and *càrritx* to reach a track. Turning right offers a shortcut to the village of s'Arracó to catch a bus.

Turn left and follow the bendy track down into a forest. Stay on the main track, passing a junction on a pronounced hairpin bend. When another junction is reached, spot 'S Elm' painted on a rock, indicating a right turn.

After a steeper descent among taller pines there are three opportunities to turn right in close succession. Take the last of these, which should be marked by a small cairn and paint marks. Quickly turn left and a cable should be stretched across the track to exclude vehicles. Rise gently along the track to reach a little house called sa Pineta.

Continue down past small fields, and the track is later patched with concrete, with fine views of sa Dragonera and Sant Elm. Pass a chain, continue down to a

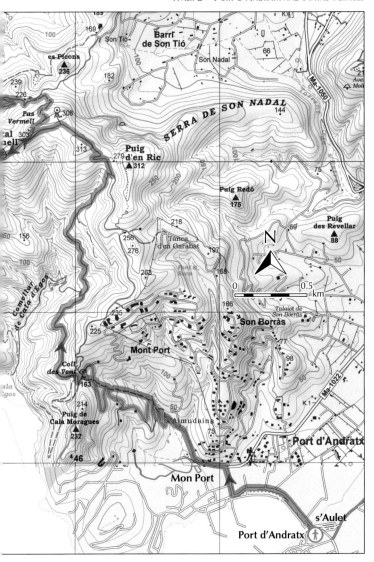

junction and turn right along a forest track. Emerge into a field and turn left along a path, then go through a gap in a wall, briefly back into forest. Cross a road at the gateway to **Castell de Sant Elm**, also known as the Torre de Sant Elm.

Originally operating as a quarantine hospital from 1342 until 1597, the building then became a watchtower. It was bought by Archduke Lluis Salvador in 1868. It was renovated in 1995 by the Fundació Illes Balears and now serves as a secluded **luxury hotel**.

Continue along a track and turn left down a flight of concrete steps. Turn right along a road, passing the Hotel Aquamarin to reach a road junction and bus stop beside a sandy beach at **Sant Elm**.

# WALK 3
*Sant Elm, La Trapa and s'Arracó*

| | |
|---|---|
| **Start** | Plaça de Mossen Sebastià, Sant Elm |
| **Finish** | Roundabout, s'Arracó |
| **Distance** | 13km (8 miles) |
| **Total ascent** | 570m (1870ft) |
| **Total descent** | 500m (1640ft) |
| **Time** | 5hrs |
| **Terrain** | Forested slopes give way to a steep, rocky slope that includes a section of mild scrambling where there may be a rope for protection. Paths climb higher, linking with tracks that allow for an easy descent. |
| **Map** | Alpina Serra Tramuntana Sud |
| **Refreshment** | Plenty of choice at Sant Elm and s'Arracó |
| **Transport** | Buses serve Sant Elm and s'Arracó from Andratx |

The walk from Sant Elm to La Trapa starts easily and is popular, but the upper parts are steep and rocky. A small community of Trappist monks settled in that remote place. The site is in ruins but there is a plan to restore part of it as a *refugi*. Paths can be followed higher to ses Basses, enjoying a wild and remote area, then a descent leads to the pleasant and quiet village of s'Arracó.

Puig des Campàs is seen on the descent to s'Arracó

Leave the last bus stop in **Sant Elm**, on Plaça de Mossen Sebastià Grau. Head inland from es Molí restaurant, where there is an old windmill, following Avinguda de La Trapa uphill. The road runs into forest and gives way to a dirt road called Camí Can Tomeví. Keep straight ahead at a junction in the forest, eventually passing near the solitary house of **Can Tomeví**.

Watch for a marker post for La Trapa and walk straight ahead on a bare, rocky path criss-crossed with tree roots. Simply follow a well-trodden path up the forested slope, passing a pair of old gate pillars and crossing other tracks. Little cairns and occasional paint marks show the way, while other paths may be blocked by branches or lines of stones. Climb past old terraces then drift left along the foot of rugged cliffs as the pines become sparse.

An easy stone-buttressed terrace path overlooks a secluded boulder-beach at Cala en Basset, with sa Dragonera in view beyond. The scrub includes rock roses, spiky broom and càrritx. The terrace gives way to a steep and rocky slope where hands must be used for mild scrambling, and one part might have a rope for protection.

Cross a rocky shoulder at 300m (985ft), pass a noticeboard and look down on old buildings and former cultivation terraces at **La Trapa**. Follow a path in that direction and cross a ladder stile to reach an access track.

Follow the zigzag access track uphill from La Trapa. A signpost and a marker post indicate that this is the way to ses Basses, but be sure to leave the track on a

49

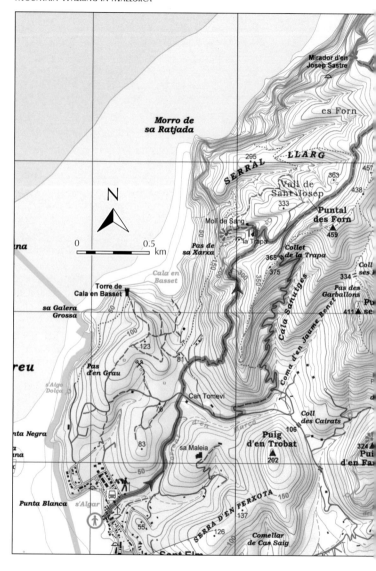

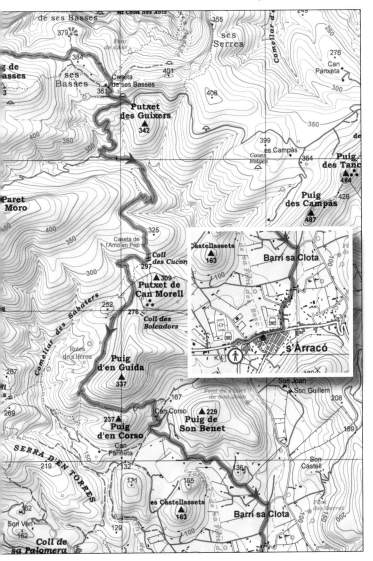

## LA TRAPA

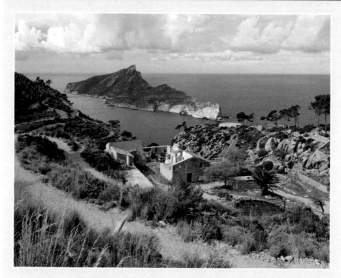

*The ruined buildings of La Trapa and the island of sa Dragonera*

A community of Trappist monks, first expelled from Normandy in France in 1789, then expelled from Zaragoza in Spain in 1808, settled in this remote valley in 1810. One monk was elected to trade with the outside world and was obliged to live separately. The site was abandoned in 1820, sold in 1853 and fell into ruins after serving as a farm. It was purchased in 1980, along with the surrounding land, by a birdwatching and environmental organisation, Grup Ornitològic Balear. Disaster struck in 1994, and again in 2013, when fires destroyed the forested upland. Trees have been replanted, but will take decades to mature. Old drystone terraces and the irrigation system have been restored. Plans to provide *refugi* accommodation have stalled.

To explore the site, simply walk down the track, passing the former monastery to reach a nearby mill. Walk down to a bare circular area that was an *era*, or threshing floor, but now bears tall pines. A little further downhill is a **mirador** with a fine view of sa Dragonera, explored on Walk 1. Double back uphill to continue the walk.

bend to follow a narrow path onwards. It is possible to follow the track over a gap and short-cut back down to Sant Elm. Pass occasional burnt and toppled pines among the dense scrub, then pass a noticeboard. Follow the path as it climbs gradually past old terraces in **Vall de Sant Josep**, becoming steeper and more rugged.

There is no sign of habitation in any direction as the path reaches 450m (1475ft) on the open slopes of **Puig de ses Basses**. When a large cairn is reached, turn left to follow a short path to the **Mirador d'en Josep Sastre**, for a fine view of sa Dragonera, then return to the cairn to continue.

The path crosses rugged terrain dotted with asphodels and rosemary. There are superb views north-east along the coast, taking in the nearby peak of Mola de s'Esclop and distant Puig Major. Head gradually down from one burnt pine tree to another. In 2013 a fire burnt many trees between here and Estellencs. When more pines are reached on a crest, turn left along a path that might be obscured by a fallen tree. Another short path on the left could be followed for a view, otherwise keep right, traversing a slope thick with *càrritx*. Enjoy coastal views and eventually reach a track beside a solitary little house at **ses Basses**.

Turn left to follow a winding track downhill, reaching a signpost and map-board at a junction around 340m (1115ft). Turn sharp right to commence the descent to s'Arracó. Following the track onwards leads to Coll de sa Gramola, where a pick-up could be organised. Descend past a few pine trees, and follow the winding track down into a valley. Keep left at a junction, but notice a limekiln among pines to the right. The track passes above a concrete dam and continues climbing across a slope. It has a buttressed edge, winds uphill and reaches a rocky, scrubby crest around 325m (1065ft).

Descend on broken bedrock, passing the solitary ruin of **Caseta de l'Amo en Pep**. Rocky, scrubby slopes are crossed on the way down past **Coll des Cucons**. Later, there might be fallen trees to negotiate on the way into a forest. The track rises and descends gently around the slopes of **Puig d'en Guida**, catching glimpses of little houses, or *casetes*, on old cultivation terraces. Cross a gentle, forested gap beside **Puig d'en Corso**, at almost 220m (720ft). Descend, and keep turning right at a triangular junction, descending to the right of a house called **Can Corso**. The track is very bendy and gives way to a tarmac road.

Simply walk straight ahead, taking note of marker posts at junctions, with occasional views towards s'Arracó. Turn right at a signposted junction at **Barri sa Clota**. Farms give way to houses as Calle del Porvenir enters **s'Arracó**. Turn right to follow the road straight through the village, passing tall buildings and the church of Sant Crist. There are cafés and bar-restaurants. Carrer de França leads to a roundabout outside the village, where there are bus stops.

# WALK 4
*Mola de s'Esclop from Ses Fontanelles*

| Start/Finish | Ses Fontanelles |
|---|---|
| Distance | 9km (5½ miles) |
| Total ascent/descent | 770m (2525ft) |
| Time | 4hrs |
| Terrain | Good tracks at first, then rugged paths are sometimes vague. The higher parts of the mountain involve short scrambles on bare rock. |
| Map | Alpina Tramuntana Sud |
| Refreshment | Basic refreshment at Ses Fontanelles |
| Transport | None |

The rugged mountain of s'Esclop can be approached from a number of directions, and the route from Ses Fontanelles is handy because it starts at a private refuge. The way is rugged and seems longer than it actually is, then the summit offers wide-ranging views. If there is no need to return to Ses Fontanelles, then descents can be made towards Estellencs or es Capdellà.

Leave **Ses Fontanelles**, at 280m (920ft), following a track as signposted up to a path. Walk up the forested valley of **Coma des Cellers** and keep left at a higher level to follow another track. Just before the track reaches a gate, switch to a narrow, rugged, cairned path, swinging left as it climbs, with views back to Pla de s'Evangèlica. Watch carefully to spot where the path exploits a breach in the cliffs at **Pas Gran**, around 450m (1475ft), crossing an old fence. Keep watching for small cairns all the way up a rocky slope dotted with pines, bushes and scrub.

The rather vague path crosses a metal ladder stile over a fence, almost touching 610m (2000ft) before descending through an area with more pines and dense *càrritx*. A house might be noticed uphill at **ses Alquerioles**, but keep watching for the cairned path, rising to cross another metal ladder stile. Turn right and pass between an old well and a ruin.

Climb, but pay great attention to the route, which is vague in places. It rises across old terraces, where burnt and fallen trees often obscure the way. In 2013 a forest fire caused extensive damage in this area.

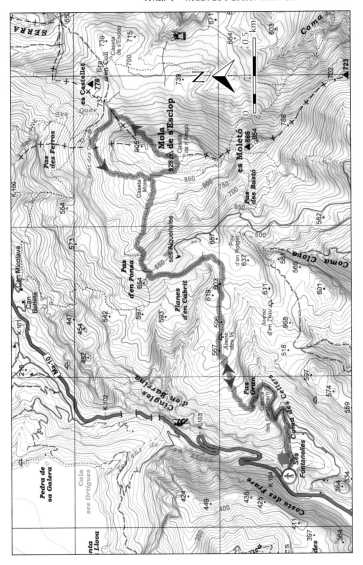

55

*Looking back while climbing a rocky slope at Pas Gran*

It is important to spot a rocky cleft in a cliff at **Pas d'en Ponsa**, which is awkwardly clogged with burnt and fallen trees. Once through, it is tempting to follow a trodden path onwards, but it leads downhill, so turn right and climb, watching for more small cairns. These show the way up another rocky slope dotted with pines. Views open up wonderfully, with the watchtower of sa Torre Nova seen far below.

Keep climbing to reach a prominent fan palm. Just beyond it is an area of short-cropped grass, with a circular *era*, or threshing floor, situated between the tumbled ruins of **Caseta de la Mola** and old terraces at 844m (2769ft).

Turn right to follow a path across terraces beneath a cliff. Turn left and tackle some mild scrambling to gain the crest of **Mola de s'Esclop**. Turn either right or left. Right leads quickly to a ruined building that once served as an observatory. Readings were taken to measure the Paris Meridian. Left leads to the summit trig point at 928m (3045ft). Splendid views stretch in all directions, with the neighbouring peak of Puig de Galatzó featuring particularly well.

Descend very roughly north-east from the trig point, watching carefully for the path across bare rock, aiming for a rocky hump called es Castellet. Don't go all the way to it, but reach a vague path junction and turn sharp left. Continuing straight ahead allows Walk 5 or Walk 6 to be used as alternative descents.

After turning left, cross a low, tumbled wall on a broad, gentle gap. Follow the path as it traverses a slope, passing above a rocky chasm above **Font des Quer**. Take care not to follow a path downhill. Climb past old terraces to return to the ruins of **Caseta de la Mola**. From this point, it is a matter of retracing steps carefully to return to **Ses Fontanelles**.

# WALK 5

*Mola de s'Esclop from es Capdellà*

| | |
|---|---|
| **Start/Finish** | Plaça de Bernat Calvet, es Capdellà |
| **Distance** | 19km (12 miles) |
| **Total ascent/descent** | 810m (2660ft) |
| **Time** | 6hrs |
| **Terrain** | Good roads, tracks and paths on the lower slopes, but steep and rocky higher on the mountain, with short scrambles on bare rock |
| **Map** | Alpina Tramuntana Sud |
| **Refreshment** | Bars and restaurants at es Capdellà, drinks machine at Finca Galatzó |
| **Transport** | Buses serve es Capdellà from Palma and Calvià |

Mola de s'Esclop can be climbed from es Capdellà via the interesting and scenic public estate of Finca Galatzó. The estate used to be private, but has been public since 2006. A long, but fairly easy ascent through a valley becomes more difficult as height is gained on the higher parts of the mountain. Alternative descents are available after enjoying wonderfully extensive views.

The name of es Capdellà derives from 'es cap d'allà', meaning 'the very end'. Start at a crossroads at Plaça de Bernat Calvet, around 130m (425ft). Follow Carrer de Galatzó, which is signposted for the Finca Pública Galatzó. A mapboard and signpost are passed at a junction with Camí del Graner del Delme. The road later becomes a track passing almond groves, olive groves and small farms, reaching a gateway on a gentle, wooded gap beside **Puig Matós**.

A track leads gently down into a marvellous valley, full of fertile red earth, flanked by the towering peaks of Mola de s'Esclop and Puig de Galatzó. Stay on the main track to reach the **Finca Galatzó**, where a huge old building, dating from the 13th century, features a courtyard, chapel, oil press and several outbuildings. It has been open to the public since 2006.

The Consell de Mallorca charge a 'tourist tax' on visitors, which for some time was used for the purchase of **private estates**, on the rare occasions they came

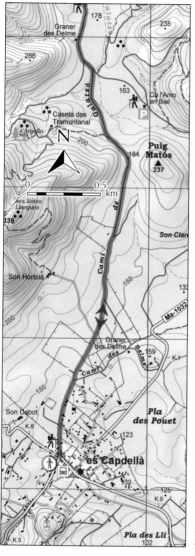

onto the market. These estates were then opened to the public. Some of the more important ones in the Serra de Tramuntana include the Finca Galatzó, Sa Coma d'en Vidal, Son Fortuny, Planícia, Son Moragues, Cúber and Menut.

Keep to the right of the main building to pass beneath an arcade and follow a walled track, which continues through almond groves. Keep to the main track at all times, which means turning right at a junction, as signposted for ses Sínies. The track drops gently into a sparsely forested valley, passing fan palms. Go through a stone gateway and pass two limekilns – one small and one large – both to the left. Wander gently up through the valley alongside the **Torrent de Galatzó**.

Watch out for a *sitja*, *carboner* hut and limekiln on the right. A picnic site is located in the shade of pine trees later, with a reconstructed *sitja* and *carboner* huts. Keep following the track to approach **Pou de ses Sínies**. There is a junction of tracks just before the *pou*, or well.

Turn right, then decide whether to make a short detour to the archaeological site of **Naveta de ses Sinies**. Later, avoid a turning to the right, then watch for a marker post and follow a path cut through *càrritx*, winding up a

58

*An easy valley track leads through the Finca Galatzó to the mountains*

rugged slope and passing above an old trough. Also watch out for a well at **Font des Poll**, hidden on the other side of the path.

A steep and rugged climb includes views of Puig de Galatzó for a while, and some parts of the path feature old cobbles and stone buttressing. There is a view back to the sea at a higher level, and the path climbs past a *sitja* and passes an occasional pine tree. Climb past another *sitja* at a higher level, noting how the course of the old path has been cleared in preference to any other trodden line. Always keep sight of the path, noting another *sitja* to the right, climbing to a sign-posted junction. Walk 9 heads right for Puig de Galatzó.

Follow the main path further uphill, eventually reaching a gap at 652m (2139ft) beside **Serra des Pinotells**. Don't cross a stile over a wall, but turn left instead. Walk 6 crosses the stile, and could be used for the descent later. The path climbs, but occasionally has burnt trees lying across it. A ruin lies to the left and an *era*, or circular threshing floor, is crossed at **Era des Coll**.

The path continues across a rugged slope covered in *càrritx*, with the rocky hump of es Castellet rising to the right. A path junction is reached beside a low, tumbled wall on a broad, gentle gap. Left leads directly to the summit of s'Esclop, but it is worth turning right and stepping across the wall instead.

Follow the path as it traverses a slope, passing above a rocky chasm above **Font des Quer**. Take care not to follow a path downhill. Climb past old terraces to reach the ruins of **Caseta de la Mola**, which features another *era* and old terraces at 844m. Turning right reveals a path descending to Ses Fontanelles, used on Walk 4. Keep left, or straight ahead, to follow a path across terraces beneath a cliff.

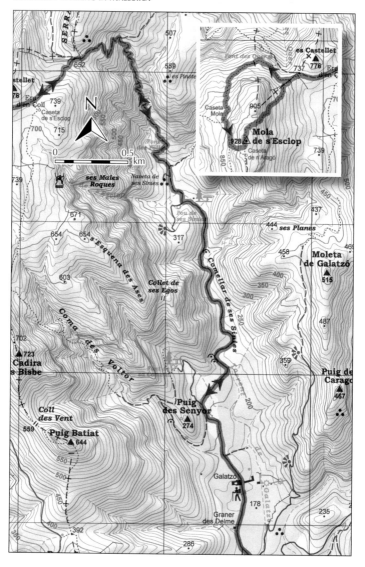

Turn left and tackle some mild scrambling to gain the crest of **Mola de s'Esclop**. Turn either right or left. Right leads quickly to a ruined building that once served as an observatory; left leads to the summit trig point at 928m (3045ft). Splendid views stretch in all directions, with the neighbouring peak of Puig de Galatzó featuring particularly well.

Descend very roughly north-east from the trig point, watching carefully for the path across bare rock, aiming for the rocky hump of es Castellet. Don't go all the way to it, but reach a vague path junction and turn right for **Era des Coll**. Simply retrace steps back to the **Finca Galatzó** and **es Capdellà** to finish.

# WALK 6
*Mola de s'Esclop from Boal de ses Serveres*

| | |
|---|---|
| **Start/Finish** | Km97 on the Ma-10 road above Estellencs |
| **Distance** | 9.5km (5¾ miles) |
| **Total ascent/descent** | 630m (2065ft) |
| **Time** | 3hrs 30mins |
| **Terrain** | Good tracks and paths on the lower slopes, but steep and rocky higher on the mountain, with short scrambles on bare rock |
| **Map** | Alpina Tramuntana Sud |
| **Refreshment** | None |
| **Transport** | None closer than Estellencs: the extra road-walking there-and-back amounts to just over 5km (3 miles). Using the signposted GR221 from Estellencs to Km97 adds 9km (5½ miles) there-and-back, although there are ways of short-cutting the distance. Limited roadside parking at Km97. |

S'Esclop is reasonably easy to climb from a recreational area at Boal de ses Serveres in the public estate of Son Fortuny, above Estellencs. It is mostly a there-and-back walk, but the summit area can be explored using a short, rugged loop, with fine views in all directions. Alternative descents lead to places such as es Capdellà and Ses Fontanelles, for anyone keen to see more of this scenic area.

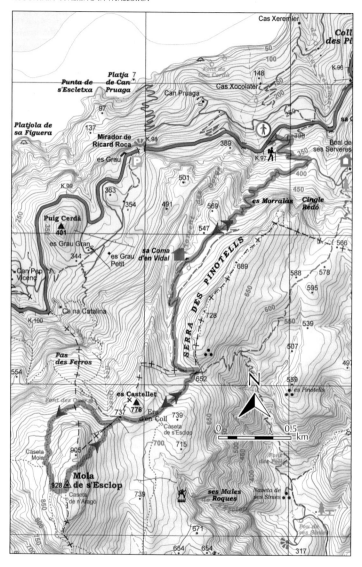

From Km97, where there is a mapboard and signpost at around 300m (985ft), walk up a dirt road onto a wooded slope. Pass a chain barrier and keep climbing, noting the mock paving underfoot while turning a bend. Reach a three-way signpost and turn right. Walk 7 turns left here.

*Cliffs above forested slopes on the way to and from Coma d'en Vidal*

Pass a water tank and follow the bendy track as it climbs, enjoying splendid views of the high cliffs of **es Morralàs**, forested slopes and the coast. The track is very steep and convoluted as it climbs, passing through a formidable wall and fence that once barred access to the mountains.

Keep climbing and pass through another gate, where the gradient eases. The track is flanked by an avenue of trees as it approaches the *refugi* of **sa Coma d'en Vidal**, around 550m (1805ft). This should have been providing accommodation when it was first acquired, back in 2002, but a permanent caretaker might be on-site from 2018. Keep following the track uphill, rising through a fire-damaged forested valley, eventually reaching a gap at 652m (2139ft) beside **Serra des Pinotells**.

Cross a stile over a wall and turn right to continue. Left leads down to Finca Galatzó and es Capdellà, described in Walk 5 and Walk 9. The path climbs, but occasionally has burnt trees lying across it. A ruin lies to the left and an *era*, or circular threshing floor, is crossed at **Era des Coll**.

The path continues across a rugged slope covered in *càrritx*, with the rocky hump of es Castellet rising to the right. A path junction is reached beside a low, tumbled wall on a broad, gentle gap. Left leads directly to the summit of s'Esclop, but it is worth turning right and stepping across the wall instead.

Follow the path as it traverses a slope, passing above a rocky chasm above **Font des Quer**. Take care not to follow a path downhill. Climb past old terraces to reach the ruins of **Caseta de la Mola**, which features another *era* and old terraces at 844m (2769ft). Turning right reveals a path descending to Ses Fontanelles, used on Walk 4. Keep left, or straight ahead, to follow a path across terraces beneath a cliff.

Turn left and tackle some mild scrambling to gain the crest of **Mola de s'Esclop**, then turn either right or left. Right leads quickly to a ruined building that once served as an observatory; left leads to the summit trig point at 928m (3045ft).

Splendid views stretch in all directions, with the neighbouring peak of Puig de Galatzó featuring particularly well.

Descend very roughly north-east from the trig point, watching carefully for the path across bare rock, aiming for the rocky hump of es Castellet. Don't go all the way to it, but reach a vague path junction and turn right for **Era des Coll**. Simply retrace steps back to **sa Coma d'en Vidal** and down to the Ma-10 road to finish.

# WALK 7
*Puig de Galatzó from Boal de ses Serveres*

| | |
|---|---|
| **Start/Finish** | Km97 on the Ma-10 road above Estellencs |
| **Distance** | 10.5km (6½ miles) |
| **Total ascent/descent** | 850m (2790ft) |
| **Time** | 4hrs 30mins |
| **Terrain** | Good tracks and paths on the lower slopes, but steep and rocky higher on the mountain, with short scrambles on bare rock |
| **Map** | Alpina Tramuntana Sud |
| **Refreshment** | None |
| **Transport** | None closer than Estellencs: the extra road-walking there-and-back amounts to just over 5km (3 miles). Using the signposted GR221 from Estellencs to Km97 adds 9km (5½ miles) there-and-back, although there are ways of short-cutting the distance. Limited roadside parking at Km97 (although, of course, walkers without cars don't need to return to their starting point and may use other routes to descend). |

Galatzó is most often climbed from an interesting recreational area at Boal de ses Serveres in the public estate of Son Fortuny, above Estellencs. A combination of paths allows a 'sort of' circular walk, but there is really only one way up and down the steep, rocky, upper part of the mountain, and this is used in common with Walk 8 and Walk 9. Views from the summit are exceptional and wide-ranging.

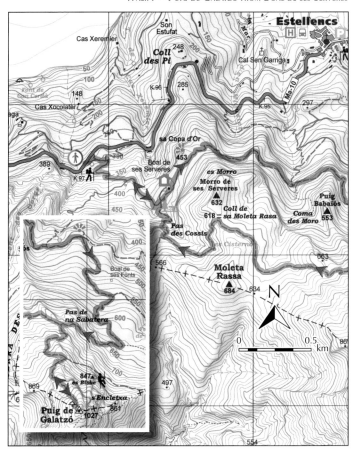

From Km97, where there is a mapboard and signpost at around 300m (985ft),
walk up a dirt road onto a wooded slope. Pass a chain barrier and keep climbing,
noting the mock paving underfoot while turning a bend. Reach a three-way signpost and turn left. Walk 6 turns right here. After an easy stretch, the track climbs
again to reach a picnic area at **Boal de ses Serveres**. There is a signpost here, as
well as *sitges* and a *carboner* hut, all around 410m (1345ft). Take the time to spot
a path behind the hut that will be used during the descent later in the day.

A path approaches a significant junction at Pas de na Sabatera

Follow the track through a gateway and keep right at a junction as marked by a post. Left leads to a tiny *refugi* building. Pass some enormous boulders, then a short spur to the left leads only to a viewpoint. The path descends in bends, which is disconcerting for an ascent route, but this is the correct way, and there are more enormous boulders. Reach a *sitja* and a signpost, but avoid a path heading downhill. The path climbs, then descends gently to 390m (1280ft), where it crosses a valley at another signpost. Again, avoid a path heading downhill.

The path mostly rises gently around the wooded slopes of **Puig Babaiós**, passing another signpost. Watch out for a clearing on the left, where there is a view down to Son Fortuny and Estellencs. Back in the woods, climb past a small ruin and pass several piles of rotting chopped logs where the woodland has been partially cleared.

Reach a three-way signpost and keep right to climb further. The other path passes Font de Dalt, and after 2.75km (1¾ miles) links with Walk 11 to Puigpunyent. The path climbs, passing a marker post beside a *sitja*, then another *sitja* has a signpost where there is a pronounced right turn. Zigzag uphill and eventually the trees thin out and the path crosses a slope of scrub bushes and *càrritx*. A three-way signpost is reached at the **Pas de na Sabatera**, around 720m (2360ft).

The three paths meeting at this point all come and go through small clefts in the rock. Turn left to follow a path up through one of these clefts, then climb as the path bends one way and another on the rugged slope. It eventually levels out for a short way, reaching the concrete base of a demolished hut, where there is a signpost around 820m (2690ft). Pause to enjoy the fine view, then turn right to keep climbing. The other path is used by Walk 8, from Font des Pi and Galilea.

The climb is steep and rugged, and occasionally involves scrambling up bare rock. Take care as height is gained, as there is a lot more rock, and some of the scrambling routes are best avoided in favour of easier and less exposed ones. Simply by climbing ever-upwards, the summit trig point on **Puig de Galatzó** is reached at 1027m (3369ft), and views are remarkably extensive.

Retrace steps carefully downhill, returning to the signpost around 820m (2690ft) and turning left. Continue down to the next signposted junction at **Pas de na Sabatera**, around 720m (2360ft) and turn left. The path is rugged, rising and falling as it crosses the slope, with bare limestone pavement underfoot before reaching a pine tree and a zigzag downhill. Note occasional *sitges*, as well as another stretch of limestone pavement.

The path crosses a slight gap at **Coll de sa Moleta Rasa**, at 618m (2028ft), then descends and passes a well while enjoying fine views. Reach a signposted junction and keep right. Walk 9 joins from the left.

The path winds steep and rugged down **Pas des Cossis** into woodland, reaching the **picnic area** that was passed earlier in the day. Turn left to follow the track downhill, keeping right at a junction with another track. Continue downhill, round a mock-paved bend, to follow a dirt road all the way down to the Ma-10 road near **Km97**.

# WALK 8
*Puig de Galatzó from Font des Pi*

| | |
|---|---|
| **Start/Finish** | Font des Pi |
| **Alternative start/finish** | Galilea |
| **Distance** | 4km (2½ miles) from Font des Pi or 10km (6¼ miles) from Galilea |
| **Total ascent/descent** | 500m (1640ft) from Font des Pi or 880m (2890ft) from Galilea |
| **Time** | 2hrs from Font des Pi or 4hrs from Galilea |
| **Terrain** | Easy roads, tracks and paths on the lower, wooded slopes, but steep and rocky higher on the mountain, with short scrambles on bare rock |
| **Map** | Alpina Tramuntana Sud |
| **Refreshment** | Bar-restaurants at Galilea |
| **Transport** | Buses serve Galilea from Palma and Puigpunyent |

Galilea is a pretty hilltop village with a bus service. It is possible to climb Galatzó from there, but motorists can get much closer by navigating a maze of roads to park at Font des Pi. Of course, motorists would have to return for their cars, but walkers who arrive by bus could finish elsewhere, such as Estellencs or es Capdellà, making the most of the interesting and scenic paths available around the mountain.

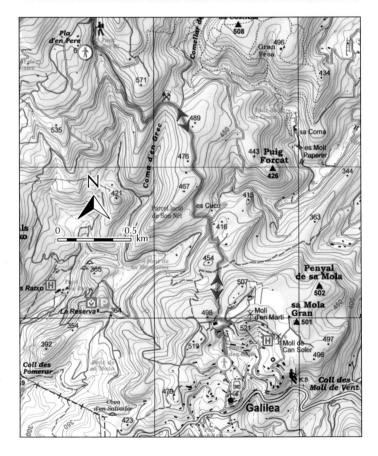

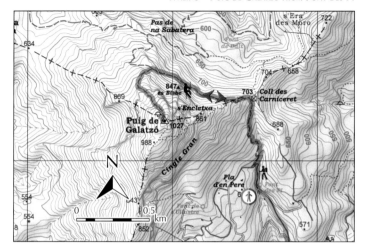

### Starting from Galilea

If arriving by bus, the driver will assume you want to get off near the church in Galilea, but stay on the bus to the highest and final stop in the village. Starting around 450m (1475ft), walk straight up the steep Camí de sa Font from a water pump. The road bends as it climbs, and when the top is reached, turn left along Camí de sa Mola Petita. When the house called Can Juan Petit is reached and the road becomes dirt, turn right along a woodland path to leave the village at 498m (1634ft).

The path soon joins another path on a bend. Turn right and follow it downhill, and it becomes rocky before suddenly reaching a road-end. Follow the road straight ahead, passing a few houses. Go straight through a crossroads at **es Cucu** and climb steeply.

Avoid other roads to right and left, but after curving around the forested valley of **Coma d'en Grec**, turn right up a stony, rocky road that becomes tarmac further uphill. Reach a parking space beside an old water trough at **Font des Pi**, around 550m (1805ft). (This is around 3km (2 miles) from Galilea.)

### From Font des Pi

A clear path climbs through woodland. When it makes a pronounced left turn, turn right up a lesser path. As height is gained, there are glimpses of a fire tower on a gap at **Coll des Carniceret**, but don't be drawn towards it. If anything, keep left while climbing and stay on the path. It is rocky underfoot, with dense scrub

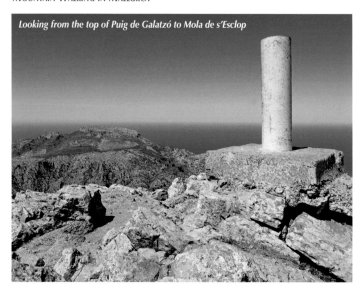

*Looking from the top of Puig de Galatzó to Mola de s'Esclop*

alongside, then cairns are reached on a rocky shoulder around 750m (2460ft). There is a view of Puig de Galatzó looking impossibly steep and rocky.

The path is rather worn, with a crumbling edge, and it needs care as it slices across the steep slopes. Cross a boulder scree, other scree slopes and rocky slopes while climbing. Pass beneath the rock tower of **es Bisbe** (it looks like a bishop wearing his mitre) then continue climbing to reach the concrete base of a demolished hut, where there is a signpost around 820m (2690ft). Pause to enjoy the fine view, then turn left to keep climbing. (Note the path running level ahead, which is used by Walk 7.)

The climb is steep and rugged, and occasionally involves scrambling up bare, polished rock. Take care as height is gained, as there is a lot more rock, and some of the scrambling routes are best avoided in favour of easier and less exposed ones. Simply by climbing ever-upwards, the summit trig point on **Puig de Galatzó** is reached at 1027m (3369ft), and views are remarkably extensive.

Retrace steps carefully downhill, returning to the signpost around 820m (2690ft) and turning right to return to **Font des Pi** and **Galilea**.

Alternatively, turn left and refer to Walk 7 for a route down to Boal de ses Serveres and Estellencs. Another option, on reaching a path junction at Pas des Cossis, is to switch to Walk 9 to es Capdellà.

# WALK 9
*Puig de Galatzó from es Capdellà*

| | |
|---|---|
| **Start/Finish** | Plaça de Bernat Calvet, es Capdellà |
| **Distance** | 23km (14¼ miles) |
| **Total ascent/descent** | 1030m (3380ft) |
| **Time** | 8hrs |
| **Terrain** | Good roads, tracks and paths on the lower slopes, but steep and rocky higher on the mountain, with short scrambles on bare rock |
| **Map** | Alpina Tramuntana Sud |
| **Refreshment** | Bars and restaurants at es Capdellà, drinks machine at Finca Galatzó |
| **Transport** | Buses serve es Capdellà from Palma and Calvià |

Galatzó can be climbed from es Capdellà via the public estate of Finca Galatzó. This used to be strictly private, but has been public since 2006. It offers a long, easy and scenic ascent through a valley, becoming more difficult as height is gained on the steep and rocky upper parts of the mountain. Alternative descents are available, offering walkers the chance to explore attractive and interesting paths on the flanks of the mountain.

The name of es Capdellà derives from 'es cap d'allà', meaning 'the very end'. Start at a crossroads at Plaça de Bernat Calvet, around 130m (425ft). Follow Carrer de Galatzó, which is signposted for the Finca Pública Galatzó. A mapboard and signpost are passed at a junction with Camí del Graner del Delme. The road later becomes a track passing almond groves, olive groves and small farms, reaching a gateway on a gentle, wooded gap beside **Puig Matós**.

A track leads gently down into a marvellous valley, full of fertile red earth, flanked by the towering peaks of Mola de s'Esclop and Puig de Galatzó. Stay on the main track to reach the **Finca Galatzó**.

The **Finca Galatzó** estate, once strictly private, was purchased and opened to the public in 2006. At its centre is an old stone building, dating from the 13th century, built around a courtyard and incorporating a chapel and oil

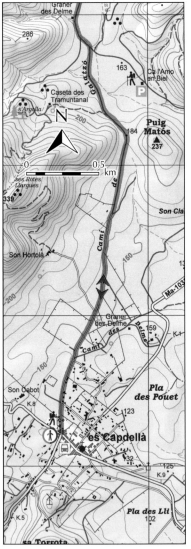

press. The estate is preserved as a traditional mountain farmstead. The valley it occupies is flanked by the mighty mountains of Puig de Galatzó and Mola de s'Esclop.

Keep to the right of the main building to pass beneath an arcade and follow a walled track, which continues through almond groves. Keep to the main track at all times, which means turning right at a junction, as signposted for ses Sínies. The track drops gently into a sparsely forested valley, passing fan palms. Go through a stone gateway and pass two limekilns – one small and one large – both to the left. Wander gently up through the valley of **Comellar de ses Sinies**, alongside the **Torrent de Galatzó**.

Watch out for a *sitja*, *carboner* hut and limekiln on the right. A picnic site is located in the shade of pine trees later, with a reconstructed *sitja* and *carboner* huts. Keep following the track to approach **Pou de ses Sínies**.

There is a junction of tracks just before the *pou*, or well; turn right, then decide whether to make a short detour to the archaeological site of **Naveta de ses Sinies**. Later, avoid a turning to the right, then watch for a marker post and follow a path cut through *càrritx*, winding up a rugged slope and passing above an old trough. Also watch out for a well at **Font des Poll**, hidden on the other side of the path.

A steep and rugged climb includes views of Puig de Galatzó for a while, and some parts of the path feature old cobbles and stone buttressing. There is a view back to the sea at a higher level, and the path climbs past a *sitja* and passes an occasional pine tree. Climb past another *sitja* at a higher level, noting how the course of the old path has been cleared in preference to any other trodden line. Always keep sight of the path, noting another *sitja* to the right, climbing to a signposted junction. The GR221 is signposted to the left, but turn right to continue towards Puig de Galatzó.

The path is steep and gritty as it climbs, then it contours across a slope and passes a *sitja*. Climb a short, steep, rocky slope among pines, then watch carefully as the path makes its way from one solitary pine tree to another while aiming for a broad gap at 588m (1929ft). The narrow path is marked by small cairns as it makes its way through *càrritx* and down to a signposted junction above **Pas des Cossis**.

Turn right to follow the path up around a valley, passing a well, then cross a slight gap at **Coll de sa Moleta Rasa**, at 618m (2028ft). The path continues and a stretch features limestone pavement, as well as passing a couple of *sitges*. There is a zigzag up to a pine tree and another stretch of limestone

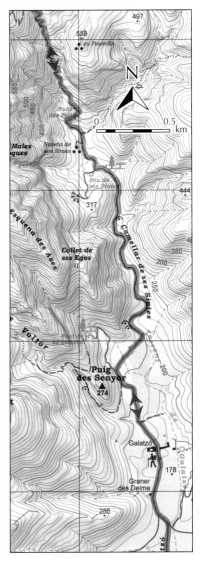

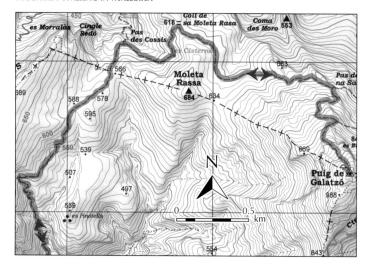

pavement. The path is rugged, rising and falling as it crosses the slope. There is a short descent to a three-way signpost at the **Pas de na Sabatera**, around 720m (2360ft).

*Leaving Comellar de ses Sinies on the way to Puig de Galatzó*

The three paths meeting at this point all come and go through small clefts in the rock. Keep right to follow a path up through one of these clefts, then climb as the path bends one way and another on the rugged slope. It eventually levels out for a short way, reaching the concrete base of a demolished hut, where there is a signpost around 820m (2690ft). Pause to enjoy the fine view, then turn right to keep climbing. (The other path is used by Walk 8, from Font des Pi and Galilea.)

The climb is steep and rugged, and occasionally involves scrambling up bare rock. Take care as height is gained, as there is a lot more rock, and some of the scrambling routes are best avoided in favour of easier and less exposed ones. Simply by climbing ever-upwards, the summit trig point on **Puig de Galatzó** is reached at 1027m (3369ft), and views are remarkably extensive.

Retrace steps carefully downhill to the signpost around 820m (2690ft), from where you can continue all the way back to **es Capdellà**.

A right turn at the 820m (2690ft) signpost offers an alternative finish to Coll des Pi, if a pick-up can be arranged, or to Galilea, to catch a bus. (Reverse the route description for Walk 8 for this route.) Another alternative is to switch to Walk 7 to descend towards Estellencs.

# WALK 10
### *Calvià to Galilea and Puigpunyent*

| | |
|---|---|
| **Start** | Bus stop, Carrer Major, Calvià |
| **Finish** | Bus stop, Galilea or bus stop, Puigpunyent |
| **Distance** | 8.5km (5¼ miles) finishing at Galilea; 9.5km (6 miles) omitting Galilea and finishing at Puigpunyent; or 12km (7½ miles) including Galilea and Puigpunyent |
| **Total ascent** | 400m (1310ft) |
| **Total descent** | 310m (1015ft) |
| **Time** | 3hrs (finishing at Galilea), 3hrs 30mins (omitting Galilea and finishing at Puigpunyent) or 4hrs (including Galilea and Puigpunyent) |
| **Terrain** | Mostly easy roads, tracks and paths with very few steep slopes |
| **Map** | Alpina Tramuntana Sud |
| **Refreshment** | Bar-restaurants in Calvià, Galilea and Puigpunyent |
| **Transport** | Buses serve Calvià from Palma; buses serve Galilea and Puigpunyent from Palma |

The walk from Calvià to Galilea is entirely flanked by private property, so there is just one line available for the path. There are good views along the way, taking in the hilltop village of Galilea, with the pyramidal peak of Galatzó rising beyond. There is an option to omit Galilea or extend the route to descend to the village of Puigpunyent.

When arriving in Calvià by bus, get off at a staggered crossroads at the bottom of Carrer Major, around 120m (395ft). Follow Carrer dels Montcada gently uphill. Turn right at the end to continue along Carrer de Son Mir, later noticing a GR221 signpost for Puigpunyent. Follow the road uphill and it becomes the Camí des Molí des Castellet, running along the foot of a well-wooded little hill called **es Castellet**.

The road leaves town and rises through **Vall Negra**, reaching a mapboard. Turn left as signposted along a broad track called Camí des Pou Nou, climb a slope covered in almond trees, then turn right along a clear path on a wooded slope. Go down through a gateway and pass a concrete *aljub*, then climb a steep and stony path. This bends and climbs along the foot of a cliff. When a path junction is reached, a left turn is signposted for **Aljub d'es Pou Nou**, which is worth visiting, otherwise keep right up a slope of dense scrub to reach an access road beside **Puig de Son Font**.

*Looking from Galilea towards the forested Puig de na Bauçana*

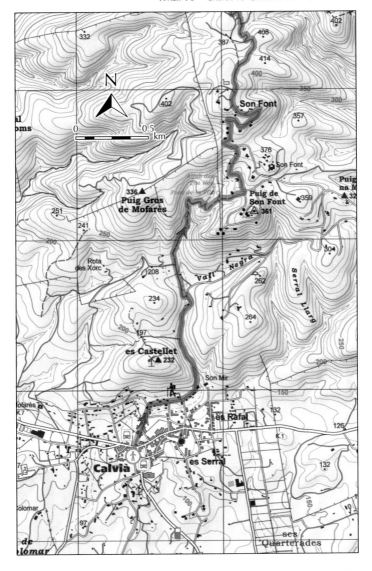

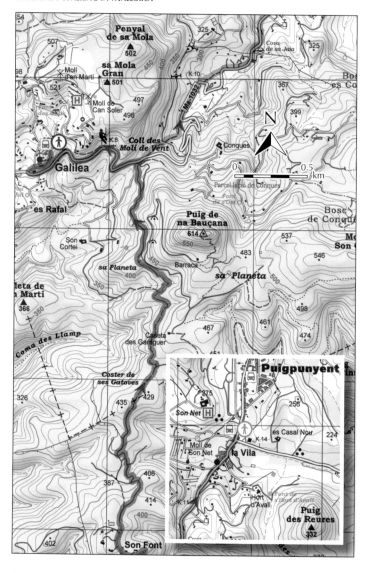

The road is the Camí d'es Pou Nou and there is a glimpse of the south coast. Climb past houses to reach a junction and turn left along Camí d'es Molí Fariner. Follow this bendy road up to another junction and turn left up the Camí de Son Font. The bendy road climbs past some fine modern houses in the **Son Font** estate.

Although a stone gateway is marked as private property, simply follow Camí de na Morruda onwards. There are stout gates at the end of the road at na Morruda, also marked as private property. If the gates are closed, step through a small gateway alongside which allows through access for walkers.

The road runs downhill and quickly gives way to a broad dirt road with a view ahead to the mountain village of Galilea, with Puig de Galatzó beyond. Stay on the dirt road and avoid all other tracks, heading downhill and uphill, with fences and forest on either side.

The track narrows and reaches a gate with a built-in stile. Beyond it, the path passes a mapboard. Continue over a forested crest at **Coster de ses Gatoves**, over 420m (1380ft), with a good view of Mola de s'Esclop and Puig de Galatzó. Keep to the clearest path, which means turning right as marked, then left, to follow a broader path, again with fine mountain views.

The path runs level and passes above some olive terraces. Join a track at **sa Planeta** and continue straight ahead and downhill across the flank of Puig de na Bauçana, reaching another mapboard where a gate with a built-in stile leads onto the Ma-1032 road at **Coll des Molí de Vent**, around 380m (1245ft). At this point, the nearby village of Galilea can be reached by turning left; otherwise turn right and follow the road towards Puigpunyent.

Visiting Galilea is simply a case of walking along the bendy road then turning right to climb to the centre, where there is a small *plaça* and a bar-restaurant beside the church. If finishing here, there is a nearby bus stop. Walking to the top of the village links with Walk 8 to Puig de Galatzó. To continue to Puigpunyent having visited Galilea, walk back along the road to **Coll des Molí de Vent**.

**For Puigpunyent**

Walk down the road a little in the direction of Puigpunyent, then step down to the left as signposted. Steps and a path drop beside a small house and an old cobbled path soon crosses a track. Continue down a broader path to reach a bend on the Ma-1032 road. Keep straight ahead down the road, round a bend, then go down a path on the left to short-cut through another bend. The road runs past orange groves and there is a view of Puig de Galatzó to the left later.

Walk down past a church to reach a crossroads in the centre of **Puigpunyent**, around 210m (690ft). There is a bus stop here, as well as one further up the road beside a modern *plaça*. There are bar-restaurants, and just beside the road to Palma are some interesting heritage structures.

# WALK 11
## Camí Vell d'Estellencs and Camí de Superna

| | |
|---|---|
| **Start/Finish** | Bus stop, Puigpunyent |
| **Distance** | 11km (6¾ miles) |
| **Total ascent/descent** | 520m (1705ft) |
| **Time** | 4hrs |
| **Terrain** | Mostly easy roads, tracks and paths with only a few steep slopes |
| **Map** | Alpina Tramuntana Sud |
| **Refreshment** | Bar-restaurants at Puigpunyent |
| **Transport** | Buses serve Puigpunyent from Palma and Galilea |

There are two interesting old highways that have partly survived modern road building around Puigpunyent. The Camí Vell d'Estellencs, which passes the splendid old house of Son Fortesa and crosses the mountains to Estellencs, links with the Camí de Superna, which crosses the mountains to Esporles. Together they offer an easy circular walk around forested mountainsides, with occasional 'surprise' views.

Start in **Puigpunyent**, around 210m (690ft), either at a bus stop near a crossroads, or a little further uphill beside a modern *plaça*. Walk straight up the Ma-1101 road through the village, and at the top it bends left, then later turns right as signposted for Esporles. Don't follow it, but walk straight ahead along another road and go through black gates to follow the Camí Vell d'Estellencs. This old road climbs towards the palatial old house of **Son Fortesa**, first seen towering above lemon terraces.

Before reaching the house, turn sharp right as marked, up through a gate and into woods. Zigzag up to a gate made of a bedstead, go through it and turn left. Climb to a track and turn right to follow a clear and obvious old track. The track has a buttressed edge as it winds uphill through a pine forest, with a glimpse of Puig de Galatzó ahead.

A broken water channel accompanies the track, so when the track suddenly bends right, follow a rugged path parallel to the old water channel, short-cutting a bend to return to the track near a ruin at **sa Teulera**. Turn left up the track, noting the ruined house of **sa Muntanya** overlooking olive terraces.

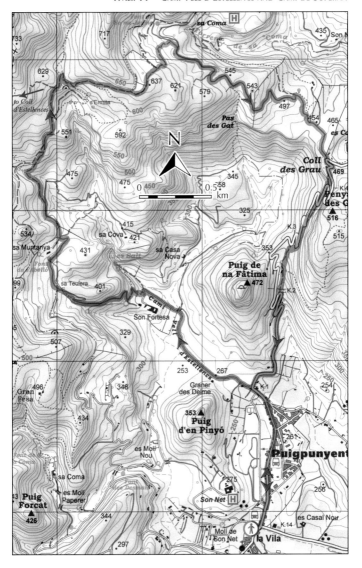

81

Keep right as marked to avoid the house and climb into dense holm oak woodland, reaching a stout gateway in a wall. Go through and turn right as marked, climbing parallel to the wall through the woods. The path is rugged, but at a higher level turn right as marked along a clearer track. When the wall drops to the right, keep climbing along the track to reach a junction on a crest, around 600m (1970ft), where there is a signpost and mapboard. It is worth stepping to the right for a view of Puigpunyent from a rocky edge. Turning left leads to Coll d'Estellencs, where a path via Font de Dalt leads towards Puig de Galatzó.

Keep straight ahead along the track, and when a sharp bend is turned, notice a limekiln. The track climbs a little more, to 637m (2090ft), then it passes through a gateway in a wall. The track is flanked by walls, and the descent passes low, overhanging cliffs with good views of nearby mountains. A straight stretch of the track is both walled and cobbled.

Join a dirt road and turn right to follow it through sparse forest, passing through gateways, sometimes with a view of the nearby *agroturismo* accommodation, sa Campaneta, above the valley of sa Coma, and sometimes with a view of Puig de Galatzó. Gates along the way bear forbidding notices, but the road is available to walkers. Descend to a signposted junction on a bend of the Ma-1101 road at **Coll des Grau**. Turn right to follow the road through a cutting at 469m (1539ft).

Emerge from the cutting and watch for a marker post on the right, where a path short-cuts a bend. Three fairly short paths offer shortcuts through the very bendy road. There is a longer path where the original old highway is completely overgrown; instead of following it, the path drops steeply for a short way to a house, turning left to reach the road a final time. The last road bends have to be followed.

Watch for ceramic plaques for *'es garrover de ses sabates'*, or the '**shoe carob**'. People visiting Puigpunyent used to hang their shoes from a nearby carob tree in order to avoid damaging them in the village!

Simply walk back into **Puigpunyent** by retracing the earliest steps of the day, returning to the bus stops in the centre of the village.

# BANYALBUFAR, ESPORLES, VALLDEMOSSA AND DEIÀ

*A view along the north coast from the Mirador de Can Costa (Walk 15)*

83

Fita del Ram as seen from the summit of Puntals de Planícia (Walk 12)

For several years, the delightful village of Banyalbufar was rather isolated from decent walking opportunities, but that changed in 2016, when a number of paths and tracks were declared public, linking the village with the nearby public estate of Planícia. The estate was once strictly private, but now offers a series of easy walking trails. A popular stretch of the GR221 trail runs through this area, from Estellencs to Banyalbufar and Esporles. There is a plan for the route to continue across the wooded plateau of Mola de Son Pacs and sa Comuna (Walk 14) to reach Valldemossa, then over the mountains again to Deià.

The coastline is rugged, but easily accessible by following a clear track between Banyalbufar and Port des Canonge. A fine circular walk can be made by heading inland to Esporles, then climbing along the Camí de Correu to return to Banyalbufar (Walk 13). Mountain climbs in this area include Mola de Planícia and Puntals de Planícia (Walk 12), which can be reached from Banyalbufar, or the mighty Puig des Teix and other fine summits, which can be climbed from Valldemossa. There are several mountain trails above Valldemossa, including some which require a permit to be obtained in advance on the 'Muntanya del Voltor' estate (such as Walk 15). Other trails are available any time, and the most notable of them is the Camí de s'Arxiduc, or Archduke's Path (Walk 16), which was constructed as a scenic mountain carriageway for the Archduke Lluis Salvador.

The hilltop village of Deià is delightful and is the resting place of the poet Robert Graves. The fisherman's village of Cala de Deià is charming. A fine, rugged coastal walk can be attempted, landslides and rock-falls permitting, and an old path which is now incorporated into the GR221 trail can be followed back to Deià (Walk 18).

# WALK 12

*Banyalbufar and Mola de Planícia*

| | |
|---|---|
| **Start/Finish** | Plaça de la Vila, Banyalbufar |
| **Distance** | 13.5km (8½ miles) or 17.5km (11 miles) including the extension to Puntals de Planícia |
| **Total ascent/descent** | 860m (2820ft) or 1020m (3345ft) including the extension to Puntals de Planícia |
| **Time** | 5hrs or 6hrs 30mins including the extension to Puntals de Planícia |
| **Terrain** | Well marked and signposted tracks and paths at first, but unmarked and sometimes vague paths in dense woodland later |
| **Map** | Alpina Tramuntana Sud |
| **Refreshment** | Plenty of choice at Banyalbufar |
| **Transport** | Buses serve Banyalbufar from Palma, Esporles and Estellencs |

The bulky mountain of Mola de Planícia rises high above Banyalbufar, but it isn't obvious how to climb it. Paths opened as recently as 2016 offer a good approach to the public estate of Planícia, but be warned that much of the ascent is densely wooded and route-finding needs care. The cliff-bound Puntals de Planícia can also be climbed as an optional extra.

Leave Plaça de la Vila in the centre of **Banyalbufar**, at 100m (330ft), and follow the Ma-10 road in the direction of Estellencs. The road rises gently and overlooks well-cultivated terraces. Turn left at a junction where there is a mapboard and signposts, both for the GR221 and local trails. Walk up the steep tarmac road, which later levels out, then climb a steep concrete access road that serves houses. Continue straight up a path, which has stone steps in places and is flanked by drystone walls. Go through a gate in a wall and follow a forested path uphill, passing to the right of the big house of **es Rafal**.

Follow a level path past olive terraces and continue across a slope of pine trees. Reach a three-way signpost and turn left, quickly reaching another three-way signpost to turn right for Planícia. A fine stretch of an old track rises and

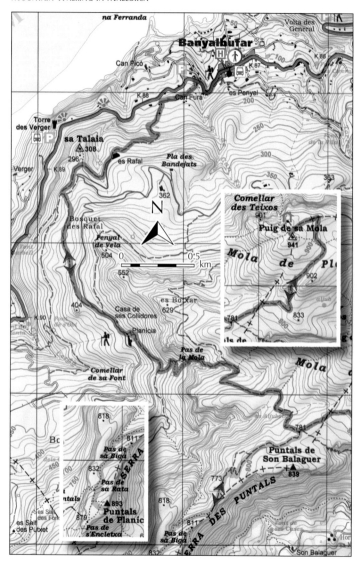

is stoutly buttressed. It gives way to a more rugged path that passes through a gateway gap in a wall. Continue rising past olives and head back into woodland.

Go through a gate in a wall, passing a mapboard. The path joins a track, and by turning right, a house is passed, followed by a gate, to reach a bend on a battered access road that reaches the big old house of **Planícia**, around 420m (1380ft), where there is another mapboard. Even if Mola de Planícia isn't climbed, there are easy signposted trails available at this point.

Go between buildings, round the back of the main house, passing a reservoir beside a huge boulder. Go through a gate and follow a track past a huge holm oak tree. Go through a gateway gap in a wall, reach a junction of tracks and turn left, climbing past a water trough fed by a channel. Pass between rocks while turning right, then take care to spot a *sitja* down to the right of the track. Next, watch carefully for a *sitja* and a couple of cairns just above the track, on the left.

Turn left to follow a cairned path up and across the wooded slope. It leads to a deep rocky cleft in a cliff at **Pas de sa Mola**. The path wriggles up through the cleft and passes through a small gateway gap. Follow the path carefully uphill, passing *sitges*, to reach a track around 660m (2165ft). Take note of this point for the return journey.

Turn right to follow the track, passing a limekiln, *sitja*, a ruin and a collapsed *aljub* (see below) in quick succession. A vague path bends to the right, becoming a clear track again. It rises, but later turns a corner and descends very gently. Watch for **es Aljubets** on the right, which are two stone-built covered water stores.

> Limestone is pervious and allows water to pass through it, seeping through cracks and settling into deep-seated underground aquifers. Throughout the centuries, settlers have dug wells (*pous*), tapped springs (*fonts*) and coaxed rainfall into **stone-built storage tanks** (*aljubs* and *cisternas*), in order to secure sources of water for use throughout the year.

Take care as the path becomes vague again, but when *sitges* are reached, it is seen very clearly as it has buttressed edges and zigzags up through another rocky cleft. Continue onwards, then after passing another *sitja*, note a vague junction of paths on a densely wooded crest above 780m (2560ft). Again, note this point for the return journey. Here it is possible to turn either left or right. Left is for the main route to Mola de Planícia, while right is for the optional route to Puntals de Planícia (see below). (Following a nearby path down to the Vall de Superna reaches locked gates preventing access to the road.)

For the main route, turn left and the path becomes a broad and obvious old track, with some of its buttressing exposed. Pass *sitges* in the dense woodland and note how the track turns distinctly to the left, then more sharply left again as it

*The steep, forested slopes of Mola de Planícia seen near es Rafal*

climbs **Mola de Planícia**. There comes a point when there is a distinct descent, but don't go any further. This point is between twin summits, which lie to the left and right. Left is the highest point, where **Puig de sa Mola** bears a trig point at 941m (3087ft). Right leads to an abrupt cliff edge overlooking Banyalbufar.

For the descent, retrace steps faithfully to the vague path junction on the crest above 780m (2560ft). Either turn right to continue the long, long descent by retracing steps to **Banyalbufar**, or if there is time, consider an extension to Puntals de Planícia.

**Extension to Puntals de Planícia**

The path running straight ahead from the junction is vague as it runs through dense woodland, but it becomes a clear old track. Be sure to follow this track wherever it exists, and follow trodden paths or lines of cairns at other times, in search of the next clear stretch. When the track becomes very stony it zigzags downhill at a gentle gradient, but is very awkward underfoot.

Watch carefully as the path drifts into a valley, then climbs past *sitges*. The path bends beside a cliff edge, close to an overhang. Pas de sa Rata descends here, for those with very good scrambling skills. Keep climbing and head for the highest point on **Puntals de Planícia**, at 893m (2930ft). There are splendid views from an abrupt cliff edge, overlooking the Vall de Superna, towards the mountain of Fita del Ram.

Unless very steep and dangerous down-scrambles are to be considered, the only safe way down is to retrace steps faithfully to **Banyalbufar**.

# WALK 13
*Banyalbufar, Port des Canonge and Esporles*

| | |
|---|---|
| **Start/Finish** | Bus stop, Banyalbufar |
| **Distance** | 24km (15 miles) |
| **Total ascent/descent** | 920m (3020ft) |
| **Time** | 8hrs |
| **Terrain** | Roads, tracks and paths through forest, along the coast, inland and across mountainsides. Mostly easy, but occasionally steep and rugged |
| **Map** | Alpina Tramuntana Sud |
| **Refreshment** | Plenty of choice at Banyalbufar, two bar-restaurants at Port des Canonge, plenty of choice at Esporles |
| **Transport** | Buses serve Banyalbufar and Esporles from Palma and Estellencs |

This is a long walk, but all of it runs along easy roads, tracks and paths. It starts and finishes in the picturesque village of Banyalbufar, taking in a coastal and upland route, but it can be cut in half by catching a bus at Esporles. The route includes interesting paths and tracks that were legally opened to the public only in 2016, after being closed for more than a dozen years.

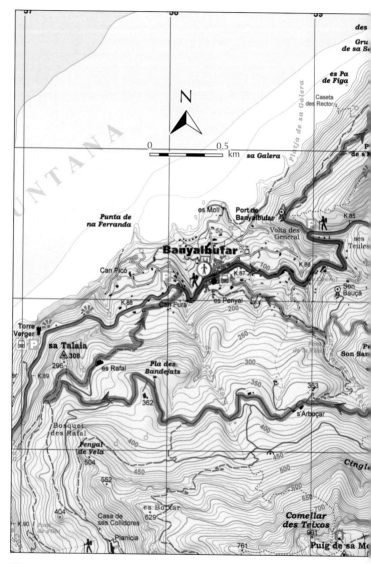

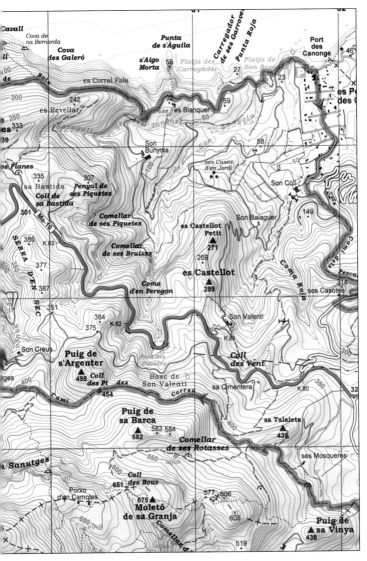

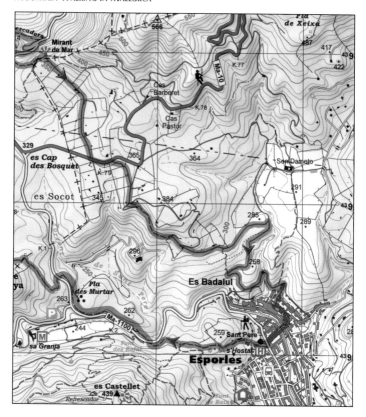

## PUBLIC PATHS

There are 'rights of way' on Mallorca, but whenever a landowner contests their use, it tends to result in years of conflict and recourse to the courts. Tracks and paths above Banyalbufar were regarded as public, but were nevertheless legally closed for many years. However, after a concerted effort and another legal judgement, they were declared public in 2016. They are fully signposted and waymarked and are already being well used by grateful walkers.

Leave the Plaça de la Vila in the lovely village of **Banyalbufar**, around 100m (330ft), by following the Ma-10 road in the direction of Palma. Use pavements where these are available, and note a 'Volta des General' signpost attached to railings on the way out of the village. There is a bus stop at Torrent d'en Roig, and starting here would save 750m (½ mile) of walking. The road is quite bendy as it climbs to a car park on a road bend 1.5km (1 mile) from Banyalbufar. Signposts point along a clear track for Port des Canonge via Volta des General and a gate and ladder stile are passed.

The track passes a couple of junctions where marker posts indicate the most well-trodden route, which is **Camí de Baix**. A boulder sits on the track, preventing vehicle access on the forested slope. Pass a *carboner* hut with a boulder for a roof, and note a *sitja* on the other side of the broad path. Massive boulders lie on a steep slope of pine trees, but the path gradient is always gentle. Take care when passing an overhanging, crumbling cliff at **es Corral Fals**, where falling boulders have smashed into pine trees below the path. The whole cliff is bound to collapse one day!

When the path joins a road, turn left downhill and look to the right to see the big country house of Son Bunyola above olive terraces. A signpost points left along a dirt road that descends gently among pines. It is bendy and very wide in places, but it ends abruptly where a rugged path continues along the coast at **Platja de Son Bunyola**, crossing a pebble beach. There are a number of paths, but keep away from crumbling cliff edges, avoid steps down to boat landings, and follow a path to a small car park at **Port des Canonge**.

*The country house of Son Bunyola on the way to Port des Canonge*

Follow the road closest to the coast, then turn right up a road offering two bar-restaurants. The road rises through several crossroads and leaves the village. When a hairpin bend is reached, turn right along a gravel track as if heading for **Son Coll**. Before reaching a gateway to the property, turn left up a lesser track that has an old water pipeline alongside it. The track later climbs steeply and joins a dirt road. Turn left along the road, then right along a path signposted for Esporles.

The path is the **Camí dels Pescadors** and it is rather rugged underfoot as it climbs a steep, wooded slope. Hardly any of its old stone paving survives, but it is clear and obvious throughout. It levels out briefly, then climbs to a road. Turn right to follow the road uphill, turning left and right bends, then watch for a marker post on the left near **ses Casotes**. A path climbs to **Mirant de Mar**, around 350m, where trees obscure the view.

Walk through a gate beside a building and follow a walled track to the Ma-10 road. Turn left and follow the road past the **Km79** marker, then turn right along a path. This soon joins a track, which in turn runs ahead to join a dirt road. Turn right to follow the dirt road, then as soon as it becomes concrete, go down a stony track that dwindles to a path, then broadens again. When it reaches a junction near a little house, keep right, and stay on the track, which loops back and forth with glimpses of Esporles.

Whenever junctions are reached, stay on the well-used track. This passes cliffs in a valley before reaching a tarmac road. Go through a car park and keep walking down to the end of the road, turning left, then right, then left again to reach the little Placeta des Pla. The GR221 trail is joined here. Turn right to follow it across a bridge and along a road called Carrer Nou de Sant Pere. This leads straight to an imposing church in **Esporles**, on the Ma-1100 road. The town offers a range of services, including buses operating from a stop on Carrer Jaume I. (At this stage 13km (8 miles) have been walked.)

To continue walking, pass to the left-hand side of the church, up the narrow street of Costa de Sant Pere. Climb around 40 stone steps and follow a path beside fields. Pass through a couple of gates and descend to the **Ma-1100** road. Cross the road and an old road bridge, then go up a path and follow a concrete watercourse. The path passes a road junction where the folk museum of La Granja can be seen. Use stone-paved ramps to cross the Ma-1100 road one last time at a rock cutting.

Follow the path into woodland and turn right as signposted to walk up a walled track. The stone paving is partly original and partly restored. The track climbs through a couple of gates and passes a limekiln. Keep left to avoid another track dropping to the nearby house of **ses Mosqueres**. The path is stony where tight zigzags climb a well-wooded slope, then a crest is crossed where there is a GR221 signpost.

The path is easy and gentle underfoot and runs down through **Bosc de Son Valenti**. A wooded gap is crossed at **Coll des Pi**, at 454m (1490ft), where there is a rugged, cobble-paved stretch of track. Later, drystone walls alongside the path have been rebuilt.

*Neat and tidy cultivation terraces flank the village of Banyalbufar*

When a signposted junction is reached, a choice is available: if time is pressing, turn right as signposted for the GR221 and descend to a nearby road, the Carrer de la Font de la Vila, and follow it straight down to the centre of **Banyalbufar**.

To continue with the main route, turn left as signposted for Planícia and have a look at a mapboard that shows paths and tracks that were opened in 2016. The old path being followed was cleared and brought back into use, contouring across a slope, then zigzagging down to a dirt road beside enormous gates. Turn left to follow the road, taking note of marker posts and signposts whenever junctions are reached. The road contours, passing properties such as former farm buildings at **s'Arboçar**. Another pair of enormous gates and a mapboard is reached and the dirt road continues ahead.

Eventually, a three-way signpost is reached. Walk 12 turns left here. By turning right, another three-way signpost is reached, where another right turn leads along the GR221. Follow the path across a slope of pine trees, followed by olive terraces, keeping to the left of the big house of **es Rafal**. Walk down a forested slope and through a gate, then go down a winding path flanked by stone walls, with stone steps part of the way.

Walk down a concrete access track and a narrow road to reach the main Ma-10 road. Turn right into **Banyalbufar** and enjoy fine views of well-cultivated terraces as the road runs gently down into the village. Finish back on the Plaça de la Vila in the centre.

# WALK 14

*Esporles to Valldemossa*

| | |
|---|---|
| **Start** | Plaça d'Espanya, Esporles |
| **Finish** | Plaça de Campdevànol, Valldemossa |
| **Distance** | 9.5km (6 miles) |
| **Total ascent** | 650m (2130ft) |
| **Total descent** | 440m (1445ft) |
| **Time** | 3hrs 30mins |
| **Terrain** | Easy roads and tracks give way to forest tracks and paths that need careful route-finding. Some slopes are steep and rocky. |
| **Map** | Alpina Tramuntana Sud and Central |
| **Refreshment** | Plenty of choice at Esporles and Valldemossa |
| **Transport** | Regular buses serve Esporles from Palma, Banyalbufar and Estellencs. Regular buses serve Valldemossa from Palma, Sóller and Port de Sóller. |

The forested mountains between Esporles and Valldemossa were supposed to be signposted as part of the GR221 many years ago. That never happened, and without waymarks, route-finding needs careful attention across Mola de Son Pacs and sa Comuna. The area is rich in stone-built structures. At the end of the day, Valldemossa's old centre is well worth exploring.

Start beside the church on the Plaça d'Espanya in **Esporles**, around 190m (625ft). Cross the main road and walk along the narrow Carrer Nou de Sant Pere. Cross a bridge and walk through the little Placeta des Pla, heading right as signposted to continue along Carrer de Mateu Font. Turn right to cross a bridge onto the Placeta de sa Taulera, then turn left to follow a road out of the village.

The road suddenly turns left, so leave it and walk straight ahead as signposted up a track. This swings left and narrows, then swings right and leads up to a road. Turn left as signposted along the road and keep straight ahead at a junction to pass a house called Can Nadal. Later, the fine old country house of **Son Dameto** can be seen well away to the left. Follow the road until it runs between stout stone gate pillars marked for **Son Cabaspre**. The 'private' notices only apply to vehicles.

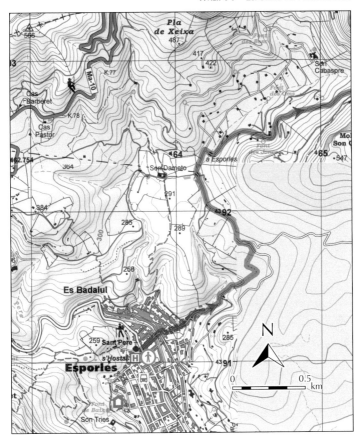

Turn right as signposted along the Camí des Bosc and rise gradually, catching a glimpse of the mansion of Son Cabaspre. The road swings left round the head of a valley, passing a solitary house called Finca Can Buades. Turn right to pass a low gateway and follow the Camí de sa Coma Llobera. This is a broken concrete track, which levels out on **Coll de sa Basseta**, at 455m (1493ft). Turn left up a track marked by a makeshift signpost for Valldemossa, but after only a few paces turn right up a vague, cairned path. There are no more obvious waymarks for the rest of this day's walk, so pay careful attention to the route description.

97

The path climbs a stony slope covered in holm oak woodland, passing a vague junction at a *sitja*, where it is best to keep left. Go up through an awkward gap in a wall and bear right soon afterwards. The path rises to another *sitja* and another junction in a shallow valley. Either direction works, but it may be clearer to turn right and follow a path that makes a rising traverse across a wooded slope. Pass another *sitja* and later join a rugged track. Turn left and later keep straight ahead at a junction.

Simply stay on the clearest track through the woods covering Mola de Son Ferrandell, passing a stone beehive-like bread oven and yet another *sitja*.

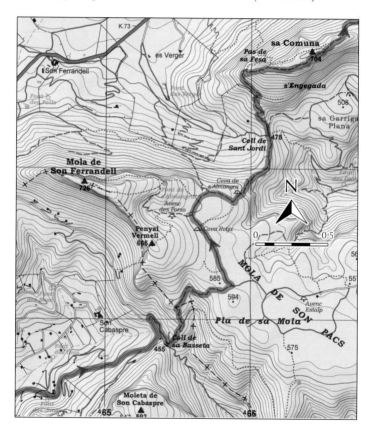

The little town of Esporles is couched in a hollow in the hills

Later, several **interesting features** are arranged well to the left of the track, and are worth a short detour. A stone shelter, Avenc des Porxo, has a barrel-vaulted roof, as does an adjacent *aljub*, where water is stored. There is also another bread oven and a number of nearby *sitges*.

Retrace steps and continue along the track, keeping right at a junction and passing a couple more *sitges*. As the track descends, a wall should be spotted to the left, and it is worth stepping across it for a view from a cliff edge. The manor house of Vistamar stands in solitary splendour among extensive olive groves. Keep walking down the track, which becomes a rugged path passing yet more *sitges*. Swing left and walk down to a wall and fence in a rocky cleft. It is important to find this cleft, which is one of the few breaches in the cliffs surrounding the wooded plateau.

At the foot of the cleft, drift left across a wooded slope, then follow a wall and fence down to **Coll de Sant Jordi** at 478m (1569ft). Turn left to go through a metal gate in the wall then turn right to climb a broad, clear path flanked at first by a wall and a fence.

The path narrows at a higher level and zigzags up a steep and rocky slope. Keep to the clearest path, although it can be vague at times. There are occasional views down to Vistamar and back to Mola de Son Ferrandell, as well as in the other direction to Palma, Randa and the distant Serra de Llevant. However, it is

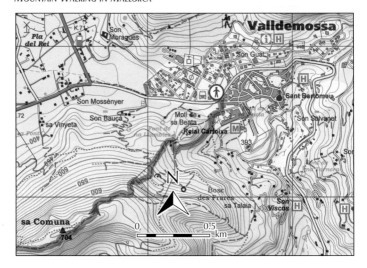

difficult to find good viewpoints on **sa Comuna**, whose well-wooded summit rises to 704m (2310ft).

Pass a couple of crude stone huts and go through a gap in a wall. Take care while following the rugged path through holm oak woodland, where thrush-hunters occasionally operate. Pass *sitges* and the path becomes much clearer, zigzagging down a steep and rocky slope. There are glimpses of Valldemossa below, but these are lost as the path passes an *aljub*.

Continue straight downhill and the path swings right across a rocky, mossy, wooded slope. Go through an iron gate in a wall and follow the path to a covered *cisterna* beside a ruined building. Turn left and the path drops straight downhill, passing through a gateway gap in a wall.

Continue downhill and pass through another gap in a wall, then the path is fenced. Catch a view of Valldemossa, then eventually, a house is reached near **Font de na Llambies**. Pass a gate, turn right down a dozen stone steps and go through a broken stone archway.

Follow a concrete road to the left, which later passes through another stone arch beside Finca Son Mossenya, passing an old windmill that has been converted to a dwelling at Es Molinet. Proceed straight ahead to visit the Reial Cartoixa, a 14th-century royal palace. (Frédéric Chopin and George Sand spent *A Winter in Mallorca* there.) Turn left along Carrer de Uruguay to reach the main road and bus stop in **Valldemossa**, around 400m (1310ft).

# WALK 15
*Valldemossa and Talaia Vella*

| | |
|---|---|
| **Start/Finish** | Plaça Campdevànol, Valldemossa |
| **Distance** | 8km (5 miles) or 9.5km (6 miles) including extension to Mirador de na Torta |
| **Total ascent/descent** | 370m (1215ft) or 420m (1380ft) including extension to Mirador de na Torta |
| **Time** | 3hrs or 3hrs 30mins including extension to Mirador de na Torta |
| **Terrain** | Good paths throughout, mostly in woodland, and occasionally rocky |
| **Map** | Alpina Tramuntana Central |
| **Refreshment** | Plenty of choice at Valldemossa |
| **Transport** | Regular buses serve Valldemossa from Palma, Deià, Sóller and Port de Sóller |
| **Note** | This route is entirely within the stewardship area and requires a 'permit', which can be obtained by making a call on tel 619 591985 and giving your details. See also the website muntanyadelvoltor.com. |

For many decades walkers used a number of paths to climb into the mountains from Valldemossa. Under the 'Muntanya del Voltor' land stewardship project, permits are now required for certain paths and visitor numbers are restricted. The woodlands are being managed and a fine old well has been restored. A mountaintop refuge stands on Talaia Vella and viewpoints have also been restored.

Leave **Valldemossa**, around 400m (1310ft), from the bus stop on Plaça Campdevànol. Walk past the taxi stand, along Carrer Rector Joan Mir, and turn right when the Camp de Futbol is reached. Climb through a crossroads and later turn left up Carrer de les Oliveres, which climbs beside olive terraces. At the very top of the road, continue up a rugged path, entering woodland and climbing to a gate with an information hut after it. This is where your permit will be checked.

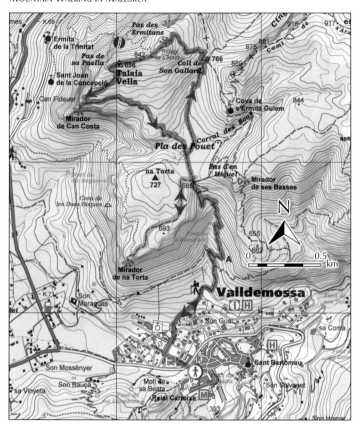

Without a permit, it is still possible to turn right on reaching the gate and follow Walk 16 or Walk 17.

The path beyond the hut is broad and bendy, climbing steadily up a wooded slope until it reaches two gateway gaps in two drystone walls that are close together, at 685m (2247ft). Go through both gaps and walk very gently downhill to reach a level area called **Pla des Pouet**. Turning right along a path after the first gap links with Walk 16 near Mirador de ses Basses. Reach a well, but also notice many heaps of stones among the woods, then watch carefully as paths head in two directions – but this isn't immediately apparent.

## LAND STEWARDSHIP PROJECT

The 'Muntanya del Voltor' land stewardship project is being watched with interest by other estates in Mallorca. Essentially, the aim is to reduce and control visitor numbers, and help the land to recover from previous overuse. There is no denying that the area above Valldemossa has improved in quality and suffers much less damage. Visiting walkers find it easy to apply for permits, and are given information about alternative walking routes if they didn't apply, or if permits weren't available on their chosen day. Be sure to check the website muntanyadelvoltor.com in advance.

Take the right-hand path and climb a wooded slope until a gap is reached at **Coll de Son Gallard**, at 766m (2513ft). Turning right up a path links with Walk 16 near Cova de s'Ermità Guiem. The gap bears notices, a signpost and a stone seat. Turn left to follow a stony path up rocky slopes with good woodland cover. The path climbs and zigzags, and it is possible to overshoot the top without realising, so watch for a path on the left leading to a summit building; the **Refugi de s'Arxiduc**. Enjoy views, then descend and continue along the crest of the mountain to climb a little to the top of **Talaia Vella**, where there is a trig point at 856m (2808ft).

Follow the path downhill, roughly along the crest at first, then it drops to one side before approaching a crenellated viewpoint called the **Mirador de Can Costa**. When seen from the main road far below, this looks like a fortress. Continue along the path, passing a *sitja* and a beehive-like bread oven. Gradually descend, passing another *sitja* on the way back to the well on **Pla des Pouet**. Keep

*The Refugi de s'Arxiduc stands high on Talaia Vella*

walking straight ahead to return to the gateway gaps in the two drystone walls that were passed through earlier.

## Extension to Mirador de na Torta

Immediately on reaching the gap in the first wall, turn right to follow a vague path that quickly becomes clearer. It rises a little, then descends gradually, eventually reaching a viewpoint at **Mirador de na Torta**. This is a splendid perch overlooking Valldemossa. Backtrack to the gaps in the walls.

From the wall gap, keep retracing steps back down to the information hut and **Valldemossa**.

# WALK 16
*Valldemossa, Puig des Teix and Camí de s'Arxiduc*

| | |
|---|---|
| **Start/Finish** | Plaça Campdevànol, Valldemossa |
| **Distance** | 13km (8 miles) or 15km (9¼ miles) including the extension to Puig des Teix |
| **Total ascent/descent** | 635m (2085ft) or 820m (2690ft) including the extension to Puig des Teix |
| **Time** | 5hrs or 5hrs 45mins including the extension to Puig des Teix |
| **Terrain** | Mostly clear and obvious roads, tracks and paths, although some short stretches are vague, steep, stony or rocky |
| **Map** | Alpina Tramuntana Central |
| **Refreshment** | Plenty of choice at Valldemossa |
| **Transport** | Regular buses serve Valldemossa from Palma, Deià, Sóller and Port de Sóller |

The Camí de s'Arxiduc, or Archduke's Path, is a remarkable 19th-century track high in the mountains above Valldemossa. It runs within easy reach of Puig des Teix and crosses other summits. It was designed by Archduke Lluís Salvador so that he could enjoy splendid views, and is planned to become part of the long-distance GR221 trail. On the descent, pause for quiet reflection at the Cova de s'Ermità Guiem.

Leave **Valldemossa**, around 400m (1310ft), from the bus stop on Plaça Campdevànol. Walk past the taxi stand, along Carrer Rector Joan Mir, and turn right when the Camp de Futbol is reached. Climb through a crossroads and later turn left up Carrer de les Oliveres, which climbs beside olive terraces. Turn right along Carrer dels Ametlers, which is also signposted as a public footpath. The road later changes its name to Carrer Hongria and descends to a junction.

Turn left to follow Carrer Xesc Forteza, which becomes Carrer Toscana. Later, turn left again along a clear track signposted as a public footpath. There are gates along this track, as well as other tracks heading right and left, but simply keep straight ahead. Steep forested slopes rise to the left and olive terraces fall to the right. Look back to catch attractive glimpses of the Reial Cartoixa palace in Valldemossa. Eventually, pass a gate and cattle grid at es Cairats, turning left at a track junction.

Pass a small ruined building at **Font de na Ropit** and keep straight ahead at a junction. The forested valley of **Coma des Cairats** features holm oaks, pines and tangled ground scrub, with cliffs towering above. The track climbs a couple of sweeping bends, passing wooden gates and a chunky stone stile.

A signpost is passed, and the track keeps climbing to the right. Pass notices explaining about limekilns and charcoal-burning. The track becomes steeper as it climbs and several tight bends are covered in concrete. Pass a picnic site at **Font des Polls** and the track climbs to the Refugi de Son Moragues (marked on maps as **Refugi des Cairats**).

The track passes a **snow-pit** that was constructed on the orders of the Archduke Lluis Salvador. Unfortunately it was built too low on the mountain, around 780m (2560ft), and failed in its purpose.

A rugged, stony path continues climbing, soon levelling out on a fine terrace with good views back down the valley. Climb again, and as the path levels out again above the forested slopes, note a couple of cairns on the right where a path heads off-route to Puig des Teix.

### Extension to Puig des Teix
The rugged path soon involves a short rock scramble, followed by an awkward ladder stile over a wall. Notices state that it is private property beyond, but watch how many walkers take any heed. The path later crosses a track then becomes rocky as it climbs. Bare rock features around a trig point at 1063m (3491ft) on **Puig des Teix**. Enjoy views towards Puig de Galatzó then retrace steps to the cairned path junction.

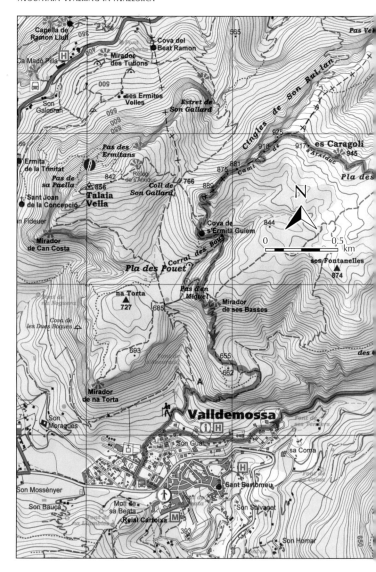

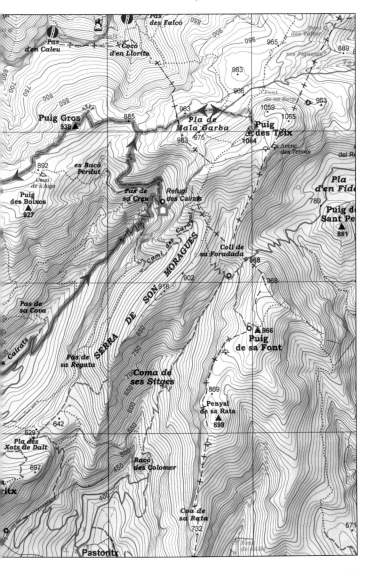

The last high stretch of the Camí de s'Arxiduc before descending

The path being followed is the Camí de s'Arxiduc, or Archduke's Path. Although rather rugged for horse-riding these days, it is very popular with walkers. Simply follow the clear path as it zigzags a short way up to the summit of **Puig Gros**, at 938m (3077ft). Views are remarkably extensive, stretching coast-to-coast as well as through the Serra de Tramuntana.

Walk across a broad dip where there are pines and *càrritx*. Continue gently uphill to a broad gap and a signposted junction beside a large cairn and a few pines at **Pla des Aritges**, at 908m (2979ft). Walk 17 is joined here and a shortcut is available by turning left to reach Mirador de ses Basses and return to Valldemossa. Turn right and follow a clear and obvious path uphill.

Cross a summit at 941m (3087ft) and look across a slight gap to a more prominent summit of bare rock. This is **es Caragolí**, rising to 945m (3100ft). Pass left of it, but note a rugged path on the right which leads to the summit in only a couple of minutes. A stone tablet commemorates Archduke Lluis Salvador.

Climb again for a short way and watch carefully for a couple of cairns and a post, where a path drops to the right. This is Walk 17, which descends to Deià. However, stay on the main path, which more or less runs along the mountain crest with only minor ascents and descents, offering splendid coastal views. The last summit is 889m (2917ft). Zigzag down a wooded slope, reaching the curious cave hermitage of **Cova de s'Ermità Guiem**. A ladder stile might be noticed to the right of the path, but this should only be crossed if a permit has been obtained. It links with Walk 15.

Follow a trodden path down a wooded slope that becomes quite rocky. Carefully turn around a rock-step and zigzag down into a valley. Reach a *sitja* where there are two paths marked for Valldemossa. The right-hand path enters an area where permits are required, but this is allowed, so long as walkers turn sharp left as indicated by a signpost, and climb to pass through a gate at **Pas d'en Miquel**. The left-hand path is more direct, starting easily by rising across a wooded slope. Go up a step of jammed boulders, then the path is squeezed, with cliffs above and below. Continue through woods and descend a little to join a clear path just above a gate at **Pas d'en Miquel**.

Follow the path uphill a short way, or maybe climb a little further to reach the rocky viewpoint of **Mirador de ses Basses**, but be sure to spot signs that indicate a path on the right, marked for Valldemossa. Zigzag steeply down a wooded slope on a gritty path.

Eventually level out, then go down past a collapsed *aljub* and a well to reach a junction with a clearer path. Walk 17 is joined here. Turn right to follow the path through a gate and zigzag down a wooded slope to reach another gate with an information hut on the other side. Walk 15 passes the hut.

Turn left to continue down a rough and rocky path to a road called Carrer de les Oliveres, passing olive terraces. Turn right at a junction, then retrace the earlier steps of the day, down the road to the Camp de Futbol, then left into **Valldemossa**.

# WALK 17
*Valldemossa to Deià*

| | |
|---|---|
| **Start** | Plaça Campdevànol, Valldemossa |
| **Finish** | Bus stop, Deià |
| **Distance** | 10.5km (6½ miles) |
| **Total ascent** | 610m (2000ft) |
| **Total descent** | 870m (2855ft) |
| **Time** | 4hrs |
| **Terrain** | Mostly along obvious mountain paths, but some stretches can be vague, as well as being steep, stony or rocky |
| **Map** | Alpina Tramuntana Central |
| **Refreshment** | Plenty of choice at Valldemossa and Deià |
| **Transport** | Regular buses link Valldemossa and Deià with Palma, Sóller and Port de Sóller |

There are at least four popular paths, plus variants, leaving Valldemossa that could be used to climb into the mountains, but there is only one path descending to Deià – and it is a truly remarkable mountain path. The following route could be varied by combining with Walk 15 (with a permit) or Walk 16 (at any time). The scenery in the high mountains is outstanding. Valldemossa and Deià are linked by the same regular bus service.

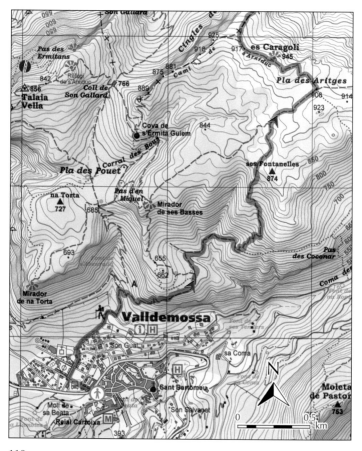

Leave **Valldemossa**, around 400m (1310ft), from the bus stop on Plaça Campdevànol. Walk past the taxi stand, along Carrer Rector Joan Mir, and turn right when the Camp de Futbol is reached. Climb through a crossroads and later turn left up Carrer de les Oliveres, which climbs beside olive terraces. At the very top of the road, continue up a rugged path, entering woodland and climbing to a gate with an information hut after it. Don't go through the gate, but turn right instead. With a permit to pass the hut, part of Walk 15 could be used as an alternative ascent.

The path is signposted for Deià and it zigzags up a steep, wooded slope with occasional views of Valldemossa. Go through a gate, where a signpost points ahead for the Ruta de Catalina Homar. Watch carefully to spot a path on the left, where Walk 16 descends, offering an alternative ascent. The path runs level, and even downhill a little as it passes wooded valleys, but later it starts climbing again.

When a *sitja* is suddenly reached, turn left up a less obvious path. This climbs steeply and is marked by cairns. Leave the woods to cross an open area of asphodels, then approach a low rock outcrop and step up through a gap, back into woodland near **ses Fontanelles**.

Later, there is a rocky area where the path is vague in places, so watch for cairns. A junction is reached with a clearer path; turn right to follow it. Turning left offers a shorter walk, descending via the Mirador de ses Basses to return to Valldemossa. The path rises clearly to a broad gap and a signposted junction beside a large cairn and a few pines at **Pla des Aritges**, at 908m (2979ft). Walk 16 is joined here.

Turn left and follow the clear and obvious path, **Camí de s'Arxiduc**, or Archduke's Path, uphill. Cross a summit at 941m (3087ft) and look across a slight gap to a more prominent summit of bare rock. This is **es Caragolí**, rising to 945m (3100ft). Pass left of it, but note a rugged path on the right which leads to the summit in only a couple of minutes. A stone tablet commemorates Archduke Lluís Salvador.

Climb again for a short way and watch carefully for a couple of cairns and a post, where a path drops to the right. This is trodden and cairned, but it needs to be followed carefully. Pass a stand of holm oaks, watching for a tight left turn into more holm oaks. It is *essential* that this path is located and followed faithfully, as it provides the only safe descent to Deià via the Cingles de Son Rul.lan.

The path turns right and begins to drop steeply. Once underway, the path features well-engineered zigzags that should be followed faithfully, whether down through woods, hugging the base of overhanging cliffs, or crossing open slopes. There are views of the village of Deià, the substantial old country house of Son Rul.lan and the distinctive pierced headland of sa Foradada.

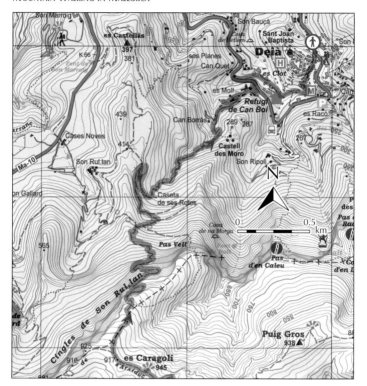

Don't follow any spur paths, but stay on the main path, which later zigzags fairly easily down a steep, boulder-strewn, wooded slope. The path crosses two *sitges* fairly close together. Go down more zigzags then turn right at a junction to pass a bread oven, *sitja* and a *carboner* hut. The path rises slightly to pass these, then, as it descends again, notice a bathtub-like water trough carved into a huge boulder on the right.

The path is broad and clear, turning left at another *sitja* with a limekiln alongside. The track finally leaves the woods and crosses ancient olive terraces with a view towards Deià. Don't go through a gateway, but turn sharp right along an obvious track to stay on the olive terraces. The track descends in long and lazy zigzags down the terraces, where a rough cobbled track could be used as a shortcut.

*A path through asphodels on the slopes of ses Fontanelles*

Watch for stone steps leading down from the track before it becomes overgrown with *càrritx*. A sloping terrace path passes a stone archway. Have a look inside with a torch to find a well at the end. The path bends left, then it is necessary to step down to the left along another old, cobbled path. The path is often overgrown with *càrritx*, while old terraces of olives and carobs are overgrown with pines. However, there is only one path and it is easy to follow, regardless of its meanderings.

Later, the path slices across the side of a valley with a view towards Deià, then the solitary house of **Can Borràs** is seen, surrounded by lemons. The path winds downhill towards it, passing through a stout stone gateway. Turn right down an access track, which becomes a narrow, winding road leading down to a hotel called **es Molí**.

When the main Ma-10 road is reached, don't be tempted to turn right for a direct approach to Deià. Instead, turn left gently downhill along a wooden walkway beside the road. Pass a bus stop just before the Restaurante Can Quet, and turn right down a minor road. Keep straight ahead at a junction and walk uphill to reach another junction. The **Refugi de Can Boi** stands to the right, around 140m (460ft).

Turn left at the junction beside the refuge to continue into Deià. On the way uphill, turn left up another road then turn left again up a flight of almost 90 stone steps, called Calle Costa d'en Topa. These overlook terraces of oranges before reaching a road called Carrer es Porxo. Walk straight ahead to pass the post office then head left to reach the main Ma-10 road near the bus stop in **Deià**, around 180m (590ft).

# WALK 18
*Deià coastal walk*

| | |
|---|---|
| **Start/Finish** | Bus stop, Deià |
| **Distance** | 13.5km (8¼ miles) |
| **Total ascent/descent** | 500m (1640ft) |
| **Time** | 5hrs |
| **Terrain** | Coastal paths that vary from easy to exposed and precarious, suffering from rock-falls and landslides. Later, easy roads, tracks and paths are followed. |
| **Map** | Alpina Tramuntana Central |
| **Refreshment** | Plenty of choice at Deià; restaurants or cafés at Cala de Deià, Béns d'Avall, Son Bleda and Son Mico |
| **Transport** | Regular buses serve Deià from Palma, Valldemossa, Sóller and Port de Sóller |
| **Warning** | This route suffers from rock-falls and landslides, making some parts dangerous. People have died when the path has been particularly bad, so it is essential to use wise judgement when faced with awkward stretches. |

Despite the potential dangers of rock-falls and landslides, this is a very popular route. The coastal scenery is particularly splendid in places. Once Béns d'Avall is reached there are places offering refreshment along the route, and options abound to alter the route by heading for Sóller, Port de Sóller, or back to Deià.

Start at the bus stop in the lovely hilltop village of **Deià** and follow the road only a short way in the direction of Sóller. Turn left down a narrow road as signposted for Sóller, and the road soon ends at a school. Continue down a track called Camí de sa Vinyeta, winding down olive terraces with plenty of marker posts.

Cross a winding road three times using stone ramps and steps. When the road is reached a fourth time, turn right along it and walk down to a linear car park. Continue down a stone-paved track to reach the lovely little rock-walled harbour of **Cala de Deià**, where there are a couple of bar-restaurants.

A beautiful, rugged little fishing cove at Cala de Deià

Walk back up the track to find a mapboard and stone steps. Climb the steps to reach a path intersection and turn left as signposted for Sóller via Béns d'Avall. Enjoy fine views from a terrace, then turn right at a path junction just before a little house. Enjoy fine views of the white rocks of **Códols Blancs**, then take care as some walkers drop steeply when they should aim to stay on a level path.

The way forward is mostly well wooded, but there are views at intervals. Pass a well, followed by a viewpoint at the foot of a private flight of steps. There is a distinct dip in the coast path, then note steps leading down to a rocky inlet, but continue along the path to pass a stone picnic table.

Watch for signposts, cross a ladder stile and pass another stone picnic table. Later, pass below a house in the woods at **es Canyaret**. This is directly below Llucalcari; a huddle of houses and a hotel best seen from the main road. Further along the rugged, wooded slope, note a slipway down to the left at **s'Escar**. Cross a ladder stile and pause to spot a viewpoint ahead, at a higher level.

### WARNING

The way ahead is subject to constant change due to landslips and fallen trees; take care when faced with a choice of paths, as some of them lead to eroded slopes, or are blocked. Always be ready to double back in search of the best-trodden paths.

Take care when climbing towards the viewpoint, as some older paths have crumbled away, and new ones have been trodden.

After the viewpoint, descend carefully to cross below a chasm. When a wall and fence are reached, descend a steep, crumbling slope with care to find a makeshift stile. Keep an eye on the path and its many obstacles, and the view ahead reveals a sheer cliff at **Penyal des Colomer**. Be sure to start climbing, taking in a very short rock scramble, in order to pass above the cliff and cross a ladder stile. There are no problems beyond this point.

Go down past a small stone hut and a ruin. Cross a ladder stile and follow a clear path, then when it ends go up stone steps to follow a more rugged path. Drop to a concrete road and follow it uphill past a few houses, passing behind the **Béns d'Avall** restaurant. After the road becomes a dirt road, watch carefully

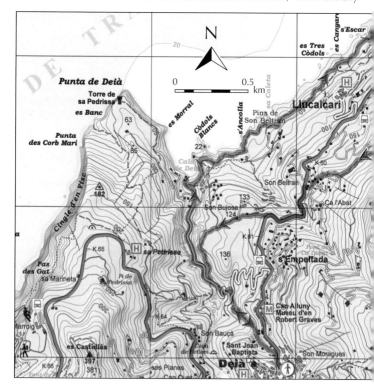

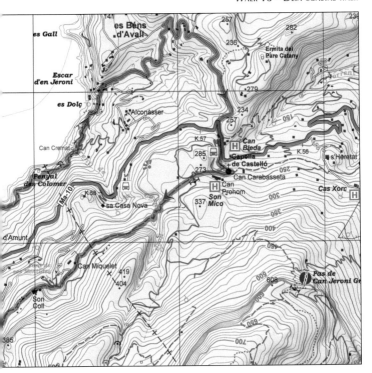

to spot a marker on the left, where a very short path with a few steps links with a tarmac road.

Turn right to follow the road uphill in broad bends, eventually reaching a signposted junction. Turning left here will allow you to follow the GR221 trail to Port de Sóller or Sóller. Turn right to reach a busy bend on the Ma-10 road, and turn left for **Son Bleda** (Can Bleda on the map) and a hotel bar-restaurant, with a bus stop nearby.

There are many ways to finish this walk and a network of old paths is available. One of these runs through the grounds of Son Bleda and descends to Binidorm, where further options are available in the Sóller valley. Cross the main road from Son Bleda, and walk up dirt road used by the GR221, reaching the **Capella de Castelló**. Turning left leads to a link with Walk 19 that can be used to reach Sóller. Turn right at the chapel and walk up to the fine old house of **Son**

**Mico**, where fresh orange juice and delicious cakes are served. The view from the garden stretches across Vall de Sóller to Puig de Bàlitx, Puig Major, Puig de l'Ofre and es Cornadors.

Follow a track from Son Mico, through a gate and up to a point where a large, bare *era* (threshing circle) lies to the right. Continue along an olive terrace and through a gateway, levelling out among pines around 310m (1015ft). Zigzag down a well-buttressed path, pass the base of a cliff and go through a rocky cleft.

Pass a *sitja* and huge boulders among holm oaks, and pass the base of another cliff. Rise near **Can Miquelet** then descend and cross a narrow access road. Continue down a rugged old cobbled path, passing a signpost where the **Font de ses Mentides** is indicated downhill.

Don't go to the *font*, but climb a restored stone-paved path, levelling out to pass the large house of **Son Coll**, followed by a small house. The path descends by degrees and later levels out on a wooded terrace, where there are views of Punta de Sóller, Llucalcari and Cala de Deià. A rugged path leads down to a road, which continues down past olive terraces. Watch for a path dropping down stone steps from a road bend, between two houses, to reach the Ma-10 road.

Turn left along the bendy road and follow it past Km60.7, where an old cobbled path is signposted on the right. Follow this and it quickly links with an access road, crossing a cattle grid to approach the fine country house of **Son Bujosa**, among orange groves. Markers show the way past a nearby building and a track continues gently downhill.

Switch to a path, crossing a level olive terrace, then follow it downhill to reach a ladder stile and a road. This point was passed early in the day, so turn left and simply follow the waymarked GR221 as it climbs, short-cutting road bends, to return to **Deià**. Alternatively, another signposted path leaves the road, formerly used by fishermen, which leads into Deià close to the Refugi de Can Boi.

# SÓLLER, PORT DE SÓLLER, FORNALUTX AND BINIARAIX

The rocky crest of Penyal des Migdia has to be followed on Walk 25

Looking from Biniaraix back to the twin peaks of es Cornadors (Walk 23)

The Vall de Sóller is one of the most popular walking areas of Mallorca. There are plenty of low-level walking routes, and some link easily with paths and tracks running high into the mountains. The whole valley is surrounded by mountains, but it isn't always obvious how to approach them. Editorial Alpina publishes a 1:15,000-scale map of the Vall de Sóller, which is very useful when unravelling a network of paths and tracks in the area. In the summer, from April to October, a bus service operates along the Ma-10 road to Cúber and Lluc, bringing even more routes within reach.

The rugged crest of Serra d'Alfàbia (Walk 23) towers above Sóller and there is really only one path offering access. Walkers sometimes attempt other approaches, but find access barred. The spectacular canyon of Barranc de Biniaraix provides splendid access to and from several mountain routes, and its stone-paved zigzag path is amazing, with the domes of es Cornadors towering high above.

The rocky peak of Penyal des Migdia towers above Fornalutx, and is the highest point that walkers can reach on Mallorca (Walk 25), with neighbouring Puig Major being occupied by the military. Bear in mind that the ascent is steep and rocky, and careful route-finding is required. The same warning goes for the circuit and ascent of Puig de Bàlitx (Walk 22), where the terrain is particularly difficult.

Several old stone-paved paths and flights of stone steps have been cleared of undergrowth and signposted as walking routes. Many of them can be combined to offer walks across the lower slopes of the mountains. Look out for them around Sóller, Port de Sóller and Fornalutx (Walks 19 and 20). Parts of these old paths and tracks have been incorporated into the long-distance GR221 trail. Another old route can be followed through the Bàlitx valley to an attractive cove at Cala Tuent (Walk 21), provided that a ferry is available, or alternative transport can be organised at the end.

# WALK 19

*Camí des Rost and Camí de Castelló*

| | |
|---|---|
| **Start/Finish** | Bus station, Sóller |
| **Distance** | 6km (3¾ miles) or 7.5km (4¾ miles) with the extension to Son Mico |
| **Total ascent/descent** | 280m (920ft) or 300m (985ft) with the extension to Son Mico |
| **Time** | 2hrs or 2hrs 30mins with the extension to Son Mico |
| **Terrain** | Easy signposted roads, tracks and paths, although occasionally steep |
| **Map** | Alpina Tramuntana Central |
| **Refreshment** | Plenty of choice at Sóller; hotel restaurant at Cas Xorc |
| **Transport** | Regular buses serve Sóller from Palma, Valldemossa, Deià and Port de Sóller; vintage electric trails serve Sóller from Palma |

Two old stone-paved paths are easily linked on the wooded slopes rising to the west of Sóller. The Camí des Rost and Camí de Castelló are splendid heritage paths that are tangled together with the convoluted course of the vintage electric train, Ferrocarril de Sóller. Halfway round the walk an extension to the lovely old house of Son Mico is possible, as well as a link with Walk 18 to Deià.

Leave the bus station in Sóller by walking back up to the main Ma-11 road, turning left at a roundabout to reach a Repsol filling station. Cross the road to find a signpost for Deià and the Camí de sa Costa d'en Llorenç. Follow the road past a hotel called **Can Coll**. The tarmac later gives way to a gravel track, which soon becomes a gravel path in woodland. Go through a gate and the path becomes more rugged, then over 200 stone steps climb, twist and turn to reach a signposted junction.

Keep right and keep climbing, and the **Camí des Rost** eventually joins a track on a wooded slope. Most turnings off this track are blocked by tall gates, so keep walking ahead as marked at a couple of other junctions. Eventually, reach a road and signposts near **s'Heretat**, where a short extension might be considered.

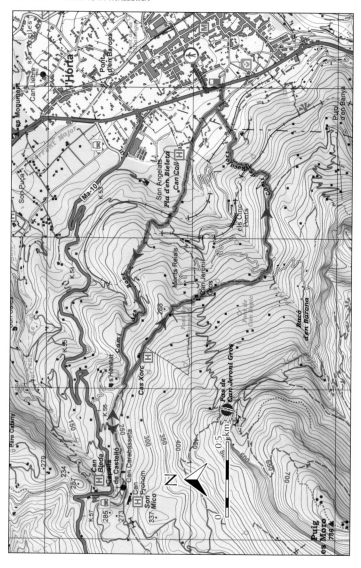

Descending past orange groves to Sóller, with mountains beyond

**Extension to Son Mico**

Cross the road and follow a track round a corner, then continue along a path on an olive terrace, with some cobbled stretches. Reach a bend on a track, where the **Capella de Castelló** stands. The track is part of the long-distance GR221 and all sorts of options become available. Turning right downhill, for instance, leads to Son Bleda and a choice of three signposted paths that lead back to Sóller or Port de Sóller. However, turn left and walk a short way up the GR221 to the fine old house of **Son Mico**, where fresh orange juice and delicious cakes are served and the view from the garden stretches across Vall de Sóller to Puig de Bàlitx, Puig Major, Puig de l'Ofre and es Cornadors. The GR221 can be followed to Deià – see Walk 18. Afterwards, retrace steps to the signpost near s'Heretat and turn right for Ca's Xorc.

If not visiting Son Mico, turn left up the road to reach **Ca's Xorc**, a fine hotel around 260m (855ft), with a lovely garden where refreshments can be enjoyed. Continue past the hotel, and the road gives way to a track that descends steadily. Watch carefully for a marker that indicates a path downhill.

Pass between two big houses at **Can Jeroni Gros**, going through a gate, then turning left downhill to find paths signposted to left and right. Turn right and follow a path past olive terraces, then rise across a slope of pines. Reach a concrete road below the gates of Can Paies.

Go down the concrete road a little, follow a path a short way, then go back onto the concrete road. This becomes a stony track, then another path continues, eventually reaching a signposted path junction. Although the Camí de Castelló can be followed further, turn left downhill along the Camí de Rocafort. The path is cobbled and bendy, soon catching views of Sóller, then crossing a bridge over a railway line.

123

## FERROCARRIL DE SÓLLER

Inaugurated in 1912, this vintage electric train runs northwards from Palma to Bunyola. It then passes through 13 tunnels beneath the Serra d'Alfàbia, the longest of which is almost 3km. It spirals down to Sóller, where it links with a vintage electric tram, opened in 1913, to Port de Sóller. It is a bone-shaking and expensive ride, but worth it at least once for the experience. For timetables, tel 971 752051 or 971 752028, www.trendesoller.com.

Continue down through a gate and the path becomes a concrete track, which joins a road. Go down the road and walk across the railway line, then follow the road down to a junction and turn right to return to the main road at the Repsol filling station. Simply walk back into **Sóller** to finish.

# WALK 20

*Sóller, Fornalutx and Mirador de ses Barques*

| | |
|---|---|
| **Start/Finish** | Plaça de sa Constitució, Sóller |
| **Distance** | 8km (5 miles) or 10km (6¼ miles) including the extension to Mirador de ses Barques |
| **Total ascent/descent** | 300m (985ft) or 400m (1310ft) including the extension to Mirador de ses Barques |
| **Time** | 3hrs or 3hrs 30mins including the extension to Mirador de ses Barques |
| **Terrain** | Mostly low-lying cultivated land, with wooded slopes rising above. Roads, tracks and paths are generally easy, but occasionally steep. |
| **Map** | Alpina Tramuntana Central |
| **Refreshment** | Plenty of choice at Sóller and Fornalutx; bar-restaurant at Mirador de ses Barques |
| **Transport** | Regular buses serve Sóller from Palma, Valldemossa, Deià and Port de Sóller. Vintage electric trains serve Sóller from Palma. Few buses link Sóller with Fornalutx. Summer buses serve Mirador de ses Barques from Sóller and Port de Sóller. |

Signposted and waymarked roads, tracks and paths link Sóller with the lovely village of Fornalutx. An easy circular walk leads through citrus groves, up and down olive terraces, as well as in and out of woodlands, often with fine views of the surrounding mountains. An optional extension climbs to the viewpoint of Mirador de ses Barques.

The Plaça de sa Constitució is in the centre of **Sóller**. Leave it by following the narrow Carrer de sa Lluna, whose pavements have been polished by constant use. Pass small shops and turn left along Carrer de la Victòria 11 Maig, signposted for Binibassí and Biniaraix. Don't cross a bridge on the left, but keep straight ahead to cross another bridge, Pont dels Ases. Continue straight along Avinguda d'Asturies and cross yet another bridge.

Turn right at a football ground, Camp d'en Maiol, as signposted for Biniaraix along Camí des Murterar, beside a bouldery riverbed. Follow the road upstream to a bridge called Pont de Can Rave, but don't cross it. Instead, turn left as signposted for the GR221, walk up the road and turn right as signposted. The route returns here later in the day. From a crest on this road, Camí de s'Ermità, enjoy a view from Penyal des Migdia, round the high mountains to Puig de l'Ofre, es Cornadors

*Morning sunlight and shadow over Sóller, on the way to Fornalutx*

125

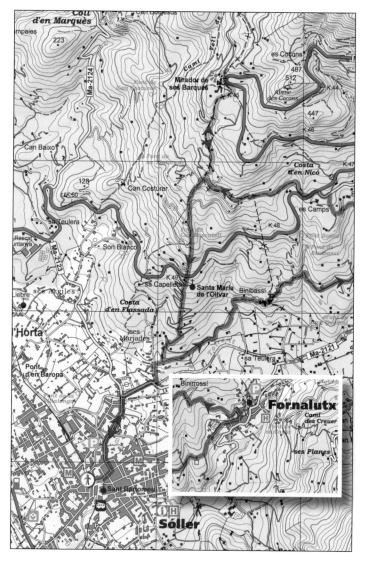

and the rugged crest of Serra d'Alfàbia, back to Sóller and Coll de Sóller, with citrus groves filling the valley. The road runs down, up and down again, to where the tarmac ends.

Turn left up a track to the gates of Can Bac, then turn right up a cobbled path to reach **Binibassí** and its huddle of charming villas. Turn left up cobbled stone steps, as signposted for Fornalutx. Keep climbing until a junction is reached, then turn right, go through a gate and walk downhill between olive terraces.

Join a concrete road and follow it straight ahead, passing the Cementiri Municipal and a village mapboard on the way into **Fornalutx**. Keep straight ahead, following the stone-paved Carrer Joan Albertí Arbona, reaching a five-way junction of streets, around 150m (490ft).

Carrer de sa Plaça leads straight to the central square, otherwise turn left up Carrer des Toros to continue walking. When the stone paving ends, turn left up a concrete road as signposted for Tuent. This is Camí de Bàlitx, which passes a big house called La Bisbala, continuing past olive terraces.

Short-cut a bend on the road by using a short flight of stone steps, then continue climbing up a longer flight of steps. Watch for marker posts to spot other shortcuts, rising past olive terraces and patchy woodlands. The narrow road leads from **Binirrossí** to another road, where a left turn leads quickly to the main Ma-10 road.

Turn left and walk a short way down the road, then turn right up a signposted path. This rises and falls gently as it follows terraces across a slope. Despite crossing land used for a multitude of purposes, there are no barriers, gates or stiles. When the path joins a concrete track, simply walk straight ahead until a junction is reached, around 300m (985ft), and a choice is available.

### Extension to Mirador de ses Barques

A signpost points right, beside a gate and ladder stile. A rugged path climbs past olive trees and goes through a gate to the left of a house. Walk up a track until a marker post indicates a right turn up some steps. A clear, rough-cobbled path climbs a partly wooded slope.

When a signposted path junction is reached, go through a gate and continue climbing towards the Ma-10 road. Turn left to walk parallel to the road, with a cable alongside. Reach a car park and bar-restaurant at **Mirador de ses Barques**, around 400m (1315ft). Climb onto a viewpoint to catch a glimpse of Port de Sóller. Walk 21 to Cala Tuent starts here. Retrace steps back downhill.

Turn left at the junction to follow a concrete track until it turns right. Walk straight down a rugged path to land on another stretch of concrete track, and follow this past a house called Son Roca. A junction is reached with another path, called the

Costa d'en Flassada, so keep left and keep walking straight downhill. The path crosses a dirt road again and again while descending, then cross the Ma-10 road.

Follow the path a short way downhill, and the gates of **sa Capelleta** stand to the left. The modern chapel in view is Santa María de l'Olivar des Fenàs, while sa Capelleta is an odd, small stone building opposite. Keep following the path straight downhill, short-cutting numerous bends on a road that is partly patched with concrete, but mostly a dirt road. Towards the bottom, turn right to follow a stretch of the road, then short-cut the final bends as marked, pass a couple of buildings and land on a tarmac road. This road was used earlier in the day; simply turn right, then left, and retrace steps back into the centre of **Sóller**.

# WALK 21
*Mirador de ses Barques to Cala Tuent*

| | |
|---|---|
| **Start** | Bus stop, Mirador de ses Barques |
| **Finish** | Jetty, Cala Tuent |
| **Distance** | 10km (6¼ miles) or 11km (6¾ miles) including sa Fàbrica detour |
| **Total ascent** | 330m (1080ft) or 480m (1570ft) including sa Fàbrica detour |
| **Total descent** | 730m (2395ft) or 880m (2885ft) including sa Fàbrica detour |
| **Time** | 3hrs or 3hrs 30mins including sa Fàbrica detour |
| **Terrain** | Mostly along easy dirt roads, tracks and paths, but some of the paths are steep and rugged |
| **Map** | Alpina Tramuntana Central and Nord |
| **Refreshment** | Bar-restaurant at Mirador de ses Barques; orange juice at Bàlitx d'Avall; bar-restaurant at Cala Tuent |
| **Transport** | Summer buses serve Mirador de ses Barques from Port de Sóller, Sóller, Lluc, Pollença and Port de Pollença; daily summer ferries (conditions permitting) at 4.55pm from Cala Tuent to Port de Sóller – tel 971 630170, barcoscalobra.com |
| **Note** | This popular walk needs careful planning. Summer buses can be caught to Mirador de ses Barques. Getting away requires a pick-up, a taxi (more than €60 to Sóller), or a ferry. Joining a guided walk with arrangements already made could be a good idea. |

Easy tracks and paths lead through a pleasant valley, passing three old country houses. After crossing a mountain gap a high-level coastal path is followed, with the option to drop down to visit an abandoned hydro-electric power station. Cala Tuent is charming, but be sure to have a sound 'exit plan' in place before reaching it.

Start at the bus stop, car park and bar-restaurant at Mirador de ses Barques, on the Ma-10 road high above Sóller, around 400m (1315ft). Climb to the top of a stone-built viewpoint for a glimpse of Port de Sóller. A signpost beside the car park indicates the path for Tuent, Sa Costera and Bàlitx, climbing stone steps. Pass a house on a concrete track, around 490m (1610ft), and walk through an avenue of holm oaks. Pass a few houses, go down through a gate and walk past olive trees, later joining a dirt road called the **Camí Vell de Bàlitx**. Turn right to follow this across a cattle grid, while drawing close to the big house of **Bàlitx d'Amunt**.

Go down through a gateway in a tall wall before reaching the house, following the dirt road until it suddenly bends left. Going down the bendy dirt road and turning left at a junction links with Walk 22 to Puig de Bàlitx. Walk along a cobbled path as marked, going down steps. Just before reaching the **Font de Bàlitx**, turn left down a slippery path, then later turn right to follow the path back down to the dirt road to pass the big house of **Bàlitx d'Enmig**.

*Bàlitx d'Enmig is the middle one of three old country houses*

The dirt road continues, passing some pines. When a small house is seen to the left, turn left as if to visit it, then turn right as signposted along a rugged path.

The path passes olives, then goes through a gateway gap in a wall to enter a forest. Zigzag down a cobbled path with steps, emerging from the trees to continue down a track, keeping to the right of the big house of **Bàlitx d'Avall**. Accommodation and freshly squeezed orange juice are available.

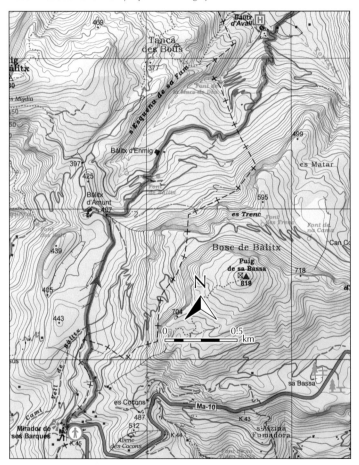

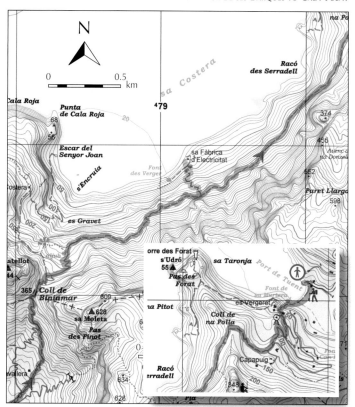

Cross a ford or footbridge across a streambed and walk up a rugged track. Turn right along a signposted, cobbled path, rising to a gateway in a wall. Don't go through the gateway, but follow the path uphill and go through a higher gateway to reach a bend on a track. Follow the track further uphill on the forested slope, keep right at a junction and cross the **Coll de Biniamar**, at 365m (1198ft).

Walk down the bendy track among holm oaks, using a cobbled path to short-cut a bend. Keep an eye on markers at junctions, and when a signpost is reached, note an arch off to the left. The path eventually leaves the woods and undulates across a steep and rugged slope. At one point, a three-way signpost points down-hill for **sa Fàbrica**, where a hydro-electric power station once operated.

**Detour to sa Fàbrica**
Anyone descending to explore sa Fàbrica will have to climb back the same way, and the path is quite rugged. The distance is less than 1km there-and-back, with an elevation change of around 150m (490ft).

The path to Cala Tuent involves some climbing as it passes along the foot of some cliffs. After passing through a succession of old gateway gaps, the path crosses **Coll de na Polla** and descends into a forest. Join a track near a house and turn left to follow it, but soon turn left down another path, back into the forest. Turn right along a track, but watch for steps down to a signposted path junction. Turn left to reach a tall mast and go down steps, passing a house to reach a road-end restaurant at **es Vergeret**.

Drop from the road as marked and the path is soon signposted as it crosses the road at a lower level. Continue down rugged steps to find a signpost beside the bay of **Port de Tuent**. The few houses that can be seen on the wooded slopes above the bay constitute Cala Tuent, and there are no services for visitors. Walk across a crunchy shingle beach to reach a small jetty and another road-end. If a ferry is due – usually at 4.55pm in summer, conditions permitting – then the sailing to Port de Sóller is an enjoyable experience, with splendid views of the coastal cliffs throughout.

# WALK 22
*Port de Sóller and Puig de Bàlitx*

| | |
|---|---|
| **Start/Finish** | Bus stop, Port de Sóller |
| **Distance** | 15km (9¼ miles) |
| **Total ascent/descent** | 750m (2460ft) |
| **Time** | 6hrs |
| **Terrain** | Easy roads, tracks and paths at the start and finish, but very rough and rocky terrain in the middle, requiring scrambling and careful route-finding |
| **Map** | Alpina Tramuntana Central |
| **Refreshment** | Plenty of choice at Port de Sóller; orange juice café above s'Illeta |
| **Transport** | Regular buses serve Port de Sóller from Sóller, Deià, Valldemossa and Palma. An electric tram links Sóller and Port de Sóller (starting and finishing at the tram adds 1.5km (1 mile) to the day's walk). |

Puig de Bàlitx is located close to Port de Sóller, and keen walkers will naturally want to climb it, but the way isn't obvious. Very few routes are open to walkers, and even those that are open prove to be very difficult to negotiate in places. The route described here is a circuit around the mountain, plus an ascent to the summit. An interesting and spacious cave, Cova des Migdia, is located high on the mountain.

*The little island of s'Illeta, seen from the orange juice café*

The bus stop at **Port de Sóller** is on a roundabout just outside the resort, and just before the mouth of the Túnel de sa Mola. If arriving on the electric tram, walk back along the line from the terminus, and turn left inland at the taxi stand, passing one roundabout to reach another roundabout where the bus stop is located.

From the bus stop, take the road signposted for Jumeirah, quickly turning right at a junction, also signposted for Jumeirah. Follow Carrer de Belgica steeply uphill, but at a left-hand bend, keep straight ahead up a narrow road. Climb past olive terraces and on **Coll de S'Illa** there is a gate on the left for Torre Picada. Visiting the tower makes a pleasant short walk for another time. There are houses along the road, but avoid their access roads. Note the leaning rock tower called **Penyal Bernat**.

The tarmac gives way to a dirt road, and when it climbs and bends, a couple of paths short-cut the bends. Some of the later bends are concrete, then a notice warns of dangers ahead. An orange juice café has a fine terrace overlooking the little island of s'Illeta. There is a locked gate alongside, but just to the right is

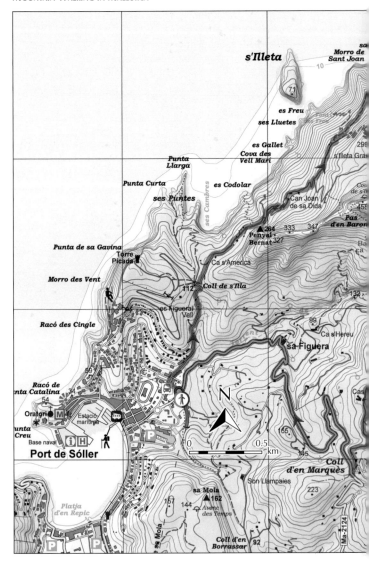

s'Illeta

sa
Morro de
Sant Joan

es Freu

ses Lluetes

299

s'Illeta Gra

es Gallet
Cova des
Vell Mari

Punta
Llarga

Punta Curta

es Codolar

ses Puntes

ses Cambres

Can Joan
de sa Dida

455

Pas
d'en Baron

264

Penyal
Bernat

333    347

327

Ba
ca

Punta de sa Gavina

Torre
Picada

Ca s'America

Morro des Vent

112    Coll de s'Illa

132

es Figueral
Vell

Racó des Cingle

99    Ca s'Hereu

sa Figuera

59

N

Racó de
nta Catalina

34

54

Oratori    M

Estació
maritima

unta
Creu

Base naval    i   H

Port de Sóller

0              0.5
                    km

145

Cas

65

Coll
d'en Marqués

Son Llampaies

223

sa Mola

sa Mola

162

157    144    Avenc
des Temps

Ma-2124

Platja
d'en Repic

Coll d'en
Borrassar    92

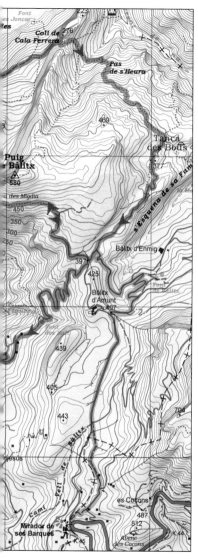

a metal hurdle that serves as a stile. Things get difficult beyond this point and progress gets very slow.

Follow the bendy track downhill and go through a gap in a wall, then fork right. An easy path traverses a forested slope around 150m (490ft), but there are fallen trees, boulders and rock-fall. Pass a cave of sorts beneath enormous jammed boulders. Cross a *sitja*, then look ahead and above to spot a rock tower. The path steps up onto bare rock and becomes very narrow. Later, it is necessary to scramble up the rock. Watch carefully to follow the path as it zigzags up towards the rock tower, passing right of it, where there is a tumbled wall on a gap at **Coll de Cala Ferrera**.

Walk down into a valley, taking great care to spot the line of the path, and also look at the rock wall on the other side of the valley, to spot where the rock is more orange in hue, and hopefully spot a diagonal line across the face. When the path rises to the rock wall, there is a scramble up a gully, which is the start of the **Pas de s'Heura**.

The path zigzags up the rock and is rather vague in places, but leads to another rock scramble. The route appears to reach an impasse, but turn left and walk carefully across sharp-edged blades of rock, then traverse through *càrritx* and scramble up another gully. There is more awkward terrain, and more scrambling above it.

A level and easy path runs through *càrritx*, past a wall, to reach a fine, stone-built, buttressed path. Unfortunately, this is very short and it only crosses a little rocky crest, with yet more awkward terrain beyond. When old olive terraces are reached, around 380m (1245ft), follow a path down past them and turn right at a junction to reach a track. Follow the track gently uphill and pass a stone hut, **Tanca des Bous**, in a pleasant hollow in the hillside.

The track was pushed into this wild area in connection with a water supply scheme, but look carefully and stretches of an old cobbled path can still be seen nearby. The track climbs and passes a gate in a wall, then levels out around 400m (1310ft), with views of Puig Major in the distance and the Bàlitx valley closer to hand. Another track drops to the left but keep walking straight ahead. The track dropping to the left links with Walk 21 and offers an exit to Mirador de ses Barques, in 3km (2 miles). Pass through tall gates to reach a junction of tracks at 397m (1302ft).

Turn right and follow the track to a big turning space. A path continues onwards up a rugged slope, turning left at a junction. Follow the path carefully to reach a **cave** with a fig tree growing out of it.

This is **Cova des Migdia**, which as its name suggests, is best entered at midday when the sun shines directly into it. It is huge and features impressive stalactites and stalagmites.

Look more carefully for the continuation of the path up a rocky, scrubby slope, passing a few pine trees. The summit of **Puig de Bàlitx** bears a trig point at 580m (1903ft). The act of stepping to the trig point reveals a sudden and vertiginous view from a cliff edge, so take care making that step! Enjoy the views, then retrace steps carefully back to the **cave**, continue down to the turning space, and follow the track back to the junction beside the tall gates.

Turn right to walk downhill from the gates. The way is vague at first, but an obvious track forms and winds its way down past olive terraces. It appears to end suddenly at **Font des Salt**. Cross a stream and walk up an enclosed path, then cross a makeshift stile that is marked as private. The path is private, but is regularly used by walkers, who must respect the property. Follow the path past olives and go through a gate near a little house, close to a large house called Can Pati.

Follow a track that is part concrete and part stony, down through gates until a minor road is reached on **Coll d'en Marquès**, around 190m (625ft). Signposts will be noticed, pointing to places as far removed as Fornalutx, Cala Tuent and Sóller. However, to finish this walk simply turn right and follow the road downhill in loops and bends to **sa Figuera**, then continue more directly back to the bus stop just outside **Port de Sóller**.

# WALK 23

*Serra d'Alfàbia and Cornador Gran*

| | |
|---|---|
| **Start/Finish** | Plaça de sa Constitució, Sóller |
| **Distance** | 16.5km (10¼ miles) |
| **Total ascent/descent** | 1200m (3935ft) |
| **Time** | 7hrs |
| **Terrain** | Steep and intricate paths lead to a high and exposed rocky crest where careful route-finding is required. The descent uses a popular stone-paved path. |
| **Map** | Alpina Tramuntana Central |
| **Refreshment** | Plenty of choice at Sóller; bar and café at Biniaraix |
| **Transport** | Regular buses serve Sóller from Palma and Port de Sóller. Few buses link Biniaraix with Sóller, and in any case they operate outside the village. Anyone desperate to avoid the 2km road-walk to Sóller could consider taking a taxi. |

This is a long and hard walk, with no options for an easy exit. For those with stamina, it provides a great challenge and splendid views on a clear day. Attention to route-finding is needed on the ascent, untangling a network of paths, and along the rocky crest, where there aren't any paths. The descent, however, is plain and obvious, through the remarkable gorge of Barranc de Biniaraix. The road-walk at the end of the route could be avoided by finishing at Biniaraix.

The Plaça de sa Constitució is in the centre of **Sóller**. Go behind the church to follow the narrow Carrer de Reial. Take the second turning left to follow Carrer de la Unió. Turn right up Carrer de Pau Noguera, noting a signpost just after a junction, for Ses Tres Creus. Pass a cemetery, or *cementiri*, and keep climbing.

Reach a junction with a track called Camí de Can Petra, where a signpost for Ses Tres Creus points up a narrow, cobbled path. Climb this, then when the signposted route turns right along a road, simply cross the road and keep straight ahead up a path. Ses Tres Creus is a monumental stone construction further up the road.

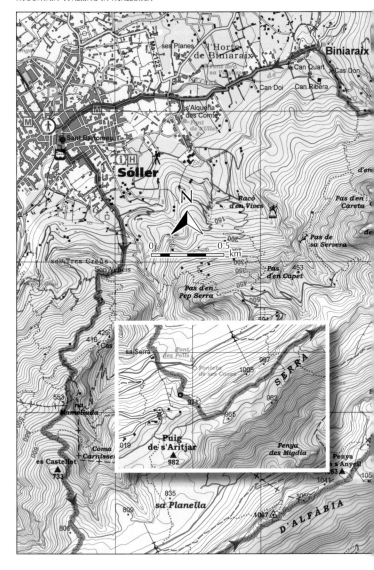

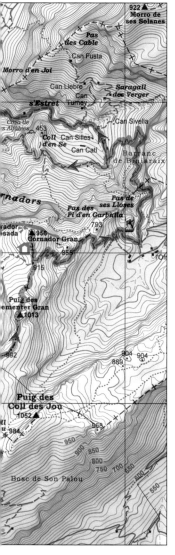

The path has rugged stone steps and later there is a tiny house, number 47. Keep climbing, drifting right and left to follow the path to a level ridge at **Son Vencis**, where there is a ruin. Keep to the right of the ruin, climbing a well-wooded slope of old olive terraces. Another little house, Ca'n Selles, lies to the left.

The path climbs further, generally drifting to the right, then pass above another little house. Keep climbing, again generally drifting right, then the path becomes rather vague as it winds uphill, but is never too far from a drystone wall. Climb past a rugged rock face among holm oaks and go through a gateway gap in a wall.

There is a more open stretch ahead, beyond **es Castellot**, but watch carefully for the path, looking for red paint dots on rocks. If these are lost, go back and find them as they offer the most reliable guidance.

The path winds back and forth as it climbs a slope of pines, scrub and *càrritx*, and there are no shortcuts. There are occasional views of communication masts on the skyline, but there are obstacles to overcome before they are reached. A level area of *càrritx* needs careful attention as the red dots are mostly hidden. Look carefully to find a rickety gate in a fence, go through it, then try and spot a path up a rocky slope.

Keep left of a little house of **sa Serra** and cross a track. Follow a narrow path uphill and cross another track, then take care finding a way through a network of vague paths on a steep, scrubby slope. Looking straight uphill, the way is barred by a rock face; keep left to pass this, then pick a way up through a rugged valley,

139

Cloud hides Corandor Gran, but leaves Puig de l'Ofre in view

where it helps to locate an old snow-pit. Looking at the communication masts, aim for a rocky gap to the left of them. A fence on the gap is easily crossed at 971m (3186ft).

Go straight down the other side, through a gap in a tall fence, down past awkward rock and càrritx, to land on a trodden path. Turn left to follow this, which is also used by Walk 30. It was once a vehicle track, but is becoming overgrown. It descends, then rises and passes through another gap in the tall fence to make a traverse of **Serra d'Alfàbia**. The path is reasonably obvious at first, and offers fine views over Sóller. When it becomes vague, look for red dots, but bear in mind they run out later. Rugged ground is crossed while passing just below a **trig point** at 1067m (3501ft).

Cross a rocky gap and the path descends and climbs rugged slopes to cross another rocky gap on the mountain crest. Following the crest onwards requires great care, primarily following small cairns among scrub and bare rock on the way past **Penya de s'Anyell**. Go through a gap in a wall and cross an expanse of bare rock, and maybe include the summit of **Puig de Son Palou** at 1044m (3425ft). Walk 30 descends to the right, towards Coll des Jou.

The correct route crosses another wall, later followed by the hump of **Puig de Sementer Gran** at 1013m (3323ft). A proper path begins to form on the descent, reaching a junction where there are stone tablets. Keep left and walk up to a small *refugi*, which offers basic shelter for those who come prepared. Keep climbing and the summit of **Cornador Gran** is crowned with a cairn at 958m (3143ft). Enjoy splendid mountain views.

Retrace steps down past the *refugi* and turn left at the path junction marked by stone tablets. There is no descent to Sóller via s'Arrom, unless keys to a locked gate have been obtained. A path zigzags downhill, first passing a small cave, then passing a pillar of rock. There are more trees further downhill, and paths to either side should be avoided. The most well-trodden path drops to a stream and crosses a footbridge to reach a signpost and a much clearer path.

Turn left along the level path and later go through a gate. Marvel at the great chasm of the **Barranc de Biniaraix**, and forget about route-finding while following the broad and obvious cobbled path as it zigzags downhill. There is a signposted junction where a choice is available; keep right at the junction, taking the most popular path, which continues down through the *barranc*, crossing and re-crossing the streambed and squeezing through a rocky gorge at **s'Estret**. (The left-hand option is clearly marked and involves an extra 60m (195ft) of ascent and descent.)

Eventually, the path leaves the *barranc* and reaches a washhouse at **Biniaraix**. Turn left to walk through the village, passing a bar and a café. A taxi could be called at this point. In the unlikely event of being in time for the last bus, it is necessary to leave the village and stop the bus at l'Horta de Biniaraix. Simply following the road straight to **Sóller** is mostly easy and level, passing orange groves and houses. Maintaining a direct line leads back to the Plaça de sa Constitució.

# WALK 24
*Fornalutx, Monnàber and Portell de sa Costa*

| | |
|---|---|
| **Start/Finish** | Plaça d'Espanya, Fornalutx |
| **Distance** | 13.5km (8¼ miles) |
| **Total ascent/descent** | 800m (2625ft) |
| **Time** | 5hrs |
| **Terrain** | A mixture of easy roads, tracks and paths into the mountains, but a steep and rugged path is used for the descent. |
| **Map** | Alpina Tramuntana Central |
| **Refreshment** | Plenty of choice at Fornalutx |
| **Transport** | Occasional buses serve Fornalutx from Sóller and Port de Sóller |

The Camí de Monnàber is regarded a right-of-way, but it has a locked gate at one point. This can be circumvented to offer a walk from Fornalutx, high into the scenic mountains and through the Túnel de Monnàber. A return can be made through the beautifully secluded valley of Coma de Son Torrella, then Portell de sa Costa offers a steep descent to Fornalutx.

The Plaça d'Espanya is in the centre of the lovely village of **Fornalutx**, around 150m (490ft). Follow Carrer Major and fork right to continue along the stone-paved Carrer de sa Font. Turn right across a bridge to follow a mock-paved road signposted for the Camí des Creuer. This bends as it climbs and offers fine views of the village, with Sóller beyond. Turn right as signposted up stone steps on a slope of olive trees. The steps give way to a stony track where marker posts indicate a shortcut through a bend. Climb more stone steps to reach a minor road and turn left.

The road is bendy, but there are two shortcuts available up more stone steps. These aren't marked or signposted, but the first one begins near a property called sa Fita, and the second one follows shortly afterwards. There is no option but to follow the road onwards, climbing gradually past houses and terraces. Watch on the right to spot a flight of stone steps, around 370m (1215ft). These steps are used later in the day when descending from the mountains. The road continues climbing, becoming steep and very bendy, without shortcuts.

*A reservoir is passed on the way into the Coma de Son Torrella*

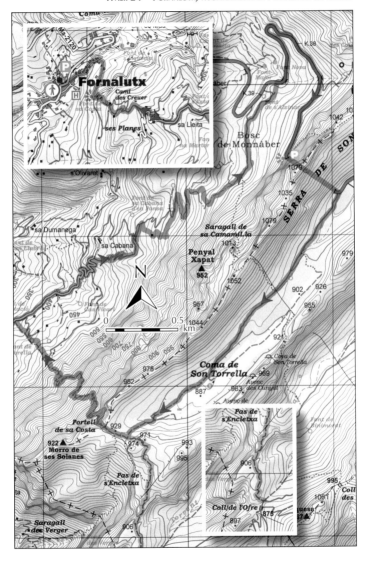

143

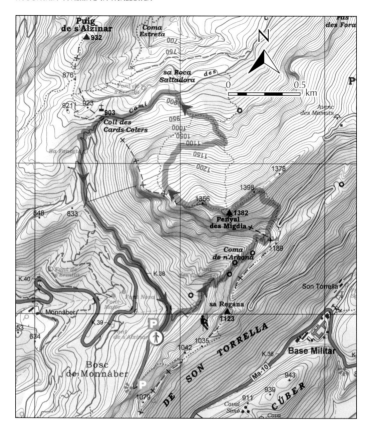

## ACCESSING THE START-POINT

When driving up the Ma-10 road from Sóller to Cúber, the mouth of the Túnel de Monnàber appears suddenly on a bend. The trick is to be aware of this in advance, and park in a dirt lay-by beforehand, on the left at Km37.6, or a tarmac lay-by closer to the tunnel mouth at Km37.3. If the lay-bys are missed, there is no option but to go through the tunnel, turn around, come back and try again.

Starting from the dirt lay-by, go straight up a path on a forested slope, joining a track. Watch carefully while climbing and keep right to cross a dry valley. As the path climbs it passes the spring of **Font des Coloms**. Keep climbing steeply and the path passes an interesting snow-pit, then another one, high in the valley of **Coma de n'Arbona**.

Follow the path carefully as it climbs further, apparently zigzagging up to a gap. However, it is very important **not** to go to the gap, but to watch carefully for a junction where a vague path climbs to the left. The reason for this route choice becomes apparent once more height has been gained, and after a rock-step has been negotiated. Walkers emerge on a steep and rocky slope high above the military road that serves nearby Puig Major and its monstrous summit radome.

Take great care climbing the slope and be prepared to use hands as well as feet. Most walkers seem to follow a vaguely trodden path that leads towards a gap on a rocky ridge. There is no need to go all the way to the gap, but once near it, swing left for a final scramble to a summit at 1398m (4587ft). This is the highest point that can be gained on Mallorca, with neighbouring Puig Major being off-limits.

Mallorcans were in the habit of climbing their highest mountain, Puig Major, until 1957. In that year a Spanish-US air defence deal was signed and Puig Major was **occupied by the military**. A road was constructed up the mountain in 1958 and two radomes were built on top, painted white. These were

*Looking towards Puig Major on the steep and rugged descent*

dismantled in 2003 and replaced by one large, camouflaged radome. The mountain is strictly off-limits, but the main road through the mountains actually passes straight through the military complex.

Enjoy spectacular and wide-ranging views through the Serra de Tramuntana, then scramble carefully along the narrow and exposed rocky ridge, passing the actual summit of **Penyal des Migdia** at 1382m (4534ft). Go down a rocky gully and note that there is a choice soon afterwards. A path on the right can be used to make an early descent, but it is worth staying high on the rocky ridge for longer. Cross a minor summit at 1356m (4449ft) and follow the rocky crest gradually downhill, bearing in mind that extensive cliffs prevent any direct descent to the road.

The only safe descent involves swinging right into a steep and rugged valley, reaching a point where it is possible to go either left or right, although the junction isn't obvious. Both ways are very rugged, but keeping right is marginally easier, traversing a slope. The important thing is not to be tempted directly down through the valley, but to watch carefully to spot a few cairns that indicate a left turn.

The path makes a short traverse past *càrritx*, then descends steep and rugged terrain towards a pine forest. A path leads through the forest to reach a track, where a left turn leads gently up to the gap of **Coll des Cards-Colers**, passing a cross at 903m (2963ft).

Descend directly from the gap and pass a water trough at **Sa Fonteta**. The gradient eases and the forest track continues gently downhill, keeping straight ahead at junctions to reach the Ma-10 road at Km38.1. Walk straight ahead up the road to return to the lay-by.

# BUNYOLA, ORIENT, ALARÓ AND SANTA MARIA

*Looking beyond Bunyola to Puig de Son Nassi early on the ascent on Walk 27*

A walled track leaves the road in the Orient valley and passes fields (Walk 28)

Bunyola is often overlooked by motorists racing between Palma and Sóller, but they can't fail to notice three impressive little mountains rising above the road. Puig de s'Alqueria (Walk 26) is the highest of these and is surprisingly easy to climb. Hidden behind it is the narrow cleft of Pas de sa Fesa. The village of Bunyola is the starting point for a fine walk exploring the forested uplands of Penyal d'Honor (Walk 27), and again the ascent is fairly easy.

The Orient valley is delightful, but on popular weekends the parking spaces fill up, and the bus service is not only sparse, but has to be booked in advance. Most walkers are only aware of walking routes to the south of the valley. One route offers a circuit linking Alaró with Orient, while also climbing to the fortified summit of Puig d'Alaró (Walk 29). Another route stretches all the way from Orient to Santa Maria (Walk 28), taking in a rugged mountain valley.

There is really only one walking route to the north of the Orient valley (Walk 30), and it isn't immediately obvious. It climbs to the rugged Serra d'Alfàbia, and is the only route available onto the range from Orient. Further along the rugged crest, options abound to descend in a number of directions. The descent to Orient is strictly a one-way affair, as the road from Comasema to the village allows an exit from the mountains, but cannot normally be used as an entry point.

The long-distance GR221 trail offers a route into the Orient valley from Puig d'Alaró, and at some time in the future it might be possible to follow a continuation to Bunyola, and even from Bunyola to Valldemossa, but at the moment there are obstacles.

# WALK 26

*Puig de s'Alqueria from Bunyola*

| | |
|---|---|
| **Start/Finish** | Bunyola or Can Penasso |
| **Distance** | 12.5km (7¾ miles) – full circuit or there-and-back |
| **Total ascent/descent** | 470m (1540ft) |
| **Time** | 4hrs |
| **Terrain** | Roads at first, then a winding track for the ascent. Steep paths on the descent, then tracks and roads |
| **Map** | Alpina Tramuntana Central |
| **Refreshment** | Plenty of choice at Bunyola; bar-restaurant at Can Penasso |
| **Transport** | Regular buses serve Can Penasso from Palma, Sóller and Port de Sóller. Regular buses serve Bunyola from Palma. Vintage electric trains serve Bunyola from Palma and Sóller (add a total of 1.5km (1 mile) to the day's walk if arriving by train). |
| **Notes** | A busy main road has to be followed for the initial section. There are obstacles to completing the full circuit – see below – although they are by no means insurmountable. Alternatively, the route can be walked as a 'there-and-back'. |

The ascent of Puig de s'Alqueria is fairly easy and the reward at the summit is a good view. However, a busy main road has to be followed first. There used to be a fairly popular circular walk, but this has been hampered by locked gates. Be sure to read the route description carefully before attempting the full circuit, otherwise simply climb to the summit and then retrace steps afterwards.

If arriving by bus, get off at the bus stops near Can Penasso, around 170m (560ft). If arriving on the vintage electric train, follow the road away from Bunyola to reach Can Penasso on the main Ma-11 road. Follow the busy main road past the bar-restaurant and only turn left to leave it when the access road for **s'Alqueria**

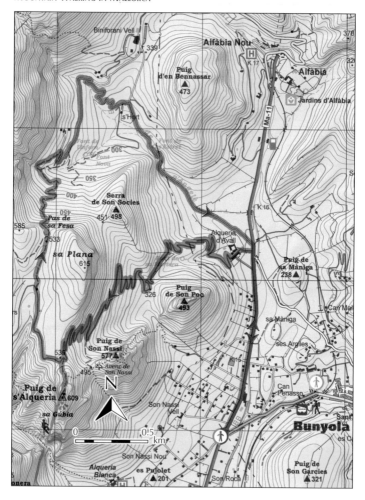

**d'Avall** is reached. There are some forbidding notices, but walkers are free to approach the substantial country house.

Pass to the left of the building, following a track between it and a large out-building. Go through a gate, then simply follow the winding track up through

*Looking from Puig de s'Alqueria towards Serra d'Alfàbia*

another gate. The way ahead can't be mistaken and is simply a case of climbing past olive terraces and passing occasional shelter huts, or *porxos*, while taking all the bends as they come. Don't look for shortcuts as there aren't any worth taking. Two of the three impressive mountains that were seen from the main road look even more impressive from behind. The highest of them, where this walk is heading, barely warrants a glance.

At the top of the track, a stone tablet is carved with 'Mirador Leandro Ximenis', after a notable Mallorcan climber. Leave the track and climb a few rugged steps and a stony path to a ladder stile. Cross this above another shelter hut and reach a trig point on **Puig de s'Alqueria**, at 609m (1998ft). The nearby mirador offers a fine view, dominated largely by the Serra d'Alfàbia. Retrace steps back to the track, then consider what to do next. The easiest thing is to walk back down the track to return to Can Penasso.

It is possible to complete the route as a circular walk, but read the following description carefully, as there are problems. Follow the track onwards and go through a gate to reach another hut. Turn right along a track that eventually peters out among olives. Keep walking ahead and stay as low as possible to pass the last olive terrace on a gap at 533m (1748ft). Immediately turn left to find the remarkable deep rocky cleft of **Pas de Fesa**. A stile halfway down it has broken, making it difficult to cross. (When it eventually collapses, the descent will be easier.)

A steep and gritty woodland path needs care on the descent. Take it slowly and avoid slipping as it winds downhill to join a track. Turn left to follow the track, descending past more olive terraces. A locked gate is reached that proves awkward to pass; some walkers have lifted up the adjacent fence to crawl beneath, rather than climbing over it.

Continue along the track, turn right at a junction and left at a bend, then another locked gate is easier to pass. Turn right down a battered and rubble-strewn concrete road. This swings left and it appears to be heading towards a big house called Biniforani Vell, but turn right at a junction to walk down a narrow road.

The road winds downhill and joins another road beside a reservoir near **s'Hort**. Turn right to continue down through the valley of the **Torrent de n'Angelè**, passing another reservoir. Continue to the main Ma-11 road and turn right to return to **Can Penasso** for a bus, or turn left at a roundabout to walk to the train station in **Bunyola**.

# WALK 27
*Bunyola and Penyal d'Honor*

| | |
|---|---|
| **Start/Finish** | Bunyola or Can Penasso |
| **Alternative start/finish** | Cas Garriguer |
| **Distance** | 14.5km (9 miles) or 8.5km (5¼ miles) from Cas Garriguer |
| **Total ascent/descent** | 750m (2460ft) or 640m (2100ft) from Cas Garriguer |
| **Time** | 4hrs or 2hrs 30mins from Cas Garriguer |
| **Terrain** | Mostly along easy paths and forest tracks, with some short, steep sections |
| **Map** | Alpina Tramuntana Central |
| **Refreshment** | Plenty of choice in Bunyola |
| **Transport** | There are three options: the centre of Bunyola is served by bus from Palma. Can Penasso, outside Bunyola, is served by bus from Palma, Sóller and Port de Sóller (add 2.5km/1½ miles total). A vintage electric train serves Bunyola from Palma and Sóller (add 1km/½ mile total). |

Penyal d'Honor is mostly forested, but has an impressive cliff face and the summit offers good views. It can be climbed from Bunyola via the Camí des Grau, then it is possible to complete either a short or a long circular walk on its higher parts. The route can be shortened by 6km by driving up a long, winding dirt road to start and finish at the recreational area of Cas Garriguer.

*Looking towards Penyal d'Honor from a cliff-edge viewpoint*

If arriving by bus from Sóller or Port de Sóller, get off at Can Penasso and follow the road into the centre of Bunyola. The road passes the vintage electric train station; anyone arriving by train should walk straight into the centre of town. If arriving by bus from Palma, it is best to use the bus that stops in the centre of town, on Sa Plaça, around 200m (655ft). Leave Sa Plaça along Carrer Major, which is the road signposted for Orient. Turn right and climb 112 stone steps up Carrer de Sant Bartomeu. Turn right at the top and follow a narrow road until a left turn can be made up more stone steps on Carreró de la Comuna. A signposted track continues, and when it becomes concrete, turn left along a stony path flanked by walls. The walls finish and the path continues up through pine and holm oak forest, and is called **Camí des Grau**.

Pass a limekiln, *sitja*, *carboner* hut and an *aljub* all close together. (Take note of heritage features such as these, as other examples will be passed.) The path climbs more steeply, becoming bendy and rugged. When a signposted junction is reached, a left turn simply drops a short way to a cliff edge **viewpoint**, looking across to Serra d'Alfàbia. Keep following the obvious path uphill, passing a limekiln at another signposted junction. There are more limekilns and *sitges* on the way up to a signposted track intersection. Turn right and pass a water tank to reach a junction with a dirt road, where there is a mapboard.

Nearby, a track leaves the dirt road and goes through a gate. The dirt road runs direct to Cas Garriguer. Follow the track up through the forest, passing a couple of *sitges*. Eventually, a signposted junction is reached where the track runs straight ahead, while paths go left and right. Turn left to follow a rugged path signposted for Penyal d'Honor. It actually leads to the rocky summit of **Penyal de Son Creus**, at 808m (2651ft). A slab of concrete on top used to be the foundation of a hut. The adjacent summit of Penyal d'Honor is slightly higher, at 813m (2667ft), but it is completely forested and difficult to access.

Enjoy the view, then walk back down to the track. For a shortcut, simply follow the other path straight downhill, and it becomes a track leading directly to Cas Garriguer. To continue with the main route, turn left to follow the track further uphill. When it starts to descend and makes a pronounced bend to the right, leave it by following a path to the left. This is rough and stony, rising a little, then it is plain and obvious as it winds down the forested slope, passing a *sitja* and *carboner* hut. When a path junction is reached, turn right. Left leads to a road on top of Coll d'Honor, offering an option for another day.

The path descends across a forested slope. There is a sharp right turn, followed by a pleasant and easy walk around a valley. A quick zigzag leads uphill, then a water tank is reached at a track junction, around 630m (2065ft). Turn right here, but along the clearest track, not a rugged one climbing just before the tank. Always stay on the main track, which runs at gentle gradients and is quite bendy, then it descends noticeably. It makes a circuit around the forested hill of **Puig des Bous**, then heads into a valley towards **Cas Garriguer**. There is a building surrounded by a picnic area, with car parking; either follow a path into the picnic area, or stay on the track, which joins a dirt road.

To continue, simply follow the dirt road away from the picnic area. Traverse a slope at around 630m (2065ft) to reach a junction with a track where there

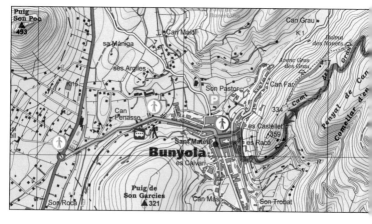

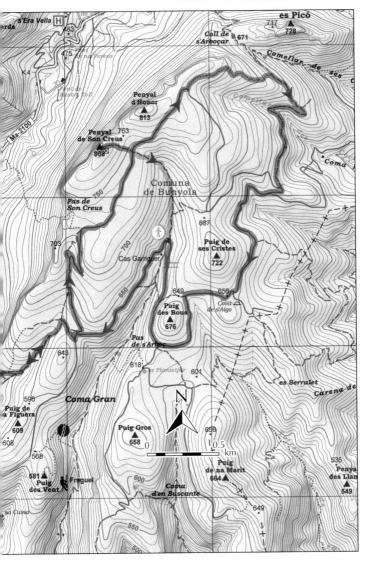

is a mapboard. This point was passed earlier in the walk. Turn right to pass a water tank, then turn left at a track intersection to follow Camí des Grau back to **Bunyola**. Towards the end, feel free to use different flights of steps for the final descent to Sa Plaça.

# WALK 28
### *Vall de Coanegra and Santa Maria*

| | |
|---|---|
| **Start** | Orient |
| **Finish** | Railway station, Santa Maria |
| **Distance** | 13km (8 miles) or 14km (8½ miles) including the extension to Avenc de Son Pou |
| **Total ascent** | 100m (330ft) or 200m (660ft) including the extension to Avenc de Son Pou |
| **Total descent** | 420m (1380ft) or 520m (1705ft) including the extension to Avenc de Son Pou |
| **Time** | 3hrs 30mins or 4hrs including the extension to Avenc de Son Pou |
| **Terrain** | Mostly obvious tracks and paths, but some parts are quite rough and rocky. There is a long road-walk to the finish. |
| **Map** | Alpina Tramuntana Central |
| **Refreshment** | Bar-restaurants at Orient; plenty of choice at Santa Maria |
| **Transport** | Occasional buses serve Orient from Bunyola, but these must be booked in advance, tel 617 365 365. Santa Maria has a railway station with trains to Palma and Inca. There is no parking for cars at Son Oliver, near Santa Maria, but a carefully timed pick-up would save the last 4.5km (2¾ miles) of road-walking. |

This popular walk from the Orient valley squeezes between the well-wooded mountains flanking the wonderfully rugged Vall de Coanegra, emerging on the plains to reach Santa Maria. At weekends, people visited a splendid cave called Avenc de Son Pou, but this was recently closed for environmental reasons. The early part of the walk is quite rugged, but it ends with a long and easy road-walk.

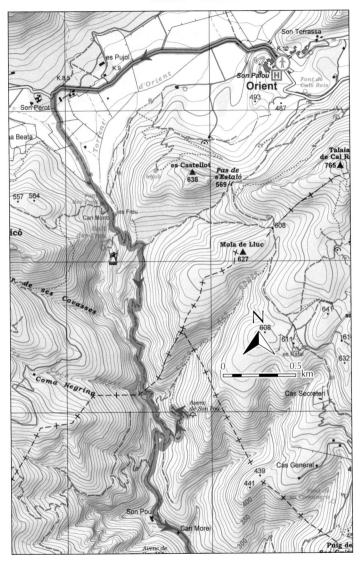

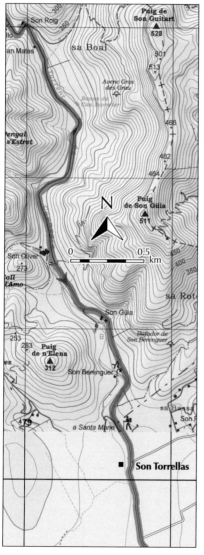

Leave the village of **Orient**, around 460m (1510ft), as if following the Ma-2100 road towards Bunyola. The road runs almost level through the valley, and there might be parked cars around Km8.5, where there is a signpost for the route to Santa Maria. Follow a track and cross a ladder stile beside a locked gate.

The track runs level between fields, passing water troughs as it runs into a wooded valley. Pass ruins at **Can Morro** and **es Freu**, cross another ladder stile beside a gate, reaching a signposted path junction at a *sitja*. A canyoning route goes down waterfalls and through pools.

The path turns left and climbs, zigzagging up to a higher junction where there is a marker post. Turn right to pass another *sitja* and a limekiln. Traverse the wooded slope and step across a *sitja* on the path, then zigzag down past another *sitja*. The path is quite low in the valley and it might be possible to hear water, or canyoners, in the rocky gorge below. Keep straight ahead at a signposted junction, quickly reaching another signposted junction and an option for a short detour.

**Extension to Avenc de Son Pou**
Turn left and climb a steep, winding path. It reaches the entrance

to the **Avenc de Son Pou**. The cave was recently closed, but if it re-opens, a narrow tunnel leads into a huge, domed space where daylight floods in through two openings. Retrace steps down to the valley path.

The rugged path descends, passing a limekiln and becoming a track. Simply follow the track through the valley until drawing close to a house at **Son Pou**. Climb left as marked up a rocky path for a short way, pass through a gate, then drop back onto the track. Pass a little house called **Can More**, then the track bends sharply left and right as it passes **Son Roig** de Coanegra and crosses a concrete slab bridge. The track simply follows the **Torrent de Coanegra** down through the valley, crossing a cobbled ford at one point.

The track gives way to a road at the house of **Son Oliver**, and gates are passed. The road is easy and virtually level, leaving the valley to reach a junction. Walk straight ahead and when a fork in the road is reached later, keep left, avoiding Camí de Ca na Cili.

The road runs straight to a signposted crossroads on the edge of **Santa Maria**, around 140m (460ft). Continue straight ahead until a level crossing is reached, and the railway station lies just to the right.

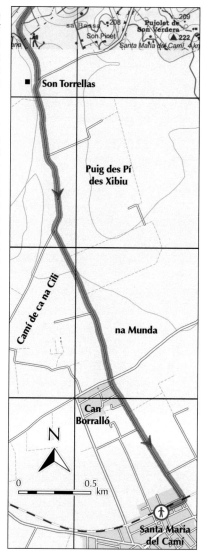

# WALK 29

*Alaró, Orient and Puig d'Alaró*

| | |
|---|---|
| **Start/Finish** | Plaça de la Vila, Alaró |
| **Distance** | 15.5km (9¾ miles) or 14km (8¾ miles) omitting es Verger |
| **Total ascent/descent** | 700m (2295ft) |
| **Time** | 4hrs 30mins or 4hrs omitting es Verger |
| **Terrain** | Mostly along easy roads, tracks and paths, although some short stretches of path are steep and rugged |
| **Map** | Alpina Tramuntana Central |
| **Refreshment** | Plenty of choice at Alaró; bar and café at Los d'Amunt; bar-restaurants at Orient; bar on top of Puig d'Alaró; bar-restaurant at es Verger. |
| **Transport** | Regular buses serve Alaró from the Consell-Alaró railway station, which is itself regularly served from Palma and Inca. Occasional buses serve Orient from Bunyola, but these must be booked in advance, tel 617 365 365. |

A fine circular walk from the lovely town of Alaró takes in a rugged pass leading to the charming Orient valley. The pretty village of Orient can be visited by a detour. The return takes in another pass, as well as climbing the fortified Puig d'Alaró. There are two options for the descent, before a road-walk returns to Alaró.

The Plaça de la Vila is in the centre of **Alaró**, in front of the church, around 220m (720ft). Walk straight through the square and gently up Carrer Calet. Turn left along Carrer d'Enmig, which is signposted for 'los Damunt'. Turn right along Carrer de Can Coxeti to reach **Los d'Amunt**, which is the old centre of Alaró. Turn left at a crossroads where there is a street plan displayed on a post. Follow Carrer de Son Durant, pass through the central Plaça de Cabrit i Bassa, then leave and pass through a small triangular *plaça*. Keep left, as signposted for Pas de s'Escaleta.

The road is narrow and pleasant, passing fine properties, including sa Font des Jardi and its assortment of millstones. Tarmac gives way to the concrete Camí de s'Estret and the road rises through a rocky valley. Eventually, a signpost is reached where a rocky path climbs to the left. Follow the path up into woodland, reaching the interesting **Pas de s'Escaleta**, where chunky stone steps climb a rocky cleft. Continue up through the woods to pass a signpost and cross a broad gap at 594m (1949ft).

The path descends with a view of the grass-floored Orient valley, with Puig de l'Ofre rising beyond. Go through a gate to reach a road, then make a choice. Turning left allows a visit to the little village of Orient in just over 1km (½ mile). Food, drink and a limited bus service are available. Turning right is for the continuation of the route, passing a hotel called **l'Hermitage**, reaching Coll d'Orient at 498m (1634ft), following the signposted and waymarked GR221 trail.

*Stone steps have been squeezed into the Pas de s'Escaleta*

Turn right as signposted through a gate, then follow a track past olives. As the track rises it dwindles to a path, then enters woodland to climb steeply. There are a few stone steps and a slope with stone paving. Reach a dirt car park and a signpost on a gap at **Pla des Pouet**, above 700m (2295ft). There is a choice at this point; either to climb Puig d'Alaró by turning left, or omit it and start the descent to es Verger by turning right. Most walkers will turn left.

## CASTELL D'ALARÓ

The mountain bore a hill fort before recorded history, and its later Moorish defences were replaced following the Conquest mounted by Jaume I in the 13th century. There were periods of building in the 14th and 15th centuries, while the current chapel, the Santuari de la Mare de Déu del Refugi, dates from the 17th century. As a site of pilgrimage, a hostatgeria was founded to offer food, drink and lodgings. This was recently restored and extended.

Walk up a stone-paved path with steps, later going down stone steps, then traverse across a steep slope and go up more stone steps. When a signposted junction is reached, turn left to climb even more stone steps. The path wriggles up through two fortified stone gateways that were built to defend the mountain-top. It looks as though only the ruins of **Castell d'Alaró** now remain, but keep climbing to discover a lovely chapel and the Hostatgeria del Castell d'Alaró. Visit the

821m (2694ft) summit of **Puig d'Alaró**, where views stretch one way to Alaró and the plains and the other way to the mountains.

There is no way off the summit except by retracing steps back down through the two stone gateways. Continue down to the signposted junction and make a choice. Keeping left, or straight ahead, allows a shortcut down a zigzag path to a road, and this saves nearly 2km (1¼ miles) of walking. Turning sharp right, however, steps can be retraced to the dirt car park at **Pla des Pouet**, where a rather patchy dirt and concrete road can be followed down a wooded slope. The road is very bendy, and while there are shortcut paths, they are rough and stony, so it is probably best to stay on the road. It reaches the Restaurante **es Verger**, around 560m (1840ft).

Continue down the winding road, passing the point where the shortcut path descends from Puig d'Alaró. Follow the road, with all its bends and loops, but watch for a couple of shortcut paths descending more directly. One path rejoins the road beside a monstrous boulder. Eventually, the road passes an old house called **Son Penyaflor**, by which time the gradients are gentle.

When a road junction is reached, turn left to follow Camí de sa Sort straight to the Ma-2100 road. Turn right and follow this road straight into **Alaró**, where Carrer de Solleric, Carrer del Pontarró, Carrer Can Ros and Carrer Petit lead back to Plaça de la Vila.

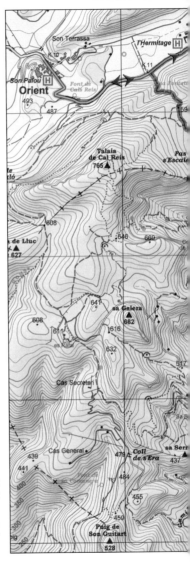

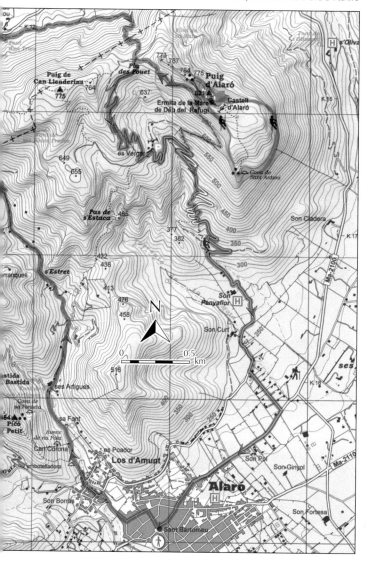

# WALK 30
*Serra d'Alfàbia from Orient*

| | |
|---|---|
| **Start/Finish** | Orient |
| **Distance** | 16km (10 miles) |
| **Total ascent/descent** | 800m (2625ft) |
| **Time** | 7hrs |
| **Terrain** | Steep and intricate paths lead to a high and exposed rocky crest where some scrambling and careful route-finding is required. The descent uses an overgrown, but well-marked path, with a long road-walk to the finish. |
| **Map** | Alpina Tramuntana Central |
| **Refreshment** | Bar-restaurants at Orient |
| **Transport** | Occasional buses serve Orient from Bunyola, but these must be booked in advance, tel 617 365 365. |
| **Note** | A locked gate at the very end of the walk is bypassed by sliding down a 'fireman's pole'! |

There is really only one path allowing the rough and rocky crest of Serra d'Alfàbia to be reached from the Orient valley. Traversing the mountain crest is a tough and challenging walk. An old, overgrown path can be used to descend to the remote country house of Comasema, but this can only be used to leave the property. Those who don't need to return to Orient can use other routes to descend elsewhere.

Leave the village of **Orient**, around 460m (1510ft), as if following the Ma-2100 road towards Bunyola. The road runs through the valley, and parked cars might be spotted around Km8.5, where Walk 28 leads to Santa Maria. Stay on the road, passing **Son Perot** to reach Km7.9. Turn right to follow an old stone-paved path up through woodland, reaching a junction with a wider path beside a pylon and a ruin. Turn right to continue and the path seems to peter out as it approaches a wall. Cross over the wall and keep straight ahead past a few *sitges*. There are a couple of broad and stony old tracks, but keep right and keep to the clearest track at all times.

*Take care with route-finding over the rocky Puig des Coll des Jou*

The track winds uphill to a gap near **Puig des Vent**, at almost 650m (2130ft). Just before the gap, turn right up another old path and keep climbing. The path is broad, has stone buttresses and eventually reaches a small rock cutting on a crest, around 730m (2395ft). There might be a cairn, but if not, turn right up a narrow path to continue up the wooded slope. It climbs steeply, then turns left and traverses, rising and falling.

Climb a very rocky slope, watching for small cairns that mark the way. There is some scrambling where more care is needed with route-finding. Above the rock, watch carefully for a path through *càrritx* near **Puig de s'Aritjar**, with several communication masts seen on the rugged crest ahead.

When a track is reached, turn right to follow it gently downhill, passing a barrier. This was once a vehicle track, but is becoming overgrown; Walk 23 also follows it. It descends, then rises and passes through another gap in the tall fence to make a traverse of **Serra d'Alfàbia**. The path is reasonably obvious at first, and offers fine views over Sóller. When it becomes vague, look for red dots, but bear in mind they run out later. Rugged ground is crossed while passing just below a **trig point** at 1067m (3501ft).

Cross a rocky gap and the path descends and climbs rugged slopes to cross another rocky gap on the mountain crest. Following the crest onwards requires great care, primarily following small cairns among scrub and bare rock on the way past **Penya de s'Anyell**. Go through a gap in a wall and cross an expanse of bare rock, but watch for any evidence of a path heading down to the right. Walk

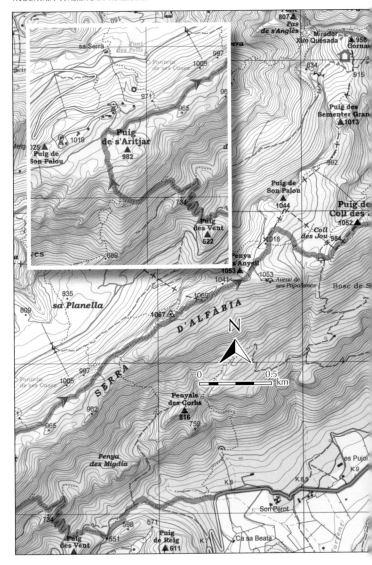

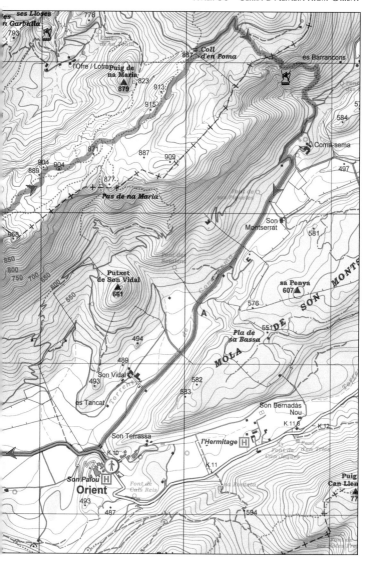

23 runs straight ahead. There are small cairns, trees and areas of *càrritx*. The path is vague, but leads through asphodels, aiming to the right of a rocky hill.

Reach a gap on the side of the hill, then turn left to climb, finding a path that makes a rising traverse with cliffs above and below. A sudden right turn leads up a rocky breach to cross the rocky gap of **Coll des Jou**. Turn left to cross bare rock and pass another rocky gap, then climb to the summit cairn on **Puig des Coll des Jou**, at 1052m (3451ft). Enjoy views and take particular note of the mountain crest ahead.

Take care coming down, crossing rocky ground, then crossing a wall and fence. Continue along a vague path through asphodels, keeping watch for any evidence of passage, such as paths or cairns while aiming to stay fairly high. The mountain crest is very hummocky and very slow-going. Don't be drawn to the right, towards Pas de na Maria, and don't be drawn left, towards Puig de na Maria.

Eventually, a stout drystone wall will be seen ahead, and when climbing towards it from a small valley, look carefully for a gap to pass through it. There is, rather surprisingly, a broken coin-operated telescope beyond, and turning left reveals a path leading to a track at **Coll d'en Poma**, at 887m (2910ft).

The track makes a loop around Puig de l'Ofre, and route choices are available at this point. By turning left, the track can be followed to Coll de l'Ofre, from where alternative finishing points as widely spread as Cúber, Fornalutx, Biniaraix and Sóller can be brought into play. See Walks 23, 24 and 31. However, to stay on the main route back to Orient, turn right along the track, as confirmed by a boulder bearing 'ORIENT' in blue paint.

Follow the track downhill, turning right and left, then almost immediately turn right down a vague path, liberally daubed with blue paint marks. The path passes pine trees and isn't always clear, but the blue paint marks are faultless guides. When a closed gate is reached, climb over it to continue out of the forest, then down a slope of *càrritx*. An old, overgrown, zigzag path needs care on a rugged slope at **es Barrancons**, so keep watching for blue paint marks. Land on a signposted track at the bottom of the slope, around 550m (1805ft).

Turn right to follow the track, reaching a notice prohibiting noise and photography. Do not approach the big house of **Comasema**, but keep to the right of it to follow its access road. There are signposts for Orient, and the access road basically runs through the valley, following the **Torrent de Comasema**.

When a stout, locked gate is reached, use four rungs to climb to the top of a gatepost, then carefully lean forward to grab a 'fireman's pole' and slide down it. This is a legitimate exit, but to enter this way requires negotiation in advance with the people at Comasema. Simply follow the road onwards, eventually reaching a junction and turning left to return to **Orient**.

# CÚBER AND
# TOSSALS VERDS

*Looking from Puig de l'Ofre to es Cornadors and Sóller (Walk 31)*

171

*Coll des Gats, with the rocky na Franquesa rising beyond it (Walk 31)*

For a remote mountain enclave, Cúber is remarkably popular with walkers. Extra car parking spaces have been created, and not only does the public bus arrive full of walkers, but additional fleets of coaches bring even more walkers. Fortunately, there are plenty of paths available and it is possible to find one or two places that remain quiet. The main thing to be aware of is that walks in any direction don't have to be followed strictly according to the route descriptions. All the walking routes link with other routes, so there are options to finish far, far away from Cúber, which would suit those using public transport.

Circular walks include a splendid route involving a scramble at Pas Llis, reaching the remote *refugi* of Tossals Verds (Walk 32). Another option is to climb high above this route and take in some rugged mountains (Walk 33). There is a popular circuit that includes a lot of bare rock, taking in a mountain crest from sa Rateta to Puig de l'Ofre (Walk 31). This route reaches Coll de l'Ofre, where alternative finishing points can be considered with reference to other route descriptions, or walkers can simply return to Cúber.

Linear routes include one that climbs onto the sprawling rocky mountain of Puig de Massanella (Walk 35). This can be reversed to Cúber, but with reference to bus timetables, it is also possible to continue to Coll de sa Batalla and Lluc, and catch a bus back to Cúber. Another linear route runs from Cúber to Tossals Verds, then continues to Solleric along a track that only became available for public use recently, and this route can be continued to Alaró (Walk 34).

# WALK 31

*sa Rateta, na Franquesa and Puig de l'Ofre*

| | |
|---|---|
| **Start/Finish** | Font des Noguer, Cúber |
| **Distance** | 11km (7 miles) or 9.5km (6 miles) omitting Puig de l'Ofre |
| **Total ascent/descent** | 600m (1970ft) or 470m (1545ft) omitting Puig de l'Ofre |
| **Time** | 4hrs 30mins or 4hrs omitting Puig de l'Ofre |
| **Terrain** | A steep, rough and rocky mountain crest with few trodden paths. More obvious paths and tracks lead to a wide-ranging choice of finishing points |
| **Map** | Alpina Tramuntana Central |
| **Refreshment** | None on the main route, but the villages at the alternative finish-points have bar-restaurants |
| **Transport** | Summer buses serve Cúber from Port de Sóller, Sóller, Port de Pollença, Pollença and Lluc |

The main part of this walk is a very rugged romp over three fine rocky mountains, for those walkers looking for a hard route with splendid scenery. Afterwards, the walk can be finished in at least four remarkably different ways. The simplest is to return to the starting point at Cúber, but for those with no need to return there, alternative finishing points include the villages of Orient, Biniaraix or Fornalutx.

There are car parks and bus stops at Cúber and while the place is quite remote, and around 750m (2460ft), it is often busy with walkers. Leaving the bus stops, walk to a gate that gives access to a road serving the reservoir, the **Embassament de Cúber**.

This **reservoir** was constructed in 1970–71, along with the neighbouring Embassament de Gorg Blau. Originally they were intended for the generation of electricity, but they now supply drinking water to Palma – despite the astonishing blue/green colouring. Water is pumped up from Gorg Blau, then flows along the concrete Canal des Embassaments to Cúber.

Simply follow the road to the reservoir dam. Stop as soon as the dam is reached and take a very careful look at the mountain across the valley from the dam, which is sa Rateta. Note the cliffs encircling the mountain, then spot an S-shaped gully that breaches them. This gully is the key to climbing the mountain, so it has to be spotted before proceeding any further.

Cross the dam and go a short way up a dirt road, only to a crest before a quarry. Turn left up a vague trodden path and follow it onto awkwardly fissured limestone. Aim for a solitary holm oak tree and find a cairn behind it. Look for more cairns across the rock, then take even more care finding a trodden path across a slope of *càrritx*.

The path is clearer as it approaches the S-shaped gully. On entering the gully, turn right and keep to the right-hand side of it to avoid scree, then scramble up rock slopes to reach a pine tree. Beyond the pine tree there is a rugged valley and a cairned route keeps to the right-hand side of it. Climb mostly across rock, then at a higher level it is a case of crossing bare rock nearly all the way to the rocky summit of **sa Rateta** at 1113m (3651ft). Enjoy fine views across the reservoir and around the mountains.

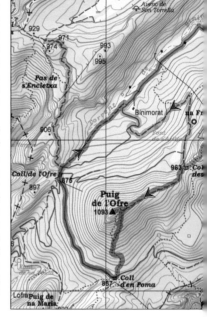

Watch carefully for cairns when leaving the summit, walking down bare rock slopes. Pass a solitary holm oak tree and swing right, passing a peculiar upstanding boulder. Aim for a gap crossed by a drystone wall, where there is short grass. The gap is **Coll des Gats** and it lies at 995m (3264ft).

A rocky peak rises ahead, so keep to the left of it, following more cairns. The cairns suddenly turn right, so climb and keep them in view, later turning left to head for the highest rocky point and a cairn on the summit of **na Franquesa**, at 1067m (3501ft). Again, follow cairns as they lead down to the next gap, which is **Coll des Cards**, at 963m (3159ft). It is possible to turn right and follow a path into the valley, omitting Puig de l'Ofre, saving 1.5km (1 mile) and 130m (425ft) of ascent/descent.

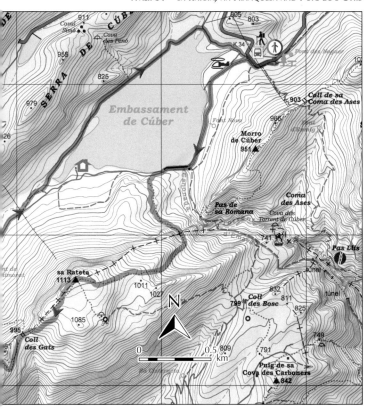

There is a pylon above the gap, and a rock-step to climb. The path appears to reach a summit, but through gaps in the trees, the true summit is seen beyond. Simply climb towards it, keeping left of an outcrop of rock, then climbing to pass a large cairn on a shoulder. Go straight up onto bare rock to reach a small summit cairn on **Puig de l'Ofre**, at 1093m (3586ft). Take a last look at the mountain panorama before descending, and bear in mind that a number of destinations are possible.

Retrace steps to the large cairn on the shoulder of the mountain and turn right to descend steeply through the forest. The path is very stony and there are exposed tree roots. Reach a track and turn right to pass through a gateway on **Coll d'en**

The Embassament de Cúber and Puig Major from the initial ascent

**Poma**, at 887m (2910ft). Turning left allows a direct link with Walk 30, which can be followed down to Comasema, to finish at the village of Orient.

Walk through the forest to reach a track junction and turn right up to **Coll de l'Ofre**, at 875m (2871ft). There is a large cairn with an ornate metal memorial cross rising from it, while nearby signposts indicate the course of the long-distance GR221.

### To finish at Biniaraix

Instead of walking all the way up to the Coll de l'Ofre, turn left down a stony path just beforehand. This is the GR221 and it has plenty of marker posts. The path drops through forest and crosses the track over and over again. Eventually, the track is followed, but only until it suddenly turns a bend, and the GR221 is signposted through a broad gap in a fence. Simply follow a rugged path, partly paved with stone, downhill and turn sharply to the right. At another signpost, it links directly with Walk 23, which can be followed down through the wonderful **Barranc de Biniaraix**, either to finish in the village of **Biniaraix**, or follow the road to **Sóller**.

### To finish at Fornalutx

From Coll de l'Ofre, follow a path uphill that twists and turns, but effectively heads northwards. When it moves onto rock it can be difficult to follow, but some parts are very obvious, despite the nature of the terrain. Pass through a gap in a wall and keep climbing, crossing a rocky crest near a rounded summit that rises to 974m (3195ft). Follow the path downhill, linking with Walk 24 and keep straight ahead towards a gap in a drystone wall at **Portell de sa Costa**. This path can be used for a steep and rugged descent to the village of **Fornalutx**.

Those who wish to return to Cúber should leave Coll de l'Ofre as signposted for the GR221, following a path straight downhill, avoiding the track altogether. Pass through pine forest with an undergrowth of juniper scrub and *càrritx*. Join the track again at a building, turning left as signposted to follow it through the largely treeless valley of the **Torrent de Binimorat**, which is grazed by sheep and horses. Pass a stone hut and eventually reach some gates.

   Go through a small gate to the left of large gates barring the track. Walk down a path signposted as the GR221, crossing a ford to continue through level, sheep-grazed terrain. The path later runs near the reservoir, the **Embassament de Cúber**, where a small locked *refugi* can be seen. The steep slopes of Serra de Cúber are dotted with holm oaks. Cross a couple of concrete channels and turn right as marked along a track, reaching a gate giving access to car parks beside the main road, with the bus stops lying a little further down the road, around a bend.

# WALK 32
*Cúber, Pas Llis and Tossals Verds*

| | |
|---|---|
| **Start/Finish** | Font des Noguer, Cúber |
| **Distance** | 11.5km (7 miles) |
| **Total ascent/descent** | 500m (1640ft) |
| **Time** | 4hrs 30mins |
| **Terrain** | Steep and rugged paths, with scrambling required at Pas Llis. Easier paths at gentler gradients later |
| **Map** | Alpina Tramuntana Central |
| **Refreshment** | Bar at the Refugi de Tossals Verds |
| **Transport** | Summer buses serve Cúber from Port de Sóller, Sóller, Lluc, Pollença and Port de Pollença |

Walking from Cúber to the Refugi de Tossals Verds was always popular. In recent years another route taking in a scramble at Pas Llis has also become popular. Combined, these routes now offer a splendid circular walk around the flanks of rugged mountains, complete with signposts and waymarks throughout.

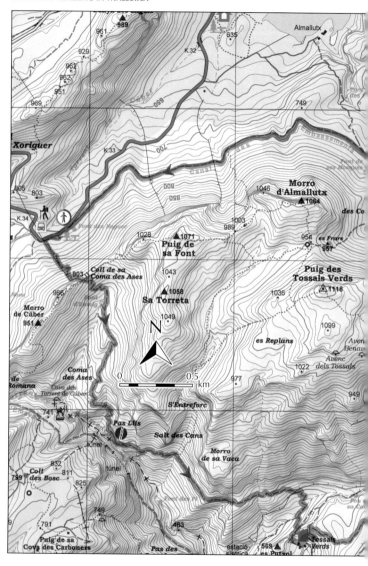

There are car parks and bus stops at Cúber and while the place is quite remote, and around 750m (2460ft), it is often busy with walkers. Leave the bus stops, enter the car park and turn right to cross a ladder stile. Follow a path to a signpost indicating the way to Pas Llis. A ruined wall rises up a slope of pines, and a zigzag path climbs steeply, rising above the pines onto slopes of *càrritx*. There are splendid views down to the Embassament des Gorg Blau, with Puig Major and Serra des Teixos rising either side of it.

Pass above the rocky **Coll de sa Coma des Ases**, at 903m (2963ft), and go down through a gap in a drystone wall for striking views of Puig de s'Alcadena and Puig d'Alaró, with Randa and the plains far beyond. A rough and stony path winds down slopes of *càrritx*, passing clumps of rosemary and later juniper bushes.

The path appears to lead deep into the exceptionally rugged Almadrà valley; however, it cuts across slopes of scree and *càrritx*, passes the base of a cliff then rather alarmingly begins to climb. A route hacked from bare rock, known as **Pas Llis**, is protected with chains, offering an exciting ascent.

Once the *pas* has been negotiated, a rugged path cuts across rocky slopes bearing a few pines. There are plenty of ups and downs, ins and outs, but essentially there is only one path to follow. When a shoulder is crossed and a little valley is seen beyond, look out to spot the rooftop of Tossals Verds, then follow the path gently down and round the valley.

Lose sight of the rooftop and pass olives and a couple of *sitges*. Climb the other side of the valley and keep right at a path junction, climbing a rugged paved path with a rustic fence alongside. Go through a gate on a rocky shoulder and walk straight down to **Tossals Verds**, around 520m (1075ft), where refreshments are available. Walk 34 leaves the *refugi* for Alaró.

Leave the building by walking straight uphill, through a gate as signposted for the GR221. Zigzag up a rugged, cobbled path on a slope of olives, following the pipe that carries water to the *refugi*. Keep straight ahead at a

179

*Walkers clutch chains beneath an overhanging cliff at Pas Llis*

path junction, climbing past pines and holm oaks, then keep straight ahead at another path junction. Cross a gentle gap covered in asphodels and juniper near the ruins of **ses Cases Velles**, at 707m (2320ft). An old well, Pou de sa Basola, lies away to the right.

Keep straight ahead and continue into woods, losing sight of Puig de Massanella, but gaining a view to the right down a valley to the plains, with the Serra de Llevant beyond. The path rises and is quite rugged. Look to the right to spot an old stone-arched aqueduct, the Canaleta de Massanella, clinging to a cliff. (This can be reached and inspected closely, but looks more impressive from a distance.)

Water flows along this old **canaleta** from Font des Prat, high in the mountains, to the distant village of Mancor de la Vall. Foreign engineers declared the construction of a watercourse an impossible task, but a local man, Montserrat Fontanet Llabrés, completed it in 1748. The water flowed in an open channel until it was modernised in 1983, with the water now being carried through a pipe.

Go through a small gate on rocky, wooded slopes and a smooth path gives way to a boulder-paved path. Use a ford or stepping-stones to cross a stream, then walk upstream a little and cross a footbridge. The path crosses a *canaleta* and some black pipes, then reaches a junction of three paths, all signposted as the GR221, at **Prat de Cuber**. A mapboard and signpost stand at a path junction. Turning right follows Walk 35 to Puig de Massanella. Turn left and zigzag up the wooded slope, reaching a gap at **Coll des Coloms** at 808m (2651ft).

Follow the path down the other side and go through a gate at the bottom. Cross a concrete bridge over a concrete water channel, the **Canal des Embassaments**, where water pumped from the Gorg Blau reservoir flows to the Cúber reservoir. A path alongside leads unerringly back to the roadside bus stops at Cúber.

# WALK 33

*Puig des Tossals Verds and
Morro d'Almallutx*

| | |
|---|---|
| **Start/Finish** | Font des Noguer, Cúber |
| **Distance** | 8km (5 miles) |
| **Total ascent/descent** | 600m (1970ft) |
| **Time** | 5hrs |
| **Terrain** | Level and easy at the start, then increasingly difficult in the mountains. Sparse and rugged paths, or no paths at all on steep, rocky, scrub-covered slopes. Hands may be required for balance at times. |
| **Map** | Alpina Tramuntana Central or Nord |
| **Refreshment** | None |
| **Transport** | Summer buses serve Cúber from Port de Sóller, Sóller, Port de Pollença, Pollença and Lluc |

Both ends of this walk tie in with the signposted long-distance GR221. While Puig des Tossals Verds is a fairly popular ascent, the neighbouring summits are less frequented and are exceptionally rugged. There are vague paths and cairned routes, but if any part seems too difficult, simply turn back and retrace steps to the start. Those who follow the entire route will be rewarded with splendid mountain views.

There are car parks and bus stops at Cúber and while the place is quite remote, and around 750m (2460ft), it is often busy with walkers. Leaving the bus stops, follow a concrete water channel as signposted for Tossals Verds and GR221. This is the **Canal des Embassaments**, feeding water into the Cúber and Gorg Blau reservoirs. There are occasional concrete bridges spanning the channel, but only cross the last one, which is signposted.

Go through a gate and follow a path up into dense holm oak woodland. A cobbled path rises and passes two *sitges*, then crosses the gap of **Coll des Coloms** at 808m (2651ft). Turn right as signposted for Puig des Tossals Verds, which is not to be confused with 'Tossals Verds' itself. The path climbs through dense holm oak and pine woodland, winding throughout and occasionally becoming a

181

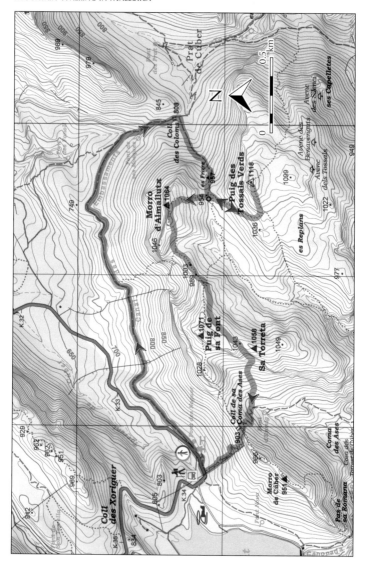

*Looking back up a steep and rugged slope to sa Torreta*

little vague. The path levels out on a gap at 954m (3130ft), where there is an old snow-pit.

Watch carefully for a narrow, cairned path rising well away from the snow-pit. There is no direct ascent available, as a rock face lies straight uphill. Instead, the path rises past a couple of small towers of rock to reach a shoulder. Once the shoulder is reached, turn left to continue climbing, still following cairns.

The summit trig point on **Puig des Tossals Verds** stands at 1118m (3668ft), with a small memorial cross nearby. Enjoy a splendid panoramic view of the surrounding mountains, but pay particular attention to Morro d'Almallutx, Puig de sa Font and sa Torreta.

Retrace steps back down to the gap and pick a way past the snow-pit to find the ruined snow-gatherers' house. Look for cairns revealing a route up a steep slope of rock and scrub. As more height is gained, it becomes more and more rugged, with the bare rock often broken and deeply fissured. The summit of **Morro d'Almallutx** bears a cairn at 1064m (3491ft), and offers fine views of the reservoirs, as well as the surrounding mountains. Bear in mind that the next stretch is difficult and awkward. There is still time to double back.

Cairns are sparse and small, but they show the way towards a neighbouring summit that might bear a pole. With care, the cairns can be followed beyond, and down a slope of rock and *càrritx* to reach a gap. Take care on the final descent to the gap, as there are unseen cliffs, but a stony path of sorts exploits a weakness. The gap is broad and features sparse woodland, a little above 970m (3180ft).

Aim to follow a path uphill along a crest, until cliffs rise ahead. Keep left of these and the path passes fairly easily, regaining a broad crest beyond. This is stony and vegetated, and it is difficult to spot a continuous trodden path, but look ahead to spot a line of cairns. Neighbouring summits bear cairns, including **Puig de sa Font**, at 1071m (3514ft), but follow the line of cairns, which show the way across a rocky crest at 1043m (3422ft), well short of the summit of **sa Torreta**.

A rather messy path descends and splits into variants on a steep slope of old scree covered in *càrritx*. Take care all the way down, and note that there are two unseen cliffs that have to be negotiated. The higher of these has a weakness that the path exploits. The path is naturally funnelled towards the lower one, deep in the valley. A rock chute, which must carry a small waterfall after heavy rain, has to be scrambled down in order to reach an obvious path.

Turn right and follow the path, which is the GR221 again. It winds uphill and goes through a gap in a wall at 903m (2963ft) on **Coll de sa Coma des Ases**. Enjoy fine views, then the path winds down a steep slope towards a road. Turn right at the bottom and walk parallel to the road, crossing a ladder stile into a car park. The gushing **Font des Noguer** lies beyond, in an extensive picnic area, while the bus stops are on the road below.

# WALK 34
*Cúber, Tossals Verds, Solleric and Alaró*

| | |
|---|---|
| **Start** | Font des Noguer, Cúber |
| **Finish** | Plaça de la Vila, Alaró |
| **Distance** | 14.5km (9 miles) |
| **Total ascent** | 350m (1150ft) |
| **Total descent** | 880m (2890ft) |
| **Time** | 5hrs |
| **Terrain** | Steep and rugged paths at first, with some scrambling involved, then easy tracks and roads |
| **Map** | Alpina Tramuntana Central |
| **Refreshment** | Small bar at Tossals Verds; plenty of choice at Alaró |
| **Transport** | Summer buses serve Cúber from Port de Sóller, Sóller, Lluc, Pollença and Port de Pollença. Buses from Alaró link with the Consell-Alaró railway station for trains to Palma and Inca. |

Options to walk from Cúber to Alaró may not be well known, but it can be done, and there are buses at either end. The route is based on the GR221 trail and it is fully signposted and waymarked. The start is quite rugged and involves a short scramble, but it becomes much easier as it follows an old highway through the scenic and interesting Solleric estate. A long road-walk leads to the fine old town of Alaró.

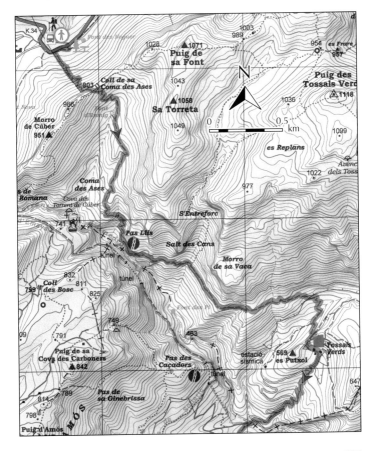

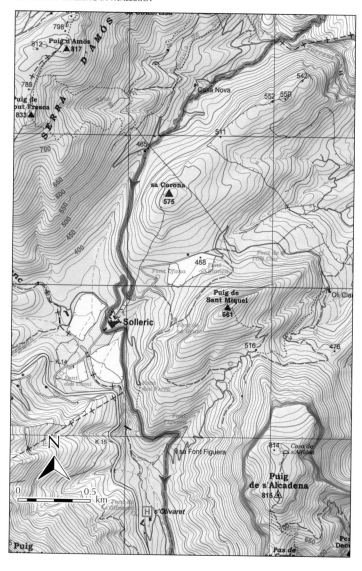

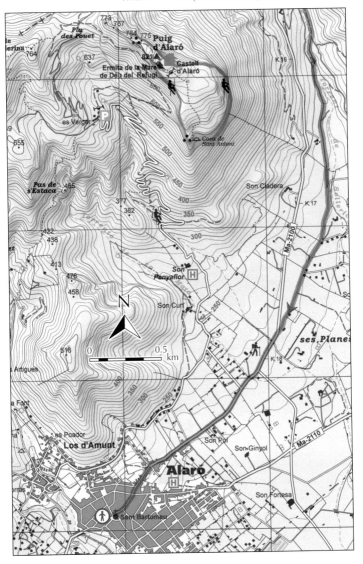

View from Tossals Verds to Puig de s'Alcadena and Puig d'Alaró

There are car parks and bus stops at Cúber and while the place is quite remote, and around 750m (2460ft), it is often busy with walkers. Leave the bus stops, enter the car park and turn right to cross a ladder stile. Follow a path to a signpost indicating the way to Pas Llis. A ruined wall rises up a slope of pines, and a zigzag path climbs steeply, rising above the pines onto slopes of *càrritx*. There are splendid views down to the Embassament des Gorg Blau, with Puig Major and Serra des Teixos rising either side of it.

Pass above the rocky **Coll de sa Coma des Ases**, at 903m (2963ft), and go down through a gap in a drystone wall for striking views of Puig de s'Alcadena and Puig d'Alaró, with Randa and the plains far beyond. A rough and stony path winds down slopes of *càrritx*, passing clumps of rosemary and later juniper bushes. The path appears to lead deep into the exceptionally rugged Almadrà valley; however, it cuts across slopes of scree and *càrritx*, passes the base of a cliff then rather alarmingly begins to climb. A route hacked from bare rock, known as **Pas Llis**, is protected with chains, offering an exciting ascent.

Once the *pas* has been negotiated, a rugged path cuts across rocky slopes bearing a few pines. There are plenty of ups and downs, ins and outs, but essentially there is only one path to follow. When a shoulder is crossed and a little valley is seen beyond, look out to spot the rooftop of Tossals Verds, then follow the path gently down and round the valley.

Lose sight of the rooftop and pass olives and a couple of *sitges*. Climb the other side of the valley and keep right at a path junction, climbing a rugged paved path with a rustic fence alongside. Go through a gate on a rocky shoulder and walk straight down to **Tossals Verds**, around 520m (1075ft), where refreshments are available.

Leave the building by walking down its access road and turn left as signposted for Alaró down stone steps. The first of these are restored, but the remainder are mostly old, cobbled and uneven. The path descends past olive terraces and rejoins the road. Turn left to continue down the road then turn right as marked. The path drops, crosses the road, drops again and rejoins the road. Turn right and follow the road down a left-hand bend. Some other time it is worth following this road down through an awesome rock gorge.

A signpost points to the right and a track crosses a bridge over the **Torrent d'Almadrà**, around 370m (1215ft). Go through gates and turn left as signposted along a path. This passes olive terraces, becoming a fine old highway, solidly built and buttressed with stone, with evenly spaced stone bollards on either side. The old road rises gently and is quite bendy in places. Keep left at a signposted junction, avoiding a spur to the derelict house of **Casa Nova**. Later, turn right up a path, short-cutting bends on the old road.

Cross the road at a higher level, then the next time it is reached, pass through a gate, cross a gap at 465m (1525ft) and reach the Placeta d'en Sion. Keep left at a junction near a small building. Go down an old tarmac road whose surface is breaking into gravel. Keep straight ahead past a signposted junction, then turn right as marked down a path. Turn right again to continue down the bendy road to **Solleric**.

Admire the old buildings and agricultural implements, as well as a collection of large pottery jars. Turn left as signposted at a junction to pass below all the buildings. Go through a gateway and later turn right as signposted through another gateway. Follow an old track with more gates, running parallel to a fearsome gorge drained by the Torrent de Solleric. The deep valley is flanked by the impressive mountains of Puig de s'Alcadena and Puig d'Alaró, which both feature steep wooded slopes and sheer cliffs.

Walk round a side valley and pass a signposted junction below a derelict house at **Font Figuera**. Note how the stone paving underfoot has been laid in two parallel lanes. The hotel of s'Olivaret sits on the other side of the valley. Pass through a couple of old gateways, then the track reaches a ford in the riverbed, where stepping-stones and a handrail are available if any water is flowing.

*Puig d'Alaró and Puig de s'Alcadena, from near Son Berga*

Continue past gates and follow the track until it joins a road. Walk straight ahead, but note the big old country house of Son Berga to the left.

Follow the road past groves of almonds and oranges, passing occasional houses. The mountains of Puig de s'Alcadena and Puig d'Alaró continue to dominate the broad and fertile valley. Keep straight ahead at road junctions, rising slightly to join and follow the main Ma-2100 road, around 220m (720ft). Walk along a generous verge while following this road, passing the Km18 marker. Keep straight ahead past carob trees, and maintain that direction for Alaró. Walk 29 also joins to finish in town.

Carrer de Solleric, Carrer del Pontarró, Carrer Can Ros and Carrer Petit lead to Plaça de la Vila in the centre of **Alaró**. For buses to the Consell-Alaró railway station, turn left before the *plaça* and walk along Carrer d'Alexandre Rosselló and Avinguda de la Constitució, then turn left onto Carrer Joan Alcover to find the bus stop.

# WALK 35
*Cúber, Puig de Massanella and Lluc*

---

| | |
|---|---|
| **Start** | Font des Noguer, Cúber |
| **Finish** | Santuari de Lluc |
| **Distance** | 16km (10 miles) |
| **Total ascent** | 660m (2165ft) |
| **Total descent** | 830m (2725ft) |
| **Time** | 6hrs |
| **Terrain** | Easy tracks at the start and finish, but steep, rough and rocky on the higher parts, with some short scrambles |
| **Map** | Alpina Tramuntana Central and Nord |
| **Refreshment** | Bar-restaurants at Coll de sa Batalla and Lluc |
| **Transport** | Summer buses serve Cúber from Port de Sóller, Sóller, Port de Pollença, Pollença and Lluc. Buses serve Coll de sa Batalla from Inca, Caimari and Lluc. |
| **Note** | A fee will be charged on leaving the property when descending in the direction of Comafreda, according to the tariff set out at www.puigdemassanella.com/en/tarifa. |

The popular and mighty Puig de Massanella can be climbed from Cúber and the summit offers extensive views. A descent can be made in the direction of Comafreda (note the fee) or alternatively, steps could be retraced to Cúber. Other options are possible by linking this route description with the course of the GR221 to reach Lluc.

There are car parks and bus stops at Cúber and while the place is quite remote, and around 750m (2460ft), it is often busy with walkers. Leaving the bus stops, follow a concrete water channel as signposted for Tossals Verds and GR221. This is the **Canal des Embassaments**, feeding water into the Cúber and Gorg Blau reservoirs. There are occasional concrete bridges spanning the channel, but only cross the last one, which is signposted.

Go through a gate and follow a path up into dense holm oak woodland. A cobbled path rises and passes two *sitges*, then crosses the gap of **Coll des Coloms** at 808m (2651ft). Go down past a path junction, through dense woodlands, passing numerous *sitges*, zigzagging to a junction where three paths are sign-posted from a mapboard at **Prat de Cúber**.

Turn left to follow a rugged path a short way down through a gap in a wall, then easier walking leads past a square corral and a couple of *sitges*, with a large *carboner* hut in-between. At a path junction there is an option to turn left to visit **Font des Prat**, returning afterwards. Cross a stone-covered channel and a stone bridge over a riverbed to continue.

The path climbs fairly gently among the woods, even levelling out as it passes a gateway between a wall and a huge, cliff-like boulder. The undergrowth is a mixture of *càrritx* and juniper. Several *sitges* can be seen, while a rock outcrop to the left allows an opportunity to look back down the valley, the **Comellar des Prat**. Pass the water trough of **Font de ses Tosses d'en Gallina**, then the path climbs from holm oaks to pines then emerges onto slopes thick with *càrritx* and stunted pines.

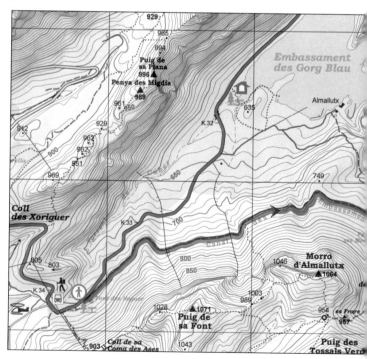

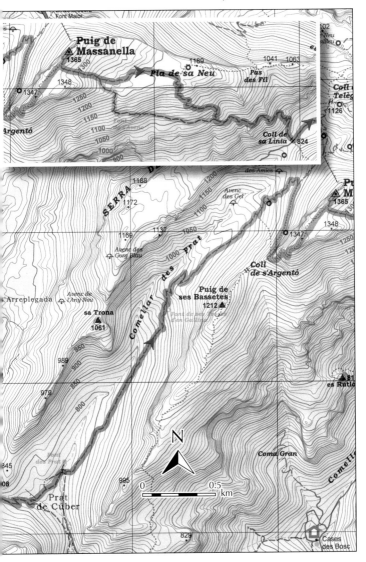

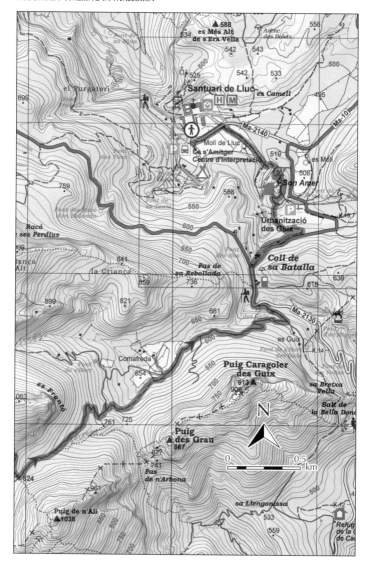

*Looking through Comellar des Prat on the way to Puig de Massanella*

Stony zigzags climb higher, passing an old snow-pit and a ruined building, then watch for a path heading off to the right afterwards. Turn right and basically contour easily across a slope at around 1180m (3870ft). The path climbs onto a rocky slope, climbing rock ledges that form big steps, to pass through the only real breach in a line of cliffs. Once through, watch carefully for the path as it swings left and climbs. The ground is steep and very rocky, but there are cairns and ample evidence of passage. Hands may need to be used.

At a higher level, the gradient eases and a summit can be seen ahead. The bare rock on top of **Puig de Massanella** rises to 1365m (4478ft). Views of the Serra de Tramuntana are exceptional, while closer to hand are cliffs and a deep hole that should be avoided. Take a good look at the slopes, especially if there are other walkers coming and going, as this will help to identify path choices later. One option is to retrace steps to Cúber.

Leave the summit and double back a short way along the rocky crest, then turn left to follow a rugged, cairned and trodden path downhill. A stone pillar is reached where there are two options. The one to the right is more rugged and descends to an interesting cave containing water at **Font de s'Avenc**. See Walk 37 for further details. Turning left follows a stony path down to the gently sloping **Pla de sa Neu**, where snow was once gathered. The path later zigzags downhill into forest, where it meets the other path from Font de s'Avenc at another stone pillar. Continue down to a track on a gap at **Coll de sa Linia**, at 824m (2703ft).

A stone pillar beside the track is carved with the words 'PUIG' and 'LLUCH'. Walk 39 reaches this gap after descending from Puig de n'Ali. Turn left to follow the track downhill, and it later becomes quite bendy. Keep right at a junction to descend further, levelling out where the farm of **Comafreda** lies to the left. Reach a gate and hut where a fee has to be paid to leave the property.

Continue down the woodland track, turning left at junctions to reach the Ma-2130 road. Turn left to follow this, crossing a footbridge and using a pavement that carries the GR222 trail. A bar-restaurant, bus stops and limited parking are available on the **Coll de sa Batalla**, around 580m (1900ft). Walks 38 and 40 also pass here.

Follow the road to a junction, cross over and turn right to follow a minor road parallel to the main road, passing the Bar Restaurant Can Gallet in the **Urbanització des Guix**. Follow the road and continue along a path as signposted for the GR222, crossing a footbridge over an old water channel. Go through a gap in a wall and up a wooded slope to join a track. Turn right down this, then left as signposted up stone steps, to reach the **Refugi de Son Amer**.

> The old mountain estate of **Son Amer** includes three fine, restored buildings. Son Amer itself now serves as a modern *refugi*, but dates from the 13th century. It stands on a hilltop with a fine view of the surrounding countryside, which is now largely wooded. In the past it would have been more agriculturally productive.

Go round the building and through a gate on the far side, to follow a zigzag path down a wooded slope. Go through another gate and continue down to a clear track. Follow this, noting a restored watermill called **Molí de Lluc** to the left. Cross a ladder stile beside a gate, then turn left along a road to reach the car park or bus stop at the **Santuari de Lluc**.

# SANTUARI DE LLUC, ESCORCA AND CAIMARI

A walker descends a reconstructed zigzag path at Voltes d'en Galileu (Walk 38)

*The Torrent de Pareis ends with an easy walk-out to Sa Calobra (Walk 36)*

Mountain walking routes abound near the monastic complex of the Santuari de Lluc. Handy bus services run up and down the mountain road between Caimari and Lluc, and summer bus services elsewhere. Nearby Escorca is the start of a classic walk down through the deep, rock-walled Torrent de Pareis (Walk 36). It needs careful planning, as well as agility and confidence on polished rock scrambles. Despite the obvious dangers, it is one of the most popular and entertaining routes on Mallorca.

Mountains that can be climbed from the doorstep of the Santuari de Lluc include the mighty Puig de Massanella (Walk 37) and its less visited neighbour Puig d'en Galileu (Walk 38). A rather long walk is necessary to climb Puig Tomir (Walk 41), while a walk around the flanks of Puig Roig (Walk 42) is only available on Sundays, due to local access arrangements. Whenever the weather is bad for mountain climbing and remote walks, there is a network of easy paths and tracks that can be linked to provide interesting circuits on rocky slopes, without expending much effort (Walk 43).

The village of Caimari sits at the mouth of a remarkable mountain valley. The Camí Vell de Lluc is an old pilgrim highway that connects the village with Lluc, and this can be used to reach Coll de sa Batalla, from where a series of rugged paths allows a circuit to be made that returns to Caimari (Walk 40). Another interesting route from Caimari climbs Puig de n'Ali (Walk 39), whose summit is a remarkable heap of enormous boulders, making it unique among Mallorcan mountain-tops.

The long-distance GR221 and GR222 trails meet at the Refugi de Son Amer, near Lluc. Parts of both routes are encountered on many of the walks from Lluc. The Refugi de Son Amer has a permanent display about the walking trails of Mallorca in its basement rooms.

# WALK 36
*Torrent de Pareis*

| | |
|---|---|
| **Start** | Bar Restaurante Escorca, Escorca |
| **Finish** | Bus stop, sa Calobra |
| **Distance** | 7km (4½ miles) |
| **Total ascent** | 50m (165ft) |
| **Total descent** | 640m (2100ft) |
| **Time** | 5hrs |
| **Terrain** | A deep canyon with polished and slippery scrambling pitches, awkward boulders and stagnant pools of water. The canyon is very dangerous when wet! |
| **Map** | Alpina Tramuntana Nord |
| **Refreshment** | Restaurants at Escorca and sa Calobra |
| **Transport** | Summer buses serve Escorca from Port de Sóller, Sóller, Port de Pollença, Pollença and Lluc. Summer buses serve sa Calobra from Port de Pollença, Pollença and Lluc. Barcos Azules ferry from sa Calobra to Port de Sóller, tel 971 630170, barcoscalobra.com |
| **Note** | Arrival and departure needs thought. It is possible to arrive at Escorca on the summer bus, descend to sa Calobra, and catch a bus to leave, but this requires careful timing. It is also possible to leave sa Calobra by ferry to Port de Sóller. Small groups of walkers who leave cars at either end of the walk can finish by shuttling everyone to where they need to be. |

The Torrent de Pareis is one of the most popular walks on Mallorca, but can prove dangerous and requires care. This is a linear walk and while most people descend the canyon, it has to be admitted that some of the scrambling is easier while ascending. The main thing is – don't attempt this walk without having a good exit plan! Anyone who feels unable to attempt this walk on their own should hire an experienced guide. With safety in mind, enjoy this truly remarkable, scenic and interesting place.

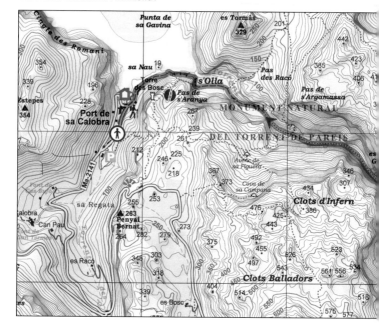

**WARNING**

Although popular, the canyon needs great care. There have been accidents and deaths in it. Mobile phones and GPS don't work deep inside it. A **rope** is useful, especially on scrambles where the rock is polished and slippery. *The canyon should never, ever be entered when it is wet.* Check the current water conditions on the website www.torrentdepareis.info

Start at the Bar Restaurante Escorca, at **Escorca**, around 640m (2100ft). There is a small car park beside a notice explaining about the Torrent de Pareis. Read the notice, and don't start the walk if there is any risk of rain, or any risk that the canyon might be flooded.

A path drops from the road and runs down through woods, with occasional views towards Puig Major. Watch for a sudden left turn, which leads to a rocky edge, then take care to follow the path faithfully as it zigzags down a slope covered in bushy scrub and *càrritx*. The path has some awkward moments, and despite being in regular use, some parts are quite overgrown, but don't short-cut. Land in the bouldery riverbed of the **Torrent de Lluc**, around 200m (655ft). Turn left, which would be downstream if there was any water – but if there is any water, abandon the walk!

The first scrambling pitch encountered, which can be avoided by using an overgrown path to the left, is a warm-up for what comes later, and the huge boulders are nothing compared to some of the monstrous boulders seen later. The Torrent de Lluc joins the **Torrent de Gorg Blau** to become the Torrent de Pareis at

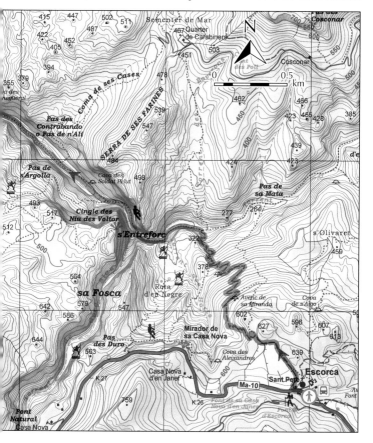

The Torrent de Pareis features several narrow, polished passages

a point known as **s'Entreforc**. By all means spend a few minutes exploring a very narrow canyon on the left, but this is not where the route goes. sa Fosca, further up the canyon, gets no direct sunlight and requires a torch to explore. Look for a signpost on the right for sa Calobra, revealing a rugged path through bushes, avoiding a massive boulder jam in the canyon.

Back on the canyon floor, the next scrambling pitch is long, complex and polished. A slip in the wrong place could result in a fall onto hard rock, or into a smelly, stagnant pool of water. Roughened steps were hammered into the rock, but these are now polished. The problem here is that one scramble follows another, and some of the moves are rather delicate. If anyone feels unable to proceed, then it is *essential* that they haven't already gone down something that they are unable to reverse. When there are groups of people around, it is customary to pass each other's packs up and down, allowing everyone a little more freedom of movement.

There is a long pitch that may or may not be equipped with a fixed rope. If the rope has gone, then it helps if you have brought your own. There is usually a short 'grab' rope at one point to provide something to hold onto while making one exposed move.

Some parts of the canyon floor are best avoided, so watch carefully to spot a path to the left-hand side of the canyon, then one to the right-hand side of the canyon, to avoid time-consuming difficulties. Next is a long but slow walk on boulders, potholed rock and mounds of water-washed gravel. Look at the rock walls and take note of where the water-line is during times of flood. Imagine how difficult it would be trying to swim through the canyon; people have drowned trying.

All of a sudden an impasse is reached, and it becomes clear that the only way is to go down through a hole in the rock. Then, after another relatively easy stretch, there is another hole, and while it is a bit more spacious there is no way out except climbing down a rock face that needs a rope for protection. (Without a rope it is best not to enter the hole, but climb a little and follow a path back down to the canyon floor.)

There is another easier stretch, but there are also a couple of bottleneck squeezes that are polished and awkward. One of these really needs a rope, but with care it can be done without one. Another is a polished corkscrew squeeze through a hole, which slender folk will slip through, but larger folk could get wedged! The last awkward manoeuvre involves straddling a polished boulder jammed in a narrow cleft. No matter how this is done, it looks ungainly, and some might need assistance getting their legs across it.

There is a long, slow walk along the boulder-strewn canyon floor, then it is best to take a path to the left to pass beneath a huge boulder, switching to the right to pass a large pool, and that really is the end of all the difficulties. All that remains is an easy trudge across masses of pebbles, finally reaching a raised beach hemmed in by the canyon walls at **s'Olla**.

Leaving the canyon involves climbing a flight of steps and passing through two tunnels lit with lights set into the floor. (Should the lights fail, a torch would be useful, but it would be possible to grope a way through.) After all the rock, effort and tears, **sa Calobra** offers restaurants and ice-creams. If leaving by ferry, head for the landing. If leaving by bus, follow the road inland to the bus stop.

# WALK 37

*Puig de Massanella from Coll de sa Batalla*

| | |
|---|---|
| **Start/Finish** | Coll de sa Batalla |
| **Distance** | 13km (8 miles) |
| **Total ascent/descent** | 820m (2690ft) |
| **Time** | 5hrs |
| **Terrain** | Easy tracks at the start and finish, but steep, rough and rocky on the higher parts, with some short scrambles |
| **Map** | Alpina Tramuntana Nord |
| **Refreshment** | Bar-restaurant at Coll de sa Batalla |
| **Transport** | Buses serve Coll de sa Batalla from Inca, Caimari and Lluc |
| **Note** | Access via Comafreda requires a fee according to the tariff set out at www.puigdemassanella.com/en/tarifa |

Puig de Massanella is one of the most popular mountains in Mallorca and its summit is an excellent viewpoint. For many years a fee has been charged for access via Comafreda, and this is the most popular approach. Most people come back the same way, but this route visits Coll des Prat, allowing two or three other descent options for for those who wish to make the most of the mountain and its surroundings.

A bar-restaurant, bus stops and limited parking are available on the Coll de sa Batalla, around 580m (1900ft). Walk down the road in the direction of Caimari, using the pavement and footbridge that carry the GR222 trail. Turn right up a

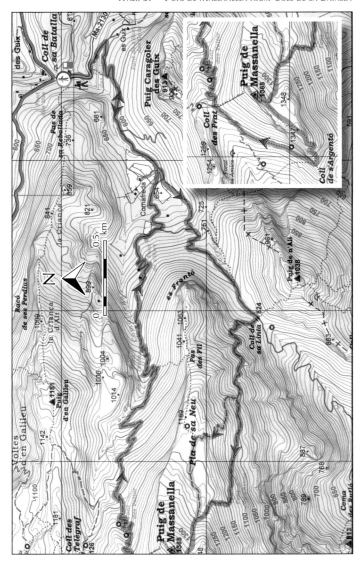

A walker picks a way along the rocky crest of Puig de Massanella

track into woodland, and when a three-way junction is reached, turn right again. The GR222 continues to Caimari, and is used in reverse on Walk 40. Follow the track uphill and keep right at another junction, eventually reaching a gate and hut where you pay a fee.

Continue along the track until a gateway is reached, where the farm of **Comafreda** lies to the right. However, don't go through the gateway, but keep left and follow the track as it climbs more steeply up a wooded slope. The well-trodden route eventually reaches **Coll de sa Linia**, at 824m (2703ft). Note the stone pillar carved with the words 'PUIG' and 'LLUCH'. Walk 39 reaches this gap after descending from Puig de n'Ali.

Turn right and follow a path up a well-wooded slope. It winds as it climbs, but drifts more and more to the right. A junction is reached where a stone pillar bears the options 'PUIG Y FONT' or 'FONT Y PUIG'. Either way leads to the summit, but it is well worth going to the *font* first. So, keep left, or straight ahead, and the trees gradually give way to expanses of bare rock. The path is vague in places, but gradually climbs as it traverses the rugged slope. The **Font de s'Avenc** is very obvious, with steps leading deep into a cave that contains water.

Watch carefully for the line of the path as it climbs a steep and rocky slope. Hands will be needed from time to time. A junction is reached with the other path at a stone pillar carved with 'PUIG' and 'FONT'. Keep climbing, following the rugged path up to a crest, then turning right to reach a summit of bare rock on **Puig de Massanella**, at 1365m (4478ft). Views of the Serra de Tramuntana are exceptional, while closer to hand are cliffs and a deep pothole that should be avoided. A descent can be made from here by retracing steps, or by turning left for a slight variance at the stone pillar.

In order to avoid retracing steps, the following route is available, but it needs care. Retrace steps from the summit, but stay fairly close to the rocky crest, heading roughly south-west. There are cairns, but it helps enormously if the weather is clear. The ground descends steeply and is very rocky, but the cairns and ample evidence of passage prove useful. Watch very carefully for the path suddenly heading to the right, exploiting the only real breach in the cliffs.

Rock ledges form big steps, along with a slope of rock, then the path basically contours easily across a slope, around 1180m (3870ft). Join a much clearer path, which is the waymarked GR221 trail, and turn right. Turning left leads to Tossals Verds or Cúber. Follow the path a short distance up to a wall and a signpost on **Coll des Prat**, over 1200m (3940ft).

The GR221 turns left on the gap and could be followed to Lluc. However, to continue this particular walk, keep straight ahead and follow a rough and stony path into a valley. As it zigzags downhill, it passes two old snow-pits near **Font des Voltor**. The path is slow going, but towards the bottom it gets easier.

Pass **Font de sa Teula** and continue into woodland, descending in long zigzags. **Font de s'Hort** is passed, then the farm of **Comafreda** is seen to the left. Pass through a gateway and keep straight ahead at a junction. (Be ready to present the ticket you paid for earlier in the day, to pass the hut and gate.) Simply retrace steps back down to **Coll de sa Batalla**.

# WALK 38
## Puig d'en Galileu from Lluc

| | |
|---|---|
| **Start/Finish** | Car park, Santuari de Lluc |
| **Distance** | 10.5km (6½ miles) |
| **Total ascent/descent** | 750m (2460ft) |
| **Time** | 5hrs |
| **Terrain** | A rugged walk with steep and rocky sections, involving short scrambles. Paths are vague on the ascent, but plain and obvious on the descent. |
| **Map** | Alpina Tramuntana Nord |
| **Refreshment** | Bar-restaurants at Lluc and Coll de sa Batalla |
| **Transport** | Buses serve Lluc and Coll de sa Batalla from Inca and Caimari. (A bus to Coll de sa Batalla from Lluc saves 2km (1¼ miles).) |

Puig d'en Galileu dominates the view from the Santuari de Lluc, and yet few observers would know its name, and even fewer may know how to climb it. The short scramble known as the Pas de sa Rebollada provides the key to a fine ridge walk to the summit. A descent is made via the restored cobbled path of Voltes d'en Galileu.

Leave the car park or bus stop at the **Santuari de Lluc**, and follow the road away, as signposted for the GR221 and GR222 for Son Amer. Turn right to leave the road as signposted, crossing a ladder stile beside a gate. A track leads gently onwards and a restored watermill, **Molí de Lluc**, stands to the right. However, keep straight ahead and the track gives way to a path up a wooded slope to a small gate. Continue up a cobbled zigzag path to reach the **Refugi de Son Amer**. The building dates from the 13th century and has been restored to provide accommodation for walkers.

Signposts and markers show the way to stone steps leading down to an access track. The GR221 turns left for Pollença and the GR222 turns right for Caimari. Turn right up the access track then turn left down an old wooded path. Go through a gap in a wall and cross a footbridge over a water channel. A path leads up to a road at the **Urbanització des Guix**.

*The Santuari de Lluc and Puig Tomir, seen from a rocky edge*

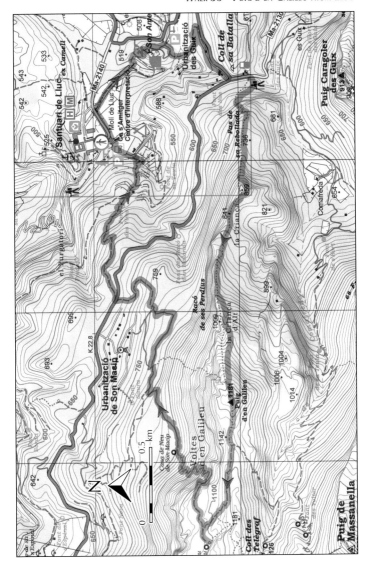

Summit cairn on Puig d'en Galileu, with Puig de Massanella beyond

Walk on a road running parallel to the main Ma-10 road, as marked and signposted for the GR222, up past the Bar Restaurante Can Gallet, to reach a road junction. Turn left to follow a path beside the Ma-2130 road, to the **Coll de sa Batalla**, around 590m (1935ft). There is a filling station with a shop and a bar-restaurant, as well as a bus stop.

Cross the road from the filling station and pass through a fence to follow a very short track up to a pig pen. Keep left to go around its electric fence, passing round the top side on a wooded slope. A vaguely trodden path might be noticed, and there are cliffs above, so take care with route-finding.

Make a sort of rising traverse across the bouldery, wooded slope, watching for a trodden path and small cairns. Once located, follow these up to the cliff. Watch carefully to spot a left turn that leads into a rocky groove, which is the **Pas de sa Rebollada**. The rock has plenty of holds and edges, which have been smoothed by use.

Once on top, holm oaks grow from bare rock and there is a view of Lluc. Watch for cairns to find a wooded valley and walk up it, passing three *sitges*. Keep left to rise past a fourth *sitja*. Again, watch for cairns on the rocky, wooded slope.

Cross a tumbled wall and climb a little, but turn left to cross a point where the wall meets a cliff. There is a steep and worn path, but scramble up the rock alongside, which is safer and easier, then keep left of the cliff. There are strands of old fence wire, which serve to lead towards a short, tumbled wall. Cross this, and maybe turn right to climb to the top of **la Criança**, at 859m (2818ft).

If not climbing the nearby summit, just follow cairns to contour across a rocky slope. Watch carefully for the cairns showing a descent to the left, which is a little easier, then cross a broad gap and keep close to the rocky crest when climbing again. The ascent is largely on bare rock, with trees some distance to either side. Some parts are in woodland, but when it is possible to reach the rocky edge, there are splendid views of Lluc and Puig Tomir. The rocky ridge is narrow and exposed, with a sheer cliff, so the path and cairns keep away from it.

The path is drawn into a rocky valley, near **la Criança d'Alt**, but always keep the cairns in view, which mark the route as it drifts left out of the valley, onto rocky slopes. There are a few trees and the last one has been bent by the wind. Watch carefully for the path when an area of *càrritx* is reached. Although there is a rocky summit ahead, the cairns pass to the left of it, and the true summit lies just beyond. The top of **Puig d'en Galileu** is rocky, but bears a cairn at 1181m (3875ft). Views are extensive, but nearby Puig de Massanella dominates by reason of its bulk.

Descend a short way on rock, then follow a stony path to a junction with the waymarked GR221 trail. Turn right to follow it across a slope of *càrritx*, rising and falling gently, reaching a signposted junction. It is worth turning left to visit the nearby snow-pit of Casa de Neu d'en Galileu. Turn right to follow a fairly level, but rough and stony path before zigzagging down the steep and rugged **Voltes d'en Galileu**. The path starts with its old cobbled stonework intact.

This splendid **mountain path** was constructed centuries ago, allowing transport across the mountains, as well as access to several snow-pits. Over time it gradually fell apart, but was faithfully reconstructed at great expense in recent years, to become part of the long-distance GR221.

The path features tighter zigzags as it drops down rugged, wooded scree slopes. When it runs through denser holm oak woodland, the path is more direct and passes *sitges* and a limekiln. The stone paving ends just above a snow-pit, giving way to a stony track. The track winds downhill, passing numerous *sitges* in dense holm oak woodland, including a big one on a bend.

After the bend, keep straight ahead as marked at a track junction, then further downhill, turn right off a sharp, steep bend as signposted, to follow a lesser track at a gentler gradient. Later, this track bends left downhill, reaching a signpost. Turn right along a path and go through a small gate in a wall. Turn left to follow another track in broad loops downhill, avoiding houses at nearby **Son Macip**. Keep left just before reaching the main Ma-10 road, crossing as signposted.

Walk down a rugged path through holm oak woodland, continuing along a broad, stony path and a restored paved path, then an old cobbled path. Pass from holm oak woodland, through a gap in a wall, onto old olive terraces where the ground is thick with cistus and asphodels.

As the path winds downhill, go through a couple of gateways, then a few steps lead down to a road at **Font Cuberta**. There is an old *font* and a bar-restaurant to the right, as well as a campsite beyond. The road leads down to a picnic area and car park, with the **Santuari de Lluc** just beyond.

# WALK 39
## *Caimari and Puig de n'Ali*

| | |
|---|---|
| **Start/Finish** | Bus stop, Caimari |
| **Distance** | 12km (7½ miles) |
| **Total ascent/descent** | 900m (2950ft) |
| **Time** | 5hrs |
| **Terrain** | Easy roads and tracks in the lower valleys. The mountain slopes are steep and rocky, and paths require attention to route-finding. Some scrambling involved. |
| **Map** | Alpina Tramuntana Nord |
| **Refreshment** | Bars and cafés at Caimari |
| **Transport** | Buses serve Caimari from Inca and Lluc |

Puig de n'Ali has one of the most unusual summits in the whole of Mallorca, being crowned with monstrous boulders. However, it stands beside mighty Puig de Massanella, so it doesn't attract the attention it deserves. The mountain is reached by way of a very scenic walk from Caimairi and its higher slopes are steep and rocky, with tricky route-finding.

If approaching Caimari from Inca or Selva, the bus stops and a small amount of parking are available just before entering the village, at 160m (525ft). (There is a very small car park near Km7.3 above the village.) Follow the road up through the village, using the narrow pavements, then continue out of the village, taking care when the pavement finishes. Pass the access for sa Rota Ca'n Casetes, but take the next turning on the left, near Km7.1, which has a prominent white and yellow paint mark to identify it.

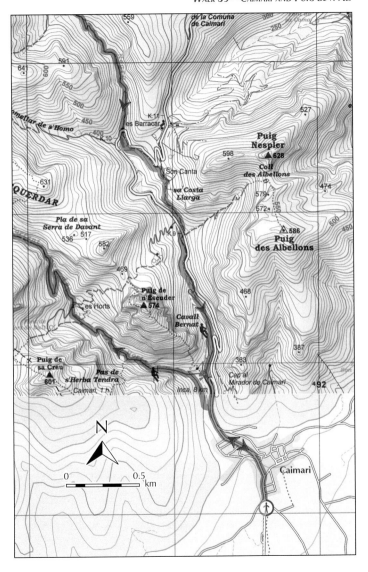

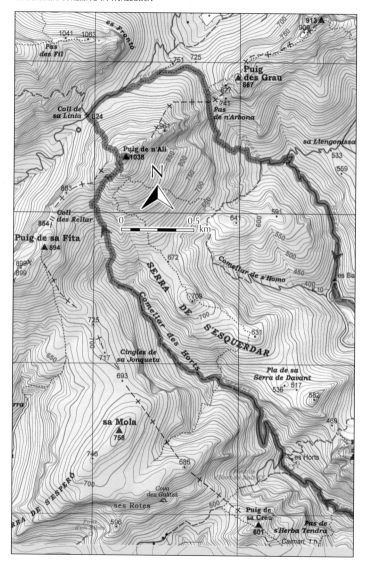

The track runs parallel to the road, then turns left and passes through a gate beside a building, then goes through another gate soon afterwards. The surrounding mountains are steep, rocky and rather eye-catching. The track stays low in the valley, beside the **Torrent des Horts**, with an overhanging cliff on the left being popular with rock-climbers, followed by an overhanging cliff on the right. The track climbs steadily with a view of the neat and tidy farm of **es Horts**.

Go through another gate and the track bends right and left as it climbs, passing a final gate. The track runs high into the valley of **Comellar des Horts**, petering out after passing an *aljub* and a *sitja*, around 650m (2130ft).

Look very carefully to spot cairns and a barely trodden path over broken rock and scrub. This is awkward when there are two or three lines of cairns, but start by crossing a small valley on the mountainside, then pick a way up the rugged slope. There are occasional paint marks on the correct route. Anyone drifting too far left will reach a wall, where it is necessary to cross and then turn right to climb further. The correct route is more direct, keeping well to the left of the rocky summit. Either way, it is necessary to climb across rock and boulders to reach the top.

> The summit of **Puig de n'Ali**, at 1038m (3405ft), is remarkable. It is made of several enormous boulders that have to be scrambled across, and one of them has a space underneath that offers a mountain-top bivouac. Views look down to the plains, and while the massive shape of Puig de Massanella is dominant, other parts of the Serra de Tramuntana can also be seen.

Take care to locate a rather vague path for the descent. Start by having Massanella in view, but it will quickly be lost among the trees. The path runs down to a gap between Puig de n'Ali and Puig de Massanella, which is **Coll de sa Linia**, at 824m (2703ft). A track crosses the gap, and there is a direct link with Walk 37 for anyone interested in adding Puig de Massanella to the day's itinerary. A stone block bears the words 'PUIG' and 'LLUCH'.

Turn right to follow the track downhill, but watch carefully on the right-hand side. The track is in a valley floor, but it drifts left away from it. However, a vague path on the right continues down through the valley, and is followed past a number of *sitges* in the woods. Keep an eye on the path, as it later drifts right and passes between the mountains at the **Pas de n'Arbona**. The path is reasonably clear throughout its descent and it eventually reaches a track on a bend. Continue down the track to a junction and turn right, now following the waymarked GR222 trail. This is Walk 40, in reverse.

Continue down through the forested valley of **Torrent de sa Coveta Negra**, where pines give way to holm oak woodland, with plenty of bare rock slopes. The track runs along the floor of a valley, passing an *aljub*, then runs beneath an

*Monstrous boulders sit on the rocky summit of Puig de n'Ali*

overhang where there is a memorial tablet. A few *sitges* are passed then gates are reached at a road bend. Don't step onto the road, but cross a ladder stile and go through an arch to reach a **picnic area**. The road is stoutly buttressed and a path has been constructed on another buttress, climbing to reach a higher bend.

Turn right to leave the road and pass the lovely old house of **Son Canta**, which stands on olive terraces. An old path winds downhill and its original cobbled surface links with reconstructed stretches, becoming quite broad as it drops to the road near the Km9 marker. Cross the road to pick up another cobbled path running parallel. When this rises to the road again, keep right as signposted for Caimari. Stone steps offer a shortcut where the track makes a big bend. Pass between a huge buttress supporting the road, and a massive boulder with trees growing on it, easily mistaken for a cliff.

The track drops as it runs parallel to the road then the road must be followed onwards from a small car park. Be careful as there is no pavement until **Caimari** is reached. Stay on the main road to return to the bus stops on the edge of the village.

# WALK 40

*Caimari, Camí Vell and ses Figueroles*

| Start/Finish | Bus stops, Caimari |
| --- | --- |
| Distance | 16.5km (10¼ miles) |
| Total ascent/descent | 630m (2065ft) |
| Time | 5hrs 30mins |
| Terrain | Mostly roads, tracks and good paths, but some of the paths in the middle of the walk are quite rugged. |
| Map | Alpina Tramuntana Nord |
| Refreshment | Bar-restaurants at Caimari and Coll de sa Batalla; hotel bar at Binibona |
| Transport | Buses serve Caimari and Coll de sa Batalla from Inca and Lluc |

The Camí Vell de Lluc is an old highway and pilgrim route, now signposted as the GR222 trail between Caimari, Coll de sa Batalla and Lluc. Old paths can be followed from the Coll de sa Batalla, down to a remote old farm at ses Figueroles, then through a mountain valley to reach the attractive little village of Binibona. The circuit concludes with a road-walk back to Caimari.

If approaching Caimari from Inca or Selva, the bus stops and a small amount of parking are available just before entering the village, at 160m (525ft). Follow the road up through the village, using the narrow pavements, then continue out of the village, taking care when the pavement finishes. After Km7.3 there is a hairpin bend and a small car park, where a track is signposted as the GR222. Also note the attractive marker stone for the Camí Vell, or 'old path'.

The track is obvious and runs alongside a steep-sided and very attractive mountain valley. Follow it and pass between a huge buttress supporting the road, and a massive boulder with trees growing on it, easily mistaken for a cliff. A flight of stone steps are marked on the right, short-cutting a bend. Keep following the track and turn left as signposted at a junction, and later cross the road near the Km9 marker. A splendid stretch of the old highway, part original and part restored, climbs to an attractive house at **Son Canta**.

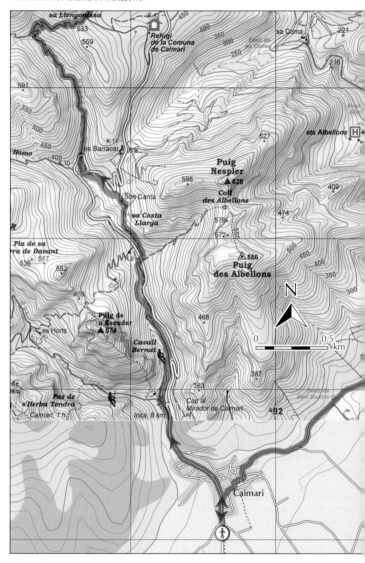

When leaving the house, don't step onto the busy road, but turn left to follow a path running parallel, down to a shaded **picnic area** on a hairpin bend. Go through an arch beneath the road and cross a ladder stile beside a gate. Continue along a track through the valley of the **Torrent de sa Coveta Negra**. Pass a couple of *sitges*, followed by an overhang with a memorial tablet. An *aljub* might be spotted. Keep right at a junction of tracks. Walk 39 joins, descending from Puig de n'Ali to Caimari.

The track climbs more steeply and a number of bends are concrete. Cross a gap at **sa Llengonissa**, at 533m (1749ft), and go down the other side to reach a junction. Turn left up a splendid stone-paved track with an intriguing patterned surface. There is a good viewpoint beside a rocky gap, where the distant Puig de Randa can be spotted between two nearby hills, as well as the Serra de Llevant. (The old track runs around 600m (1970ft), while the modern road below is around 450m (1475ft).) Go through a striking cleft at **sa Bretxa Vella**, where there is a cliff to the left and a pinnacle of rock to the right.

Pass some bouldery rock-fall and damaged sections of the old track. Pass an unfinished building at **es Guix** and simply keep walking ahead, noticing the stout oaks alongside the track. Keep right at junctions, descending to a road, signposts and mapboard. Cross a footbridge over the **Torrent de Comafreda** and walk up to a filling station, shop and bar-restaurant at **Coll de sa Batalla**, at 576m (1890ft).

Face the bar-restaurant and follow a track to the right of it, through a gate, quickly passing into woodland. There are views of Puig de Massanella and neighbouring peaks. Keep left at a junction, gradually climbing, and the track narrows to a path, ending on rocky ground at **Pas d'en Bartomeu**, around 660m (2165ft).

Go through a gap in a wall and a path continues. It is quite rugged, crossing broken ground flanked by *càrritx*, but it is fairly well trodden and obvious. It becomes easier as it descends through pine forest, passing through another gap in a wall. Pass an *aljub* at **sa Rota** then head back among pines. Go through another gap in a wall and make a sudden left turn to pass within sight of an old farm at **ses Figueroles**, around 330m (1080ft).

Don't approach the farm, but follow its overgrown access track away, which is little more than a path. Keep right at a junction, and while the route basically runs down through the valley of the **Torrent des Picarols**, be prepared for it to

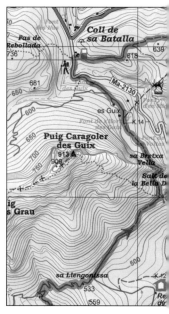

*View towards Puig de Massanella from the Pas d'en Bartomeu*

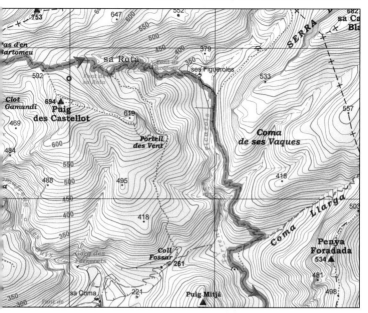

climb, as well as being rocky underfoot in places. Later, as it descends through woods into the valley of **Coma Llarga**, the path broadens into a track and passes a limekiln. Later, another limekiln is passed, then keep straight ahead at a track junction where there is a large boulder.

Pass yet another limekiln, then turn right at a junction, down an old track that crosses a riverbed. Continue through a little rocky gap, following a path as it crosses another riverbed, which is the **Torrent de Sant Miquel**. Step up onto a dirt road at almost 150m (490ft) and turn left. All that remains is a long road-walk to Caimari.

The road becomes tarmac at the gates of the Finca-Hotel Albellons. Follow the road straight past olive groves on the way to the Ca'n Beneït Finca-Hotel. This is closely followed by a huddle of fine stone buildings and hotels at **Binibona**. From here, follow the road straight ahead as signposted for cyclists to Caimari.

The road passes cultivated slopes and rises, then runs into **Caimari**. Follow the cycling signposts for Mancor de la Vall, passing through the central Plaça Major. The Carrer de Ca s'Hereu leads to the main road at the bar Els Ares. Turn left to return to the bus stops at the edge of the village.

# WALK 41
## Puig Tomir from Lluc

| | |
|---|---|
| **Start/Finish** | Car park, Lluc |
| **Distance** | 19km (12 miles) |
| **Total ascent/descent** | 950m (3115ft) |
| **Time** | 8hrs |
| **Terrain** | Easy paths and tracks at the start and finish, but steep, stony and rocky on the mountain, with overgrown paths in the valleys. There are some sections of scrambling, including two for which a chain is provided for assistance. |
| **Map** | Alpina Tramuntana Nord |
| **Refreshment** | Bar-restaurants at Lluc |
| **Transport** | Buses serve Lluc from Inca and Caimari. Summer buses serve Lluc from places as far removed as Port de Sóller, Sóller, Pollença and Port de Pollença. |

Puig Tomir is a splendidly isolated mountain, and it used to be possible to park high on the Coll des Pedregaret to climb it. These days a long walk-in is required. The mountain is steep and rugged, with awkward paths, while making a circuit by returning through adjacent valleys involves rugged and overgrown paths.

This route is formed of two circular walks that join briefly in the middle. Either walk would serve as a good day's walk; together they make for a long and hard day. There are car parks beside the Ma-10 road that would allow the distance to be shortened, but the walk is more satisfying if it starts and finishes at Lluc.

Leave the car park or bus stop at the **Santuari de Lluc**, and follow the road away, as signposted for the GR221 and GR222 for Son Amer. Turn right to leave the road as signposted, crossing a ladder stile beside a gate. A track leads gently onwards and a restored watermill, **Molí de Lluc**, stands to the right. However, keep straight ahead and the track gives way to a path up a wooded slope to a small gate. Continue up a cobbled zigzag path to reach the **Refugi de Son Amer**. The building

*Walkers pick their way across the pathless top of Puig Tomir*

dates from the 13th century and has been restored to provide accommodation for walkers.

Signposts and markers show the way to stone steps leading down to an access track. The GR222 turns right for Caimari and the GR221 turns left for Pollença. Turn left and keep an eye on the markers to pass a car park, then walk parallel to the main road. Cross it using the gates provided, then continue walking parallel to it. Later, veer away from the road and turn right to cross a stone-lined channel.

A clear path leads up a slope of scrub to join a track going through a gateway in a wall. Climb through mixed forest containing pines, holm oaks, arbutus and tree heather. Follow the bendy track until a path is marked off to the left. This rises to the restored chapel of **s'Ermità de Son Amer**, where there are a few little terraces, *sitges* and a view of the mountains flanking Puig de Massanella.

Walk up to a track and turn left further uphill, passing more *sitges* and a lime-kiln. Keep right at a junction, then further up the track, head right as marked and cross a ladder stile over a wall and fence on **Coll Pelat**, around 690m (2265ft). A path leads quickly to a track, which is followed straight ahead past a few *sitges* in rocky woodland. Turn right at a signposted track junction. The track runs gently up and down before passing a gap in a wall beside **Serra d'en Massot**, where there is a view of bulky Puig Tomir ahead.

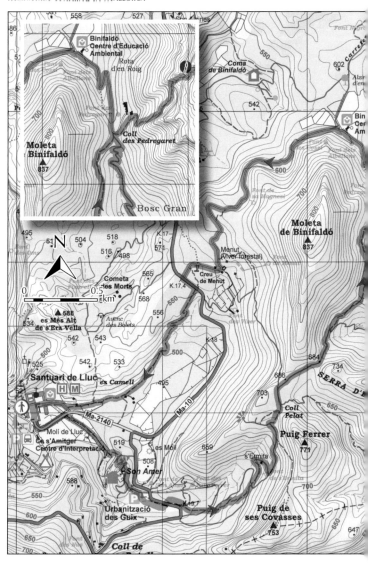

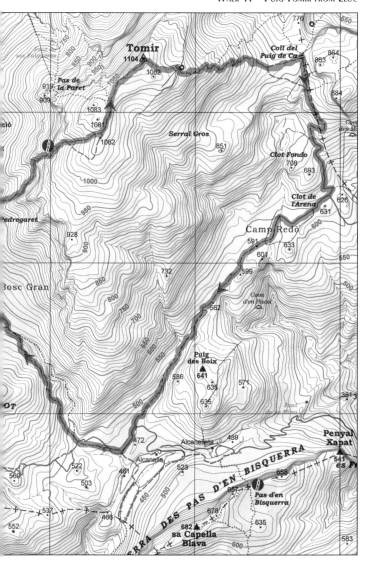

*A narrow path runs through a rugged valley to Alcanella*

Walk down the track but when it bends sharply right, keep straight ahead as signposted along a narrow, rugged path. This features plenty of ups and downs as it passes *sitges* and a ruin, but remains clear and obvious as it crosses a forested slope to reach the broad **Coll des Pedregaret** at around 650m (2130ft). For a short walk (9.5km, 3hrs), omitting Puig Tomir, walk straight along the road and pick up the route description for Lluc below.

Cross a stone stile beside a gate and turn right to follow a signpost for Puig Tomir. Walk up a wooded slope between a fence and drystone wall, then swing left to follow the fence, passing above the old Água Binifaldó water bottling plant. The path turns right before reaching a scree slope. It climbs steeply and is often worn to bedrock, then it runs along the top of the scree, with cliffs above it. A few marker posts confirm the route, then there is a rock scramble, followed by a scramble with the aid of a chain.

Aim for a small rocky gap above, crossing it to find a gully full of scree. Keep to the right-hand side and climb all the way to a rock face at the very top. Another chain and two metal rungs assist on another scramble. Afterwards, keep climbing and keep watching to spot small cairns. The slopes aren't steep, but they are very rocky and it can be difficult to see a trodden path. Nearby humps should be avoided, and the true summit of **Puig Tomir** bears a trig point at 1104m (3622ft). Enjoy extensive views, but look more closely to hand when it is time to leave.

Head towards a jumble of drystone walls, where there is an old snow-pit and a ruined house. Look further downhill to spot a distant grassy gap with a few trees. The route is heading that way, but look closer to hand to spot cairns and the fragmentary remains of the old snow-gatherers' path. There is an unseen cliff between the snow-pit and the gap, and if a breach can't be found, then head left, then head right to reach the gap. A fence stands on the gap of Coll de Fartàritx, at 800m (2625ft), so cross it using a ladder stile.

Follow a track downhill, and it later twists and turns and is surfaced with concrete, passing a gate and a ladder stile. When a junction is reached among a few trees, turn right to follow another track. This serves **Camp Redó**, an area enclosed by a wall and fence, so ladder stiles have to be crossed to enter and leave it. The path beyond is narrow and not always easy to see ahead due to dense *càrritx* or bare rock, but it is often well trodden and marked with cairns.

Later, the valley narrows and there are some substantial holm oaks. Cross another ladder stile and follow the path to link with a track. Turn right and go past a gateway, noticing an old house to the left at **Alcanella**. At one point there is a *sitja* in the middle of the track, and at that point a path can be followed on the right. (Don't worry if this isn't spotted, as the track goes through a gateway and the path crosses it soon afterwards.) Follow the path through a rocky area where there is a fine *aljub*. The path crosses the track again where a big holm oak tree stands.

Take care, as the path becomes vague, and watch carefully as it crosses a streambed. Cairns and paint marks show the way up and across a rocky, scrub-covered slope, but it can be difficult and awkward. A couple of *sitges* are passed, then the path – if it could even be called a path – passes through a gap in a fence into woodland. There is a descent towards a streambed, at a point where a track crosses it.

Turn right and follow the track uphill. It crosses the stone stile beside a gate on the **Coll des Pedregaret**, used earlier in the day. Follow the road ahead and downhill. It bends left and right and passes an educational centre at **Binifaldó**. Walk 44 turns right and leads to Pollença. The road gradually rises, then descends and goes through a gate to pass the forestry house of **Menut**. The stone cross of **Creu de Menut** is seen later on the left, while a limekiln stands to the right. Gates are reached at a junction with the Ma-10 road.

Turn left along the road, then right past gates and a ladder stile, as signposted for Lluc. A broad and stony track descends and becomes quite bendy, then it heads straight to a gritty sports ground. Cross this and reach a road, turning right to follow it through an arch to return to the **Santuari de Lluc**.

# WALK 42
## Mossa, Puig Roig and Lluc

| | |
|---|---|
| **Start** | Mossa gate, Km15.3 on the Ma-10 |
| **Finish** | Car park, Santuari de Lluc |
| **Distance** | 17.5km (10¾ miles), plus 2km (1¼ mile) extension |
| **Total ascent** | 420m (1380ft) |
| **Total descent** | 450m (1475ft) |
| **Time** | 5hrs or 5hrs 30mins |
| **Terrain** | Fairly good paths, but rugged and vague in places, ending with a long walk along a dirt and tarmac road |
| **Map** | Alpina Tramuntana Nord |
| **Refreshment** | Bar-restaurants around Lluc |
| **Transport** | Buses serve Lluc from Inca and Caimari. There are no Sunday buses between Lluc and the Mossa gate. There is very limited roadside parking at Km15.3 on the Ma-10 road near the Mossa gate. (It is only worth parking if another car can be parked at Lluc.) Taxi Escorca, tel 608 631707 or 639 287055 |
| **Note** | Due to local access arrangements, walking around Puig Roig is only possible on Sundays. The route is open-ended, with no Sunday bus service, leaving walkers facing a long road-walk unless a taxi is used, or a vehicle parked at each end. |

Despite the difficulties in regard to access and transport, this walk is very popular, and it is well worth the effort involved in organising it. The coastal cliff scenery is superb, as is the sight of Puig Major dominating the view later. A remote police barracks and cave houses at Cosconar are interesting possible stop-offs.

On Sundays only, go through the pedestrian gate beside the vehicle gate and follow a winding concrete and dirt access road towards the remote farm of **Mossa**. There are signposts for Puig Roig at junctions, and before reaching the house a signpost directs walkers to the right, up through a gate and up a steep flight of stone steps.

Go through a gate and turn left to follow a path above the house, turning right at another signpost to follow a more rugged path. This picks its way across a low cliff, but later makes a rising traverse across a higher cliff face, where the path was blasted from the rock. Holes beside the path used to hold the posts of a safety fence, but that has long disappeared, so take care. Reach the broad gap of **Coll des Ases**, around 620m (2035ft), beside a pine tree.

Look for cairns to follow the rugged path through *càrritx*, then the path should quickly become plain and obvious. Although the surface may be very stony or rocky, it is gently graded and gradually rises across the slope. Looking ahead, it often displays a stone buttressed edge. An *aljub* is passed at the base of a cliff. Later, look back to see Puig Tomir framed by the gap of Coll des Ases.

Turn a sudden corner at **Pas d'en Segarra** for splendid coastal views, taking in the headland crowned by the Torre de Lluc, with the striking Morro de sa Vaca headland beyond. The path passes through a walled enclosure, rises to around 700m (2300ft), and has cliffs above and below. It begins a gradual descent and is obvious most of the time, but there is a slope of dense *càrritx* below **Cingle Pla**, where it is easy to lose the line. If this happens, look for the biggest tree on the slope, then look up towards the cliff, and the stone buttressed edge of the path should be visible.

Later, the buttressing has collapsed, leaving an awkward rock step with a downward scramble. Look down towards the ruined Torre de Lluc, but continue across the slope, keeping an eye on the path, especially when there is a lot of

*The Quarter de Carabiners building with Puig Major rising beyond*

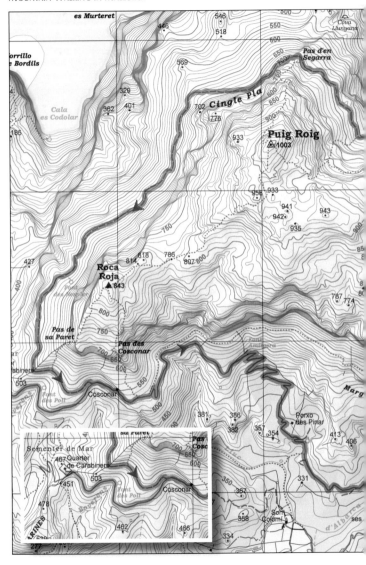

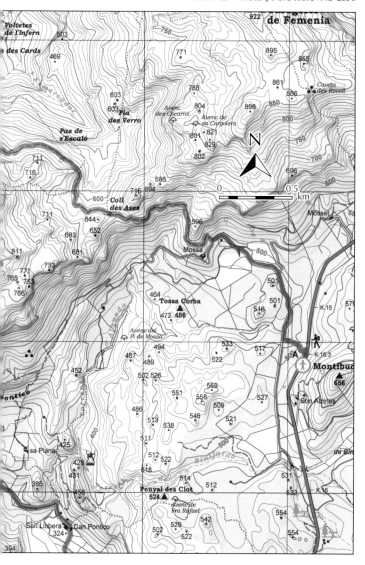

*càrritx* around. A solitary building comes into view; a former police barracks, situated in this remote place to keep a lookout for smugglers. The massive bulk of Puig Major rises beyond. The path stays high, passing pines to reach a gateway gap in a wall. (With some difficulty, the wall could be followed down to the building.)

The path contours round the slope, around 530m (1740ft), then suddenly drops steeply a short way to a dirt road. At this point, an optional extension is possible by turning right and following the road to the barracks, or Quarter de

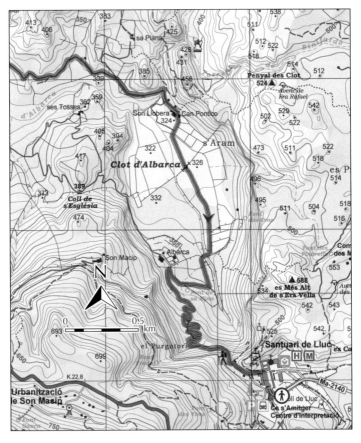

Carabiners. The distance there-and-back is 2km (1¼ miles). If not visiting the barracks, turn left up the dirt road to pass some curious cave houses at **Cosconar**.

The dirt road climbs a little, but later descends in sweeping bends and passes a gate at **Font Amitgera**. Follow the road across a broad, level area largely planted with olive trees, around 330m (1080ft). Keep to the road at all times and it leads to a house, followed by a ford in a riverbed. A footbridge is available, in the rare event of any water flowing.

Follow a tarmac road past houses at **Son Llobera** and continue through fields, crossing cattle grids. A big cross on the skyline shows where Lluc is located. The road makes more sweeping bends as it climbs past the big house of **Albarca**. The road passes through a gate on a wooded slope, although there are views at one point. After passing a sewage works the road suddenly reaches the **Santuari de Lluc**.

# WALK 43
*Lluc, Binifaldó and Menut*

| | |
|---|---|
| **Start/Finish** | Car park, Santuari de Lluc |
| **Distance** | 9.5km (6 miles) |
| **Total ascent/descent** | 250m (820ft) |
| **Time** | 3hrs |
| **Terrain** | Mostly easy roads, tracks and paths, but some paths have short, rugged stretches |
| **Map** | Alpina Tramuntana Nord |
| **Refreshment** | Bar-restaurants around Lluc |
| **Transport** | Buses serve Lluc from Inca and Caimari. Summer buses serve Lluc from places as far removed as Port de Sóller, Sóller, Pollença and Port de Pollença. |

There are some interesting signposted paths and tracks that explore the rugged karst landscape around Lluc. A combination of these routes can stretch to Binifaldó and Menut, offering fine views of the surrounding mountains, as well as exploring some peculiar landforms along the way. Towards the end, the cave of Cova de sa Cometa des Morts can be entered, for a brief exploration underground.

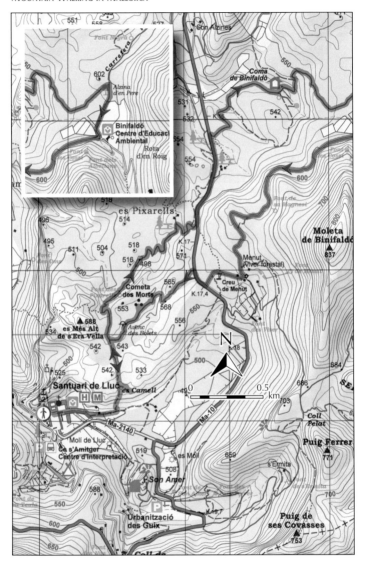

*Passing asphodels near Binifaldó, with Puig Tomir beyond*

Leave the car park or bus stop and go into the courtyard of the **Santuari de Lluc**, almost to the front door. Turn right and go through an arch and follow a road, then turn left at a mapboard and follow a short track to a sports ground. Cross this, then cross a footbridge and follow a very rocky path and crude stone steps uphill.

Reach a level area where there is a *sitja*, and turn right as signposted for **es Camell**. The 'camel rock' is very distinctive and worth the short detour, but return to the signpost afterwards and continue up a broad path until it joins a track.

Turn left to follow *itinerari* 5 along the easy track, reaching a couple of stone seats at a viewpoint looking towards Puig Roig and Puig Caragoler. The track winds downhill and passes remarkable limestone outcrops, then heads into dense holm oak woodland, where the rock is mossy, grotesquely contorted and full of holes. Rise to a car park and shelter at **es Pixarells** and follow a bendy access road up to the main Ma-10 road.

Turn left and follow the road past an entrance for 'Menut I' and continue to an entrance for 'Menut II'. Turn right to leave the road, passing a gate and ladder stile to follow *itinerari* 6. The track features a couple of concrete bends, then it later passes the **Refugi de sa Coma de Binifaldó**.

The track rises and some stretches are concrete, while others are stony. Emerging from the woodland, cross a broad area of asphodels to reach a track junction at 600m (1970ft). The sprawling mountain of Puig Tomir rises beyond. Walk 44 follows the track left to Pollença.

235

The track is the Camí Vell de Pollença, and by turning right it leads past a huge 500-year-old holm oak tree, **Alzina d'en Pere**. Continue onwards until the track reaches a road near the attractive restored buildings of an education centre at **Binifaldó**. Turn right and the road gradually rises, then descends and goes through a gate to pass the forestry house of **Menut**. The stone cross of **Creu de Menut** is seen later on the left, while a limekiln stands to the right. Gates are reached at a junction with the Ma-10 road.

Turn right along the road, then left down a track into another wooded area. Note a signpost on the right for Cova de sa Cometa des Morts; a cave that can be entered, but a torch is needed to explore deep within it. The track continues to a signposted junction. Turn left and follow a broad but rugged path that was followed earlier in the day. It gets more rugged after the signpost for **es Camell**, dropping to a footbridge. Turn right through the sports ground, along a short track, then right again along a road to return to the **Santuari de Lluc**.

## SANTUARI DE LLUC

According to legend, a small statue of the Virgin was discovered beside a stream by a shepherd-boy called Lluc. He showed it to a monk, who took it to a chapel at Escorca. The next day the statue disappeared and was found again beside the stream. This happened three times, as if giving a strong hint about the sacredness of the location, so a chapel was built beside the stream. History sheds little light on the foundation of the chapel, although it was documented twice in the 13th century and was already a place of pilgrimage. The site grew in importance throughout succeeding centuries and the current structure largely dates from the 17th century. Great honours have been bestowed on the monastery by bishops, princes and popes, and today's visitors are enchanted by the voices of the adjoining school choir, who perform briefly each day in the richly decorated Basilica. Dressed in blue robes, they are nicknamed 'Els Blauets' and are recruited from around Mallorca.

The ground plan of the monastery is extensive, and while some parts are private, there is a high degree of access around the site. Be sure to visit the herb garden behind the school, and take a stroll around the stone-paved Camí dels Misteris del Rosari, which encircles a rocky knoll and offers splendid views of rugged mountains arranged around a fertile plain. There is also a fine museum with exhibits stretching back to prehistoric times, see www.lluc.net.

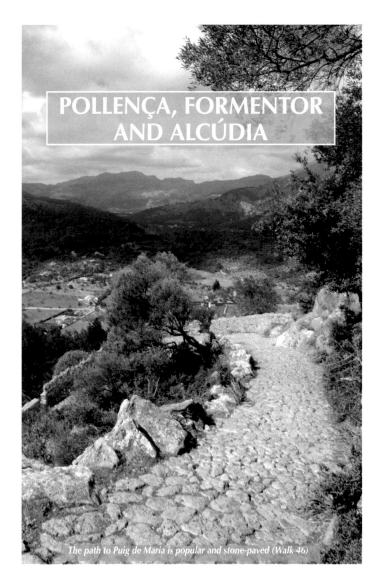

# POLLENÇA, FORMENTOR AND ALCÚDIA

*The path to Puig de Maria is popular and stone-paved (Walk 46)*

237

Looking east from Calvari, over Pollença, towards Formentor (Walk 44)

The Serra de Tramuntana extends all the way through the northern part of Mallorca, then runs far out to sea as the Formentor peninsula. The old 'Camí Vell' can be used to walk from Lluc to Pollença (Walk 44). Anyone finding themselves in Pollença for a couple of hours could climb the miniature mountain of Puig de Maria (Walk 46), which has long been crowned with religious and defensive structures, and is a splendid viewpoint.

Explorations of the Torrent de Mortitx (Walk 45) appear alarming as there are notices warning that people have died there, but this really refers to a canyon not included in this guidebook. The traverse of the rocky ridge of Serra del Cavall Bernat (Walk 47) involves some exposed and difficult scrambling, and it is definitely not for the faint-hearted, inexperienced or those who suffer from vertigo. Anyone who starts, but later realises they have taken on too much, should retreat immediately.

Out on the Formentor peninsula, two notable little mountains offer interesting walks. Rising behind the Hotel Formentor, the rugged na Blanca (Walk 48) can be climbed from sea level as a circular walk. The ominous overhanging peak of el Fumat (Walk 49) can best be explored using a truly remarkable zigzag path that was originally constructed to serve the remote lighthouse of Far de Formentor.

Another mountainous peninsula juts into the sea from Alcúdia. A fine circular walk (Walk 50) takes in two notable heights, including a scramble to the top of Penya des Migdia, which is naturally fortified, and a traverse of Talaia d'Alcúdia, which is the highest point on the peninsula and bears a ruined watchtower. Mapboards in this area detail plenty of other signposted trails, so there is a lot to explore.

# WALK 44

*Lluc to Pollença*

| | |
|---|---|
| **Start** | Car park, Santuari de Lluc |
| **Finish** | Plaça Major, Pollença |
| **Distance** | 19.5km (12 miles) |
| **Total ascent** | 330m (1080ft) |
| **Total descent** | 760m (2495ft) |
| **Time** | 6hrs |
| **Terrain** | Mostly easy tracks and paths, ending with long road-walks into town |
| **Map** | Alpina Tramuntana Nord |
| **Refreshment** | Bar-restaurants around Lluc; plenty of choice around Pollença |
| **Transport** | Buses serve Lluc from Inca and Caimari. Summer buses serve Lluc from places as far removed as Port de Sóller, Sóller, Pollença and Port de Pollença. Regular buses serve Pollença from all the nearby coastal resorts. |

The Camí Vell is an old highway, now signposted as the GR221 trail between Lluc and Pollença. Walkers who follow this pleasant and easy route are surrounded by mountains at first and follow paths and tracks between them. Towards the end, a river is followed through a flat, low-lying valley, with the finish being in the bustling and interesting town centre of Pollença.

Leave the car park or bus stop at the **Santuari de Lluc**, and follow the road away, as signposted for the GR221 and GR222 for Son Amer. Turn right to leave the road as signposted, crossing a ladder stile beside a gate. A track leads gently onwards and a restored watermill, **Molí de Lluc**, stands to the right. However, keep straight ahead and the track gives way to a path up a wooded slope to a small gate. Continue up a cobbled zigzag path to reach the **Refugi de Son Amer**. The building dates from the 13th century and has been restored to provide accommodation for walkers.

Signposts and markers show the way to stone steps leading down to an access track. The GR222 turns right for Caimari and the GR221 turns left for Pollença. Turn left and keep an eye on the markers to pass a car park, then walk parallel to the main road. Cross it using the gates provided, then continue walking parallel to it. Later, veer away from the road and turn right to cross a stone-lined channel.

A clear path leads up a slope of scrub to join a track going through a gateway in a wall. Climb through mixed forest containing pines, holm oaks, arbutus and tree heather. Follow the bendy track until a path is marked off to the left. This rises to the restored chapel of **s'Ermità de Son Amer**, where there are a few little terraces, *sitges* and a view of the mountains flanking Puig de Massanella.

Walk up to a track and turn left further uphill, passing more *sitges* and a lime-kiln. Keep right at a junction, then further up the track, head right as marked and cross a ladder stile over a wall and fence on **Coll Pelat**, around 690m (2265ft). A path leads quickly to a track, which is followed straight ahead past a few *sitges* in rocky woodland. Turn right at a signposted track junction. The track runs gently up and down before passing a gap in a wall beside **Serra d'en Massot**, where there is a view of bulky Puig Tomir ahead.

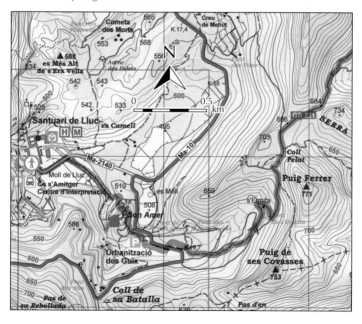

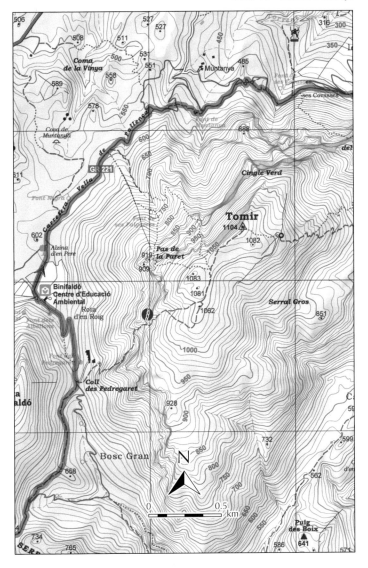

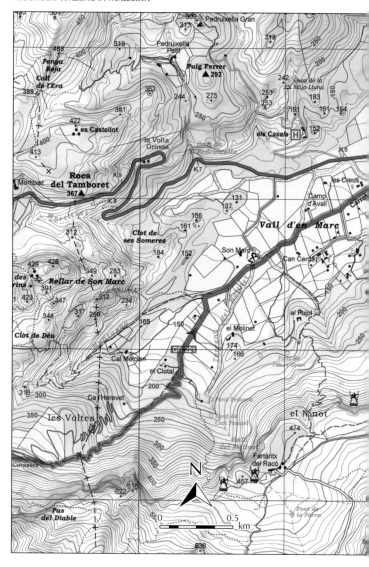

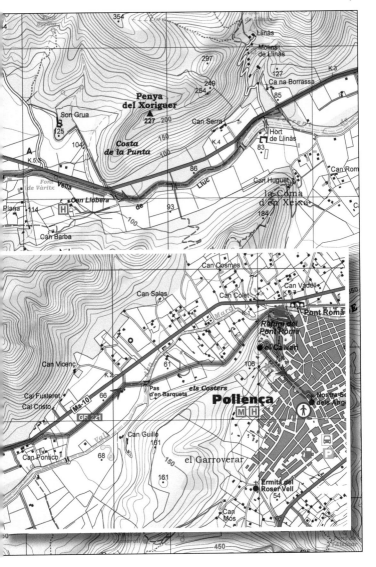

The Santuari de Lluc, as seen from the Refugi de Son Amer

Walk down the track but when it bends sharply right, keep straight ahead as signposted along a narrow, rugged path. This features plenty of ups and downs as it passes *sitges* and a ruin, but remains clear and obvious as it crosses a forested slope to reach the broad **Coll des Pedregaret** at around 650m (2130ft). Cross a stone stile beside a gate and follow the road ahead and downhill. It bends left and right and passes an educational centre at **Binifaldó**.

Turn right at a ford and stepping-stones to follow a track, where notices alongside are available in braille. Fields rise on the right towards Puig Tomir, while stony scrub stretches to the left. Mountains form a complete circle including Puig Tomir, Moleta de Binifaldó, Puig de Massanella, Puig Roig and Puig Caragoler. A holm oak tree of considerable girth stands on the left of the track. It is known as Alzina d'en Pere and is estimated to be 500 years old!

The track rises gently and is joined by the Camí Vell, or 'old road', from Lluc. Walk straight ahead and gently down into a forest with limited views. Pass through gates and follow the track beneath the rocky face of Puig Tomir, heading down through sparser woodland with an undergrowth of heather and cistus. The track is broad, rough, stony and increasingly bendy. Views range from the rugged Ternelles region to the spiky peaks of the Formentor peninsula in the distance, with Cuculla de Fartàritx closer to hand.

Watch for marker posts, stepping down a cobbled path on the left to short-cut a bend from the track. Cross the track and go down a winding path that features old cobbles and restored surfaces. Pass the **Font de Muntanya** and land on the track again beside a bridge. Continue straight ahead downhill until a path is sign-posted away from the track. Use this to short-cut a bend, then continue along the track. Watch for another path short-cutting another bend, and land on the track again further downhill.

Follow the track until a hairpin bend is reached at **ses Covasses**, where a narrow path is signposted straight ahead. When a *sitja* is reached, step down to the left as marked. Walk down across a wooded slope alongside a wall and go through a wooden gate. The path runs down a steep, rugged, bouldery, wooded slope, becoming incredibly convoluted further downhill. Pass a couple of *sitges* and a limekiln and continue roughly parallel to a wall. Fork right as marked, and follow the woodland path downhill beside a tall fence.

Turn right along a tarmac access road as signposted and continue down mock-paved concrete bends. After passing through a gateway, the mock paving gives way to a narrow tarmac road. Simply follow this straight ahead, bending right to pass **Son Marc** and **Camp d'Avall**, on the way past fields, orchards and nut groves in **Vall d'en Marc**. Eventually cross a bridge over a river to reach a junction with the main Ma-10 road.

Turn right as signposted for the GR221, following a riverside path rather than the main road. The **Torrent de la Vall d'en Marc** is followed closely, and the path is quite rugged in places. Sometimes, there is no water in the river, while at other times it may carry enough water to flood low-lying parts of the path, in which case it is best to double back and follow the road. The riverside path crosses a track beside some tall plane trees, where the big house of **Can Serra** can be seen across the nearby main road. There might be changes here in the future, and the route might cross to the southern bank of the river.

Keep to the northern bank of the river, but note that the route is suddenly diverted left to a ladder stile, reaching the main road. Turn right to walk beside the main road, passing **Can Pontico**. A signpost indicates a right turn to a track, which in turn leads to a road. Further along, turn left along a track that runs parallel to the river, but some distance from it. Turn right as marked at a junction and cross a footbridge over the river at **Pont d'en Barqueta**. Continue straight along a road, which leads unerringly to the **Refugi del Pont Romà**, around 60m (195ft), on the outskirts of Pollença. The *refugi* occupies a former slaughter house. Pont Romà is a crumbling arched bridge a little further downstream.

Leave the *refugi* and turn right along Carrer de l'Horta. This road could be followed straight into town, and is signposted as such, but a more impressive alternative is available. Turn right up Carrer de Gruat, a winding road that is also signposted as the GR221. The road is flanked by the Stations of the Cross, which lead to the hilltop chapel of **Església del Calvari** at 125m (410ft). From there, after enjoying views across town to Puig de María, walk down 365 stone steps into the Plaça dels Seglars at the foot of the hill. Continue down the narrow Carrer de l'Ombra to reach the open Plaça Major in front of the church in the middle of **Pollença**.

# WALK 45

*Mortitx and Rafal d'Ariant*

| | |
|---|---|
| **Start/Finish** | Mortitx gate, Km10.9 on the Ma-10 |
| **Distance** | 7.5km (4¾ miles) or 10km (6¼ miles) there-and-back for the alternative walk to ses Basses |
| **Total ascent/descent** | 300m (985ft) |
| **Time** | 4hrs or 3hrs for the alternative walk to ses Basses |
| **Terrain** | Apart from easy tracks at the start and finish, vague, arduous and rugged paths that require careful route-finding, and a canyon requiring some scrambling. By contrast, the alternative walk is very easy. |
| **Map** | Alpina Tramuntana Nord |
| **Refreshment** | None, unless sampling the wine at Mortitx Vinyes |
| **Transport** | Summer buses pass the Mortitx gate, from Port de Sóller, Sóller, Lluc, Pollença and Port de Pollença. However, this is not a recognised stop and it would be necessary to negotiate with the driver for a drop-off and pick-up. |

Facing a notice saying that people have died on this walk is alarming, but this really refers to a dangerous canyon off-route. That said, this is quite an arduous walk to a remote, ruined farmhouse, and there is a splendid canyon to negotiate on the return that requires occasional scrambling. However, it isn't as tough as the Torrent de Pareis. There is an easy alternative available, which simply follows a clear track to an area noted for its population of black vultures.

Start at Km10.9 on the Ma-10 road at the Mortitx gate, around 390m (1280ft), where there is very limited parking. If the gate is locked, use the steps nearby to reach the access track, then follow it past a tennis court. Watch for a building on the right, and cross a ladder stile with a gate on top of it. Follow a track through a vineyard to reach a gate for the Finca Publica de Mortitx. The gate is locked and surmounted by a tall fence, and bears a sign warning that people have died in this area. It all seems calculated to deter the casual visitor. If deterred, double back and enjoy the easy alternative walk instead.

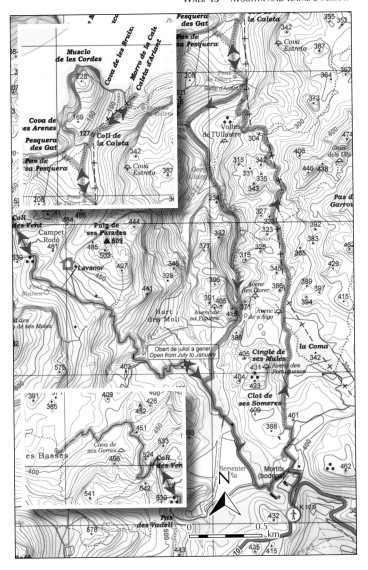

*The route can be extended a little beyond the ruins of Rafal d'Ariant*

Turn left and follow a track, but watch carefully to the right and a ladder stile will be spotted, crossing the wall and fence. Once across, turn right and follow the track on the inside of the locked gates. The track turns left at a junction, then when it turns left again, leave it on the right to follow a vague, cairned path.

Take great care to follow the trodden line and cairns, despite them weaving about among trees, rocks and *càrritx*. If the path is lost, stop and find it again. It leads through a gateway in the corner of a wall, then there are some rocky stretches ahead, and some easy scrambling at times.

The path descends a little, rises again, and some short stretches of stone buttressing are seen from time to time. Cross a rugged gap, descend a little and rise, then descend again and maybe spot a notice to the right.

The path zigzags down beneath a cliff face at **Voltes de l'Ullastre**, and a solitary, ruined building can be seen below. The aim is to go to the ruin, but only by following trodden paths, which are not always easy to spot or follow. The ruin is **Rafal d'Ariant**, standing around 150m (490ft).

At this point the route turns left, but anyone in the mood to explore could follow a route to an alarmingly sudden cliff edge at **Pesquera des Gat**, or pick a way down towards the sea at **Caleta d'Ariant**. Both options are very worthwhile extensions, but steps have to be retraced to the ruin.

To continue on the main route, walk past fig trees to reach a rubble-strewn riverbed. To the right is a rocky constriction at **Gorg des Bec d'Oca**. Canyoners are sometimes seen heading this way, carrying ropes and hardwear, but the route becomes very dangerous for ordinary walkers. So, turn left and walk along the riverbed, crossing boulders while walking towards a lesser rocky constriction at **Gorg Llarg**. A rock pool is passed easily, but the next rock pool is more of a problem. It is best to keep left of it and scramble carefully across the rock to get past. A slip means a ducking!

Two rugged canyons meet and several cairns suggest that walkers should take the one on the left, which is the **Torrent de Mortitx**. Some parts are walkable at a slow pace, while other parts involve squeezing past boulders, or climbing over them. There are some short scrambles. Don't be tempted to follow a path climbing out of the canyon, which only leads to awkward terrain that was crossed earlier in the day.

Follow the canyon bed as closely as possible, and it later broadens, but there is also dense *càrritx* that tends to obscure the path. The way becomes clearer again as the canyon narrows, but looking ahead, it appears to finish with rock walls all around. In fact, there is a sudden turn to the right, and a final climb leads out of the canyon, onto a level path through a broad area of *càrritx*. Follow the path carefully, crossing a streambed in order to reach a clear track with little difficulty.

Turn left to follow the track past olive groves. Turning right allows the walk to be extended, but see the note below. A stone hut is reached, where there are notices, a mapboard, and a ladder stile beside a gate. Follow the track past vineyards, with the massive hump of Puig Tomir rising beyond. The track climbs past the entrance to Vinyes Mortitx, where wine is sold, then it continues uphill, passing the tennis court to return to the Ma-10 road.

## Alternative walk to ses Basses

Walkers who start the main walk and then realise that the terrain is far too difficult should retrace their steps immediately. Instead of abandoning Mortitx, it is worth following the vehicle track as far as it goes.

In brief, the track descends past Vinyes Mortitx and passes vineyards. Cross a ladder stile beside a gate to pass a mapboard, notices and a stone hut. After a level stretch past olive groves, the track begins to climb and is quite bendy, with some stretches surfaced with concrete. Pass a junction and signpost, keeping right and descending a little to cross a dam. The bendy track climbs, reaching a gateway on what appears to be a gap beside a tower of rock. In fact, the track climbs further into a forest.

When a junction is reached, a right turn leads down to a *refugi* at Lavanor, while keeping straight ahead through the forest is prohibited between January and July. Outside that time, the track can be followed over the **Coll des Vent** to reach an area known as **ses Basses**. The reason for the seasonal prohibition is to protect black vultures while they are nesting and rearing their young. At any point, simply turn around and retrace steps all the way back to **Mortitx** and the Ma-10 road.

# WALK 46
## *Pollença and Puig de Maria*

| | |
|---|---|
| **Start/Finish** | Plaça Major, Pollença |
| **Distance** | 5.5km (3½ miles) |
| **Total ascent/descent** | 275m (900ft) |
| **Time** | 2hrs |
| **Terrain** | Easy roads and paths, but steep in places |
| **Map** | Alpina Tramuntana Nord or Mallorca Nord |
| **Refreshment** | Plenty of choice in Pollença; bar-restaurant on the summit |
| **Transport** | Regular buses serve Pollença from all the nearby coastal resorts. There are also summer buses from Port de Sóller, Sóller and Lluc. |

Puig de Maria is a small mountain that dominates Pollença. It is easily climbed from the town centre, and its summit bears an old chapel and defence fortifications. It is a natural viewpoint, taking in the town, countryside, Serra de Tramuntana and the rugged coastal peninsulas. Pilgrims climb to the summit on Easter Monday.

Leave Plaça Major in the centre of **Pollença**, walking along Carrer de Sant Isidre, turning right at the end to reach the leafy Jardins Joan March Servera. Walk past the tourist information office and *museu*, continuing straight along a road, then turn left along Carrer del Bisbe Desbach. Take the second turning on the right, along Carrer del Puig de Maria. This reaches a Repsol filling station on a busy road, opposite the Bar Ca'n Bach.

Cross the busy road to follow what appears to be a dead-end road. However, turn right and left along a track, reaching the main Ma-2200 road. Cross this road with care and follow Camí del Puig de Maria straight ahead. This narrow road rises and turns sharp right and left past a few houses and terraced gardens. The road becomes even narrower, with tarmac giving way to concrete, climbing in steep zigzags past holm oak, pines, carobs and fan palms.

At the end of the road a wide cobbled path with steps continues climbing and leads unerringly to the summit. However, there is another path on the way

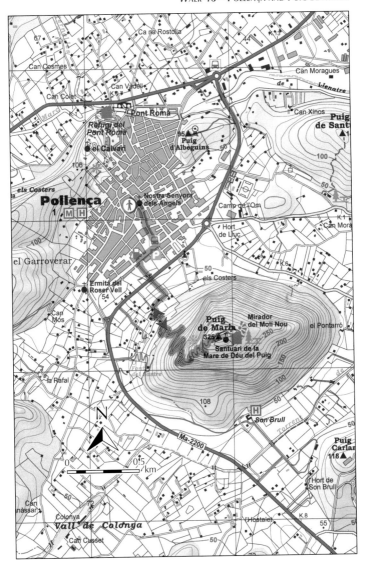

*Fortifications, a church, a bar and accommodation sit on the summit of Puig de María*

uphill, heading off to the left to the Mirador del Molí Vell. This offers a splendid a bird's-eye view of Pollença. The top of **Puig de María** is entirely built-up, around 325m (1065ft).

> A **chapel** has existed on the summit since 1348, and by 1362 this was tended by the first female hermits in Mallorca. As a place of pilgrimage, the site expanded to include accommodation and dining facilities. A particularly spacious room was once a refectory. In 1988 the last of the elderly nuns who ran the place retired, but the chapel remains open.

Go through a gate into a courtyard to face a chapel and enjoy excellent views from a parapet wall. Go through a gate to the left of the chapel to reach a **picnic site** behind it. Explore the buildings, noting that there is usually access between the chapel and the adjoining hostatgeria. Bygone artefacts can be studied in a small *museu*.

When explorations are completed, simply retrace steps back down to **Pollença**.

# WALK 47

*Serra del Cavall Bernat*

| | |
|---|---|
| **Start/Finish** | Carrer de Joan XXIII, Port de Pollença |
| **Distance** | 9.5km (6 miles) |
| **Total ascent/descent** | 450m (1475ft) |
| **Time** | 5hrs |
| **Terrain** | Easy roads and paths at first, then steep and rugged paths, followed by some very exposed scrambling that requires great care. Easy paths at the end |
| **Map** | Alpina Mallorca Nord |
| **Refreshment** | Plenty of choice around Port de Pollença and Cala de Sant Vicenç |
| **Transport** | Regular buses serve Port de Pollença from all the nearby resorts |
| **Warning** | Although popular, this walk is potentially dangerous and requires a head for heights and confidence on rocky, exposed terrain. There are no easy escapes from the rocky ridge. |

This walk is dangerous, but also quite popular with those who have a head for heights, who like to scramble and are looking for a challenge. Access is easy from Port de Pollença or Cala de Sant Vicenç, but the paths are rugged and the rock scrambles need great care. With safety in mind at all times, enjoy the rock scenery, the sheer and overhanging cliffs, and the exhilarating feeling of exposure.

Start on the seafront at **Port de Pollença**, at the roundabout where there is also a taxi stand. Follow the road straight inland as signposted for Palma, which is Carrer de Joan XXIII, and also the GR221 trail. When a big roundabout is reached at the Eroski supermarket, turn right and use a pedestrian crossing, then follow the busy main road to a small stone building. Turn left along Carrer de les Roses, and left again at a junction. The road then turns right and left, leaving the houses to run beside a field. Turn right again at a junction marked for Síller, still running beside the field.

The road reaches a junction, where a dirt road continues straight ahead, eventually passing through gates beside a house. Follow a clear track onwards, keeping left at a junction, then turning right along a well-trodden path. This weaves as it climbs, but is clearly heading for a low gap between the mountains. The path becomes a track and passes a covered reservoir on the **Coll de Síller**, at 82m (269ft).

Keep right, or straight ahead, at a junction to reach a roundabout built around a pine tree. Follow a road downhill, but only as far as a pronounced left bend. If starting from Cala de Sant Vicenç, walk up this road, which is Camí de Cala Carbó. A path leaves the road on the right, but it isn't obvious at first. It is partially trodden and cairned as it climbs a slope of *càrritx*, but keep watching as it is possible to lose it.

The slope gets steeper and rockier as height is gained, with good views across Cala de Sant Vicenç. Looking uphill, two drystone walls can be seen among jumbled rocky outcrops, and both of these need to be passed. The summit of **Talaia Vella**, at 353m (1158ft), is bare rock, with views along the Formentor peninsula, as well as far beyond to the Serra de Llevant and Serra de Tramuntana.

Take a good look ahead at the rocky crest of the Serra del Cavall Bernat, and decide whether continuing in that direction is a good idea. (Retrace steps if you have any doubts.) Immediately to hand, there is a rocky ridge descending from Talaia Vella, with a small valley full of *càrritx* beside it. There is a trodden path down through the valley, but it is worth scrambling down the rocky ridge, just to get a feel of what is to come later. Either

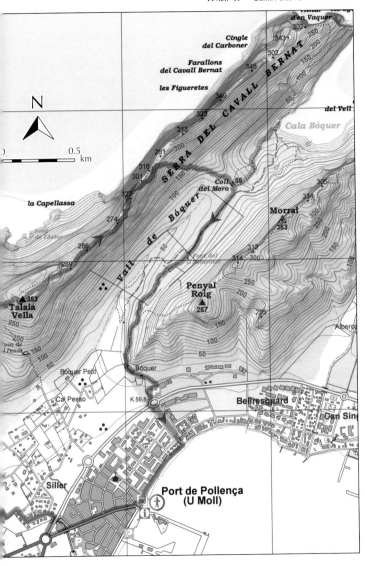

The steep and rocky Serra del Cavall Bernat from Talaia Vella

way, watch carefully for the path as it crosses a gap on the crest, and bear in mind that there is no escape from the ridge ahead, until a path is followed downhill much later.

Watch carefully for the line of the path, which is sometimes obvious, but sometimes virtually absent. There are small cairns to mark the route, but these need to be looked for very carefully at times. The path, such as it is, traverses the mountain flank overlooking the Vall de Bóquer, and only occasionally reaches the actual crest of the ridge, where there are always spectacular views of the cliffs and sea. Hands begin to be used more and more, and an early gap is easily identified because it has a peculiar, small, level slab of rock on it. Leave this gap by traversing a rocky slope.

Further along the slope and below the ridge there is an awkward rocky corner to negotiate by scrambling. Further along again there is more scrambling, and if the small cairns are followed faithfully, the route appears to reach an impasse at a huge boulder and an imposing rock face. Look up and a cairn can be seen. There is no doubt that the rock face has to be climbed. Fortunately there are good holds for hands and feet. Do not climb if you feel unable to reverse it, should any problems be encountered later. Keep following the cairns, and if there is any doubt about where to go, pick a way up to a rocky summit at 327m (1073ft), stopping to admire the view, but also to study the rest of the ridge very carefully.

For once, the actual rocky ridge can be followed with care, but it soon leads to a gap that ordinary walkers and scramblers should not cross. Although it can't be seen from this point, the ridge ahead has a hole through it – a rock 'window'.

It is necessary to descend the steep and rocky slope with care, watching all the time for little cairns, and traverse far below the ridge. Looking ahead, one of the key points to aim for is a cairn sitting on a boulder, which in turn sits on a flat rock platform on a shoulder. Getting there involves plenty of scrambling, as well as squeezing past scratchy fan palms, and it all proves arduous and awkward.

Once the key point is reached, a sloping rock ledge beyond also needs care. However, this ledge ultimately leads to a path that descends from the ridge to safe ground in the valley. The path is marked with cairns, crossing rock, scree and scrub. Keep following it to link with a very well-trodden path beyond **Coll del Moro**, at 85m (279ft). The path is usually busy with walkers, heading to and from the nearby beach of Cala Bóquer, which is only 600 metres there-and-back.

Turn right to follow the broad and clear path through the **Vall de Bóquer**, passing through gateways in and out of a large, walled enclosure. Look up to the ridge to spot the rock 'window'. The path passes between truly monstrous boulders with ease, then the way is flanked by dense bushes. Gates are passed, on either side of the old house of **Bóquer**, and a dirt road runs down to a busy round-about on a bypass. Simply cross to the other side and walk through a linear park into **Port de Pollença**, flanked by parallel roads. At the end, the short Avinguda de Bocchoris leads straight to the beach. Turn right and follow the pedestrianised promenade past bar-restaurants, hotels and shops to return to the roundabout where the walk started.

*Rock climbers follow the crest of the Serra del Cavall Bernat, while scramblers keep low on the right*

# WALK 48
## Formentor and na Blanca

| | |
|---|---|
| **Start/Finish** | Formentor car park, Km8.8 on the Ma-2210 road |
| **Distance** | 8km (5 miles) |
| **Total ascent/descent** | 350m (1150ft) |
| **Time** | 3hrs |
| **Terrain** | Easy tracks give way to rugged mountain paths, ending with a road-walk and coastal paths. |
| **Map** | Alpina Mallorca Nord |
| **Refreshment** | Beach bars (the Hotel Formentor facilities are for residents only) |
| **Transport** | Summer buses serve a large car park at Formentor, from Port de Pollença, Alcúdia and Can Picafort. La Gaviota ferries from Port de Pollença land only a short distance from the car park, tel 971 864014 |

The rugged little mountain of na Blanca offers a fine walk with good views. Its higher parts are a world removed from the Hotel Formentor complex at its foot, along with a popular beach. This circular walk looks at the mountain from all directions, and it can also be tied with Walk 49, over el Fumat, using an obvious linking track.

The Ma-2210 road has a junction where a signpost points straight ahead for Formentor, and left for Cap de Formentor. Summer buses stop here, and there is a large, sheltered car park. Walk all the way through the car park to reach tall gates and a ladder stile, bearing in mind that these might be hidden behind parked cars. Don't worry about the 'private' notice, and follow a clear track onwards into woodland. A limekiln stands at a junction, where blue and green arrows point right. Turn right and follow the track up past a cave as it bends left. Go straight ahead through a broad, open area where there are heaps of rubble.

Follow the track straight ahead through the forest. Don't take any tracks heading left, which lead back to the road, and don't take any tracks heading right, which reach dead-ends. Occasional blue and green arrow markers point the way ahead. The track runs through a gentle valley called **Pla del Pujol**, and the arrows

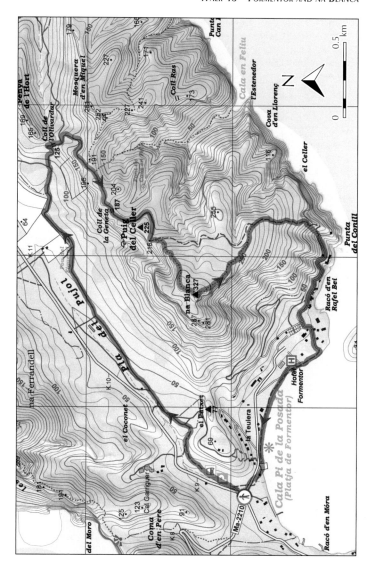

point right at a junction, avoiding a cultivated area and vineyard to the left. Follow the most obvious track gently uphill through the forest, turning right at a signposted junction that also has a green arrow marker. The track that joins at this point links directly with Walk 49, for el Fumat and Cala Murta.

*The walk finishes with a pleasant and easy coastal path*

The track soon swings right as it climbs and it is very stony. It later levels out and is much more pleasant as it passes a few pines. It descends a little to a gap at **Coll de la Geneta**, where there are views to the end of the Alcúdia peninsula, with the Serra de Llevant beyond. Climb again around the slopes of **Puig del Celler** and the track suddenly dwindles to a path.

Watch very carefully, as the path soon splits into two, and while both options are cairned, the split isn't obvious. Be sure to turn right, as the left-hand path misses na Blanca summit completely. Both paths join again, but well beyond the summit. Climb from a scrub-covered slope onto a more rocky slope. Watch the cairns carefully and they eventually lead to a larger summit cairn on **na Blanca**, at 327m (1073ft). Views stretch from the Formentor and Alcúdia peninsulas, to the Serra de Llevant and part of the Serra de Tramuntana.

For the descent, note that there is absolutely no way to go directly down to the Hotel Formentor. Instead, look towards the Alcúdia peninsula and walk as if heading for its furthermost tip. At the same time, watch for cairns while negotiating awkward, broken rock. As more and more pines begin to feature, the path is clearer, and a junction is reached where another path joins from the left.

Walk straight ahead, and there is really only one path down a steepening slope of pines. It winds downhill and eventually reaches a locked gate in a fence, where a house sits on **Punta del Conill**. Turn right to follow the path steeply downhill and it reaches a road beside a stout gate. Turn right to follow the road and cross a chain barrier. Later, pass a private car park, then when a road junction is reached, turn left and walk down to a turning area beside Club de los Poetas.

A short path leads to the coast, where turning right reveals a pleasant coastal path. Pass a couple of large gates that allow residents access to the **Hotel Formentor** grounds, and follow a paved path for a while, followed by a path so worn that the roots of pine trees are exposed. A sandy beach-walk passes beach bars, as well as a jetty where La Gaviota ferries land, offering a splendid way to return to Port de Pollença. However, anyone catching a bus, or returning to the Formentor car park, will have to leave the beach and head inland to the road.

# WALK 49

### *el Fumat and Cala Murta*

| | |
|---|---|
| **Start/Finish** | Cala Figuera car park, Km13 on the Ma-2210 |
| **Distance** | 10km (6¼ miles) |
| **Total ascent/descent** | 400m (1310ft) |
| **Time** | 3hrs 30mins |
| **Terrain** | Mostly easy roads, tracks and paths, but the highest parts are steep, rocky and require more care |
| **Map** | Alpina Mallorca Nord |
| **Refreshment** | None |
| **Transport** | None, but using a taxi would avoid a road-walk through a tunnel. |
| **Note** | It is best to start this walk reasonably early in the morning, before there is much traffic heading out along the Formentor peninsula. |

Out on the Formentor peninsula, the peak of el Fumat leans so ominously that the road was tunnelled beneath it. When the lighthouse was constructed at the end of the peninsula, it was served by an older road called the Camí Vell del Far de Formentor. A remarkable zigzagging stretch of the old road passes behind el Fumat.

From the dirt car park, around 100m (330ft), the road needs to be followed uphill and through a tunnel, to reach a point between Km14.3 and Km14.4. If arriving by taxi, go through the tunnel to be dropped at a viewpoint with a small car park

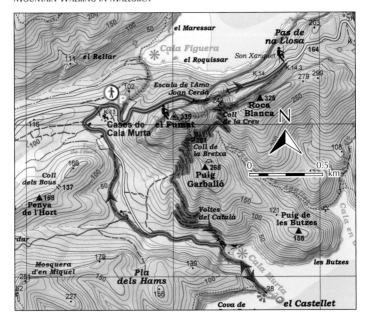

at Km14.9, then walk back along the road to Km14.4. The path starts awkwardly from the road, being steep and worn, but only for a short distance.

The old Camí Vell is distinguished at first only by the scant remains of its stone buttressing, but a trodden path follows it. Despite the steepness of the slope beneath **Roca Blanca**, the path gradient is remarkably gentle. For the sake of its heritage, and to avoid damaging the path, don't short-cut and faithfully trace as many old zigzags as possible. A gap is reached around 240m (790ft) at **Coll de la Creu**.

### To climb el Fumat

Anyone intending to make a summit bid should do so from here. A trodden path marked with cairns climbs stony and rocky slopes. The summit of **el Fumat** bears a trig point at 335m (1099ft), where views of the Formentor peninsula are of course splendid. There is a choice; either to retrace steps down to Coll de sa Creu and follow the zigzag path onwards, or descend rather more steep and rocky terrain towards Coll de la Bretxa. The latter route is cairned, but not as obviously trodden, and it needs more care.

Those who intend following the remarkable Camí Vell from Coll de la Creu, across a valley to Coll de la Bretxa, will be amazed at the apparently endless zigzags, and the whole thing was constructed slowly and patiently by hand.

> A '**Camí Vell**' is simply an 'Old Road' and there are plenty around Mallorca that bear the name. This particular old road was constructed around 1860 to serve the lighthouse at the end of the Formentor peninsula. Its apparently endless zigzags ensure that gradients are easy, no matter how steep the slopes. It was constructed with horses and carts in mind, and it is a great shame that it is suffering damage and becoming overgrown. With care and attention, it would be a splendid heritage feature.

Resist the temptation to short-cut, and follow the zigzags as faithfully as possible, although admittedly some parts are choked with scrub. At **Coll de la Bretxa**, at 251m (823ft), a rocky notch was cut to accommodate the path, and the remains of telegraph poles can be seen.

Once again, the endlessly zigzagging Camí Vell is seen making its way down a very steep slope with the gentlest of gradients. It is a joy to follow, and if it was ever to be restored it would be a monument to the men who constructed it. Pine trees are reached and the old path turns round a corner to traverse a slope. A final set of zigzags is known as the **Voltes del Català**. The last part runs into the grounds

*Looking down from el Fumat towards Cala Murta and beyond*

of a house, so the final descent is a steep and awkward scramble to a road. The straight-line distance from road to road is only 1.3km (¾ mile), but the zigzag Camí Vell is 5.5km (3½ miles)!

Turn left and step off the road to follow a track to **Cala Murta**, where there is a picnic area beside a bay. A signpost indicates the Camí del Castellet, which is a well-trodden path picking its way across a rocky, pine-covered slope to reach the end of a point. The little islet of **el Castellet** can be inspected, then it is necessary to retrace steps to the road, and start following it inland.

The road can be followed through the pine forest and up to the main road, but part of it can be avoided. Simply watch for a well-trodden path that starts running parallel to the road, and as it drifts away from the road, it has a wooden fence alongside. It loses sight of the road, but by keeping straight ahead at a junction at a limekiln near a white house, it gradually returns to the road. At the junction, a track climbs for 1km (½ mile) to join Walk 48 at Coll de l'Olivardar.

The road leads up past the Campament Santa Maria de Formentor, and **Cases de Cala Murta**, passing a gate to reach a junction with the Ma-2210 road. Turn right and walk up the road to return to the car park, or to wait if phoning a taxi. The car park might well be busy with people visiting the nearby Cala Figuera, which is reached by a short, popular path that has been pounded to white dust. It is less than 1km (½ mile) there-and-back, with 100m (330ft) of ascent/descent.

# WALK 50
*Penya des Migdia and Talaia d'Alcúdia*

| | |
|---|---|
| **Start/Finish** | Bar s'Illot, La Victòria or Ermita de la Victòria |
| **Distance** | 13km (8 miles) |
| **Total ascent/descent** | 700m (2295ft) |
| **Time** | 5hrs |
| **Terrain** | Mostly good tracks and paths; some scrambling involved on Penya des Migdia and some very stony paths on Talaia d'Alcúdia. |
| **Map** | Alpina Mallorca Nord |
| **Refreshment** | Bar s'Illot is at the start and finish, and there is a restaurant at the Ermita de la Victòria. |
| **Transport** | Regular buses serve Alcúdia from all the nearby coastal resorts, and taxis are available to reach the start of the walk. |

The Alcúdia peninsula contains a wonderfully compact range of hills, of which Talaia d'Alcúdia is the highest, bearing the remains of a watchtower. However, the lower peak of Penya des Migdia is more remarkable, as it is naturally fortified and its summit bears a cannon. A fine circular walk makes the most of these hills.

Either drive from Alcúdia, or take a taxi, towards La Victòria. The walk starts at a small car park near the Bar s'Illot, which is below the youth hostel of **Alberg Juvenil la Victòria**. There are two ways to find the initial path. One is to set off up the youth hostel road, but immediately drop to the left into a valley. The other is to start on the coast near the bar and go through a tunnel beneath the road to enter the valley.

Follow a path up through the forested valley. It runs along the bed of the **Torrent de s'Aladernar** for a while, but whenever this becomes too rugged, use paths running parallel. The streambed splits, so keep left as marked and climb steeply, eventually reaching a path junction. Turn left and climb further, suddenly reaching a car park near the **Ermita de la Victòria**. The car park near the *ermita* offers an alternative start/finish point. There are signposts and information boards worth studying.

Follow a broad dirt road uphill, keeping right near a restaurant to pass a barrier. A signpost points left for **ses Tres Creus**, which is a viewpoint, otherwise keep climbing along the dirt road. A path will be spotted on the left that climbs parallel to the dirt road and has a rickety fence alongside; it leads to Penya des Migdia, and could be counted as an optional detour, but it really is well worth including at this point. The fence soon ends and the path rises and falls as it crosses the steep, forested slope. Watch carefully for a path junction and keep left, or straight ahead. Turning right leads to a gap where Penya des Migdia looks like an unassailable tower of rock. The path runs along narrow ledges of rock at the base of a cliff.

There is an alarming moment when the path narrows and a rocky corner has a peculiar little tunnel built onto it, where it is necessary to crouch to pass through, and it is very important not to slip. There is a chain to hang onto when leaving the tunnel. Pass a couple of *aljubs* and climb a slope that is mostly steep and rocky, requiring short scrambles. Continue all the way to the top of **Penya des Migdia**, at 358m (1175ft), where there is a small cannon and fine views.

The summit of Penya des Migdia overlooks two bays and has an obvious **military advantage**. It is naturally fortified by sheer cliffs and it was a simple matter to control access along the only path leading onto it. Defensive structures

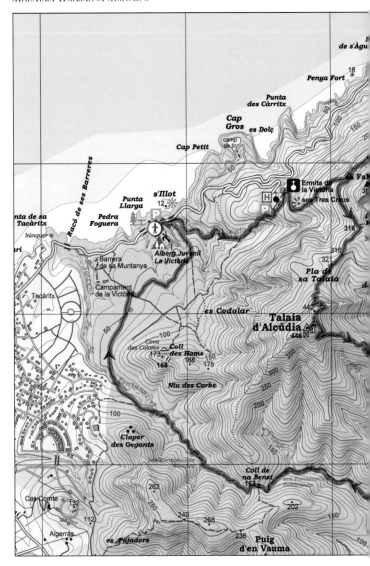

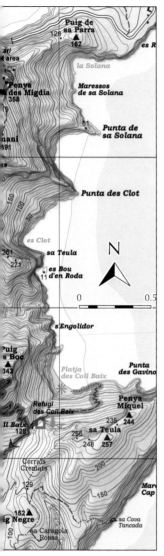

are obvious, dating from the 16th to 18th centuries. Cannons were mounted in some places, and the summit itself is effectively a platform for a cannon placed there in 1630, which remains to this day. The end of the peninsula is a military zone.

Follow the route all the way back to the dirt road and continue climbing. Pass a gate on **Coll des Pedregaret**, at 316m (1037ft), and keep straight ahead at a junction. The track follows a forested crest then it ends at **Pla de sa Talaia**. A well-trodden path zig-zags uphill, and when cliffs rise above the steep slope, the path features buttresses and rocky ramps, climbing with relative ease. A signpost is reached where turning right leads quickly to the summit of **Talaia d'Alcúdia**, at 446m (1463ft). A trig point sits on the stump of an old watchtower and views extend far beyond the summit, embracing the Serra de Llevant, the Formentor peninsula and Serra de Tramuntana.

Walk back down to the signposted junction and turn right, following a rugged path which later zigzags down a rock-strewn ridge to reach a gap at **Coll de s'Engolidor**, at 286m (938ft). The path appears to be heading for the next summit, which is Puig des Boc, but it only climbs a short way before zigzagging downhill. It lands on **Coll Baix**, at 128m (420ft), where there is a *refugi* and a picnic area. A path takes a convoluted course down to Platja des Coll Baix, becoming vague and rocky towards the bottom. It is 2km (1¼ miles) there-and-back, with 130m (425ft) of ascent/descent.

Head inland from the *refugi*, down an obvious dirt road that passes a barrier. Watch for a signposted path on the right, and follow

*An exposed path leads to and from Penya des Migdia (photo: Jaume Tort)*

it into a forested valley. It runs along the dry streambed of **Coma de s'Egua**; it also rises from it, crosses it back and forth, but is well-trodden, cairned and equipped with marker posts. The path climbs through the valley and passes another signpost on the broad **Coll de na Benet**, at 163m (535ft).

Cross the gap and walk down the other side into another valley, following the **Torrent de ses Fontanelles**, and pass a pool cut into the streambed. As well as signposts, there are also marker posts bearing a red strip or arrow, for a Nordic walking trail. Follow the posts faithfully, keeping right as the path becomes a track.

Turn right at a junction (left leads to a youth camp called **Campament de la Victòria**), then soon afterwards turn left as indicated by the Nordic walking trail marker. More of these posts indicate a path that eventually descends and leads all the way back to the road near the Bar s'Illot.

# APPENDIX A
*Glossary*

**Pronunciation tips**

Castilian Spanish is pronounced exactly as it is spelled, so once the rules are grasped a reasonable attempt at pronunciation is possible. Stress is normally on the last-but-one syllable unless an accent indicates otherwise. There are plenty of English–Spanish phrasebooks available, and every effort should be made to use the language. Opportunities for English speakers to learn Catalan are limited but resources can be found online.

**Castilian Spanish**

The following is a basic reference guide, but it is best to listen to people speaking the language in real life.

| | |
|---|---|
| *a* | between a in lass and in father – adiós – goodbye |
| *b* | as in English – banco – bank |
| *c* | used before i and e, like th in thin – cinco – (thinco) – five |
| | used before anything else, as in cat – cliente – customer |
| *ch* | as in church – chico – boy |
| *d* | used at beginning of word, like d in dog – dos – two |
| | used at the ends of words, like th in though – verdad – true |
| *e* | as in men, but at end of word as in day – leche – milk |
| *f* | as in English – fácil – easy |
| *g* | used before a,o,u, or consonants, as in gas – gasolina – petrol |
| | used before e and i as ch in loch – gente – people |
| *gu* | used before a, like gw – agua (agwa) – water |
| *h* | is always silent – hombre (ombre) – man |
| *i* | between i in bit and in machine – litro – litre |
| *j* | like ch in loch – ajo – garlic |
| *k* | as in English – kilo – kilo |
| *l* | as in English – libro – book |
| *ll* | like lli in million – me llamo – I'm called |
| *m* | as in English – mantequilla – butter |
| *n* | as in English – naranja – orange |
| *ñ* | as ni in onion – los niños – the children |
| *o* | between top and for – oficina – office |
| *p* | as in English – pan – bread |
| *q* | like English k – quizás – perhaps |

| | |
|---|---|
| r | pronounced slightly rolled – el norte – the north |
| rr | pronounced strongly rolled – carretera – main road |
| s | voiceless hiss, as in sin – seis – six |
| t | as in English – tienda – shop |
| u | as in boot – usted – you |
| v | like a soft English b – vaso (baso) – glass |
| x | used at end of word, like tch – Felanitx (placename) |
| | used between vowels, like gs – taxi (tagsi) – taxi |
| y | like y in yes – mayor – bigger |
| y | the word y, as the i in machine – y – and |
| z | as th in thick – manzana (manthana) – apple |

The three double letters *ch*, *ll* and *rr* are considered as separate letters by the Spanish Academy so they have separate sequences in Spanish dictionaries.

## Catalan

The sounds are broadly the same as for Spanish, including those pronounced as in English, but with a few notable exceptions. Mastering the rules ensures that placenames will be pronounced correctly.

| | |
|---|---|
| c | used before e or i is soft, otherwise hard, never lisped – cinc (sink) – five |
| ç | sounds like s in English – plaça (plassa) – square |
| g | used before e or i is soft, otherwise hard |
| j | is pronounced soft the same as the French pronounce Jean |
| ll | like lli in million |
| l.l | sounds like ll in English, as in – col.laboració – collaboration |
| ny | is always used in Catalan where Spanish uses ñ – Bunyola/Buñola |
| qu | used before e or i like k, but before a or o like kw |
| r | is pronounced rolled at the start of a word |
| v | used at the start of a word sounds like b, otherwise sounds like f |
| z | is pronounced like an English z and is never lisped |

## Placenames

| | |
|---|---|
| Andratx | *an-dratch* |
| Biniaraix | *bini-a-raitch* |
| Lluc | *l'yook* |
| Mallorca | *my-orka* |
| Pollença | *pol-yen-sa* |
| Puig | *pooj (with a soft j)* |
| Sóller | *sole-yair* |
| Valldemossa | *vall-day-moh-sah* |

**Basic words and phrases**

Some very basic words and phrases are included here because it can be useful to have them without having to carry a phrase book. Note that question marks and exclamation marks are always used upside down at the beginning of a question or exclamation in Spanish.

| English | Spanish | Catalan |
|---|---|---|
| hello | *hola* | *hola* |
| good morning | *buenos días* | *bon dia* |
| good afternoon | *buenas tardes* | *bones tardes* |
| goodnight | *buenas noches* | *bona nit* |
| goodbye | *adios* | *adéu* |
| see you tomorrow | *hasta mañana* | *fins demà* |
| see you later | *hasta luego* | *fins després* |
| yes/no | *sí/no* | *si/no* |
| please | *por favor* | *per favor* |
| thank you | *gracias* | *gràcies* |
| that's all right | *de nada* | *de res* |
| thank you very much | *muchas gracias* | *moltes gràcies* |
| excuse me | *perdón* | *perdoni* |
| I'm sorry | *lo siento* | *ho sento* |
| I'm English (man) | *soy ingles* | *sóc anglès* |
| I'm English (woman) | *soy inglesa* | *sóc anglesa* |
| I don't understand | *no comprendo* | *no ho entenc* |
| would you repeat please? | *¿puede repetir, por favor?* | *ho pot repetir, per favor?* |
| more slowly, please | *más despacio, por favor* | *mès lent, per favor* |
| what did you say? | *¿qué ha dicho usted?* | *que m'ha dit vostè?* |
| what is that? | *¿qué significa ésto?* | *què vol dir això?* |
| do you speak English? | *¿habla inglés?* | *parla anglès?* |
| I don't speak Spanish | *no hablo español* | *no parlo espanyol* |
| I don't speak Catalan | *no hablo catalán* | *no parlo català* |

| English | Spanish | Catalan |
|---------|---------|---------|
| there is/are, is/are there | *hay* | *hi ha* |
| is there a bank here? | *¿hay un banco aquí?* | *hi ha un banc d'aquí?* |
| where is...? | *¿dónde está...?* | *a on és...?* |
| ...the post office? | *¿...la oficina de correos?* | *l'oficina de correus* |
| ...the toilet? | *¿...los servicios?* | *...el banyo?* |
| men | *señores/hombres/ caballeros* | *homes* |
| women | *señoras/mujeres* | *dones* |
| open/closed | *abierto/cerrado* | *obert/tancat* |
| today/tomorrow | *hoy/mañana* | *avui/demà* |
| next week | *la semana próxima* | *la setmana que ve* |
| where can I buy...? | *¿dónde puedo comprar...?* | *a on se pot comprar?* |
| ...a newspaper/stamps | *¿...un periódico/ los sellos* | *un diari/segells* |
| I'd like that | *quiero eso* | *voldria OK* |
| I'll have this | *me llevo ésto* | *m'en duc aixó* |
| how much? | *¿cuánto cuesta?* | *quant val?* |
| do you have a room? | *¿tiene una habitación?* | *té alguna habitació?* |
| double/single | *doble/individual* | *doble/individual* |
| tonight | *esta noche* | *aquesta nit* |
| for two/three nights | *para dos/tres noches* | *per dues/tres nits* |
| how much is the room? | *¿cuanto cuesta la habitación?* | *quan val l'habitació?* |
| with bath/without bath | *con baño/sin baño* | *amb bany/sense bany* |
| anything else? | *¿algo más?* | *qualque cosa més?* |
| nothing more, thank you | *nada más, gracias* | *res més, graciès* |
| the bill, please | *la cuenta, por favor* | *el compte, per favor* |
| packed lunches | *los picnics* | *picnics* |
| two packed lunches | *dos picnics* | *dos picnics* |
| for tomorrow | *para mañana* | *per demà* |
| by car/on foot | *en coche/a pie* | *en cotxe/a peu* |

| English | Spanish | Catalan |
|---|---|---|
| how do you get to Sóller? | ¿cómo se llega a Sóller? | com es va a Sóller? |
| where is...? | ¿dónde está...? | a on és...? |
| ...the bus station? | ¿...la estación de autobúses? | ...l'estació d'autobusos? |
| ...the bus stop? | ¿...la parada de autobús? | ...la parada d'autobús? |
| ...for Pollença? | ¿...para Pollensa? | ...per Pollença? |
| how much is the fare? | ¿cuánto vale el billete? | quan val el bitllet? |
| return | ida y vuelta | d'anada i tornada |
| single | sencillo/solamente | idanomés anada |
| where is the footpath to...? | ¿dónde está el camino a...? | a on és el camí a...? |
| may we go this way? | ¿podemos pasar por aqui? | se pot passar per aquí? |
| is it far? | ¿está lejos? | està lluny? |
| how far? | ¿a qué distancia? | a quina distància? |
| how long? | ¿cuánto tiempo? | a quans minuts? |
| very near? | ¿muy cerca? | molt proper? |
| to the left/right | a la izquierda/a la derecha | a l'esquerra/a la dreta |
| straight on | todo recto | tot recte |
| first left | la primera a la izquierda | la primera a l'esquerra |
| second right | la segunda a la derecha | la segona a la dreta |
| in front of the church | en frente de la Iglesia | davant l'església |
| behind the hotel | detrás del hotel | darrera l'hotel |
| at the end of the street | al final de la calle | al final del carrer |
| after the bridge | después del Puente | passat el pont |
| where are you (singular/plural) going? | ¿adónde va/van? | a on va/van? |
| I'm going/we're going to... | voy a/vamos a... | vaig a/anam a... |
| a right of way | derecho de paso | dret de pas |
| private hunting | coto privado de caza | àrea privada de caça |
| please close | cierren, por favor | tancau, per favor |
| dogs on guard | cuidado con el perro | alerta amb el ca |

273

| English | Spanish | Catalan |
|---|---|---|
| Monday | *lunes* | *dilluns* |
| Tuesday | *martes* | *dimarts* |
| Wednesday | *miércoles* | *dimecres* |
| Thursday | *jueves* | *dijous* |
| Friday | *viernes* | *divendres* |
| Saturday | *sábado* | *dissabte* |
| Sunday | *domingo* | *diumenge* |
| Help! Fire! | *¡Socorro! ¡Fuego!* | *Ajuda! Foc!* |
| Police | *Policía/Guardia Civil* | *Policía/Guardia Civil* |
| there's been an accident | *ha habido un accidente* | *hi ha hagut un accident* |
| call a doctor quickly | *llamen a un medico rapidamente* | *cridin al metge ràpidament* |
| it's urgent! | *¡es urgente!* | *és urgent!* |

### Eating and drinking

| English | Spanish | Catalan |
|---|---|---|
| drinks | *las bebidas* | *begudes* |
| breakfast | *el desayunoberenar* | |
| lunch/dinner | *la comida/cena* | *dinar/sopar* |
| I'd like/we'd like | *quiero/queremos* | *voldria/voldriem* |
| I'll have/we'll have | *tomo/tomamos* | *prendré/prendrem* |
| a black coffee | *un café solo* | *un café sol* |
| two black coffees | *dos cafés solos* | *dos cafés sols* |
| white coffee | *un café con leche* | *un café amb llet* |
| three white coffees | *tres cafés con leches* | *tres cafés amb llet* |
| tea with milk | *un té con leche* | *un tè amb llet* |
| tea with lemon for me | *un té con limón para mi* | *un tè amb llimona* |
| beer | *una cerveza* | *una cervesa* |
| the house wine | *el vino de la casa* | *el vi de la casa* |
| a glass of red wine | *un vaso de vino tinto* | *un tassó de vi negre* |
| white wine | *un vino blanco* | *un vi blanc* |

| English | Spanish | Catalan |
|---|---|---|
| a dry sherry | un jeréz seco | un xerès sec |
| a bottle of water | una botella de agua | una botella d'aigo |
| fizzy/still | con gas/sin gas | amb gas/sense gas |
| orange juice | el zumo de naranjas | uc de taronja |
| starters | el primer plato | primer plat |
| soup | la sopa | sopa |
| eggs, egg dishes | los huevos | ous |
| fish, fish dishes | los pescados | peix |
| sea food/shellfish | los mariscos | marisc |
| meat, meat dishes | la carne | carn |
| game | la carne de caza | carn de caça |
| vegetables | los verduras/legumbres | verdures/llegums |
| I'm vegetarian | soy vegetariano | sóc vegetarià |
| cheese | el queso | formatge |
| fruit | la fruta | fruita |
| ice-cream | el helado | gelat |
| desserts | los postres | postres |
| sandwich | un bocadillo | panet |

**Local specialities**

| | |
|---|---|
| Angules | small eels fried whole in batter |
| Arròs brut | rice soup with meat |
| Bacallà | dried codfish with tomatoes in a casserole |
| Butifarra | Catalan spiced sausage |
| Calamars | squid, served a la romana or deep fried, in rings |
| Caldereta de peix | fish soup with rice and slices of bread |
| Capó a lo Rei en Jaume | capon, cock or turkey stuffed with marzipan and sweet potatoes and lightly fried |
| Cargols | snails cooked in garlic mayonnaise sauce |
| Xocolata calenta (Chocolate a la taza) | thick hot chocolate for dipping pastries such as ensaimadas or cocas de patatas |
| Coca de trempó | looks like a pizza without cheese |

| | |
|---|---|
| *Coca de patata* | light round bun (looks like a potato) for dipping in chocolate |
| *Ensaimada* | a light, flaky, spiral bun sprinkled with icing sugar, often eaten for breakfast or on picnics |
| *Escaldums* | a casserole of chicken and potatoes in an almond sauce |
| *Espinagada* | savoury pie of eels and seasoned vegetables |
| *Frit Mallorquí* | a fry-up of liver, kidneys, onions and garlic |
| *Gambes* | prawns |
| *Gazpacho* | a cold soup made from tomatoes, onions, peppers, cucumbers, garlic, oil and vinegar |
| *Greixonera de peix* | fish with vegetables and eggs |
| *Greixera* | mixed pressed cold meats with egg, artichokes, peas, beans and herbs |
| *Guisantes a la catalana* | peas fried with ham and onions |
| *Laccao/Saccao* | trade names for a hot or cold chocolate drink like cocoa |
| *Llangosta a la catalana* | lobster sautéed in wine and rum with herbs and spices |
| *Llenguat* | sole, usually grilled with fresh herbs |
| *Molls* | red mullet |
| *Musclos a la marinera* | mussels cooked in a spicy sauce |
| *Napolitanas* | like sausage rolls but filled with chocolate or custard (crema) |
| *Pa amb oli* | bread drizzled with oil, may also be rubbed with tomato and garlic, and may be served with sliced meat |
| *Paella* | cooked to order for a minimum of two people and take at least half an hour, combining rice with various seafoods, meat and vegetables |
| *Paella catalana* | spicy sausage, pork, squid, tomato, chilli pepper and peas |
| *Paella marinera* | fish and seafood only |
| *Paella valenciana* | the traditional dish with chicken, mussels, shrimps, prawns, peas, tomatoes and garlic |
| *Panada (Empanada)* | meat and/or vegetable pie |
| *Porcella rostida* | roast suckling pig (a famous speciality) |
| *Sobrassada* | pork-liver sausage, bright red with pimento |
| *Sopes Mallorquines* | very filling soup, almost a stew, made from garlic, onions, vegetables in season and bread |

| | |
|---|---|
| *Trempó* | a summer salad with mixed vegetables |
| *Truita* | can mean trout or omelette in Mallorquí, hence: |
| *Truita a la navarra* | trout stuffed with bacon or smoked ham |
| *Truita de patates* | |
| *(Tortilla española)* | omelette with potatoes |
| *Tumbet* | a type of ratatouille with layers of aubergines, peppers, tomatoes and potatoes cooked in olive oil |
| *Xoriç (chorizo)* | a strong spicy sausage |
| *Zarzuela* | a stew of various fish in a hot spicy sauce |

**Topographical terms**

This glossary is given in Catalan and English only, to assist walkers to unravel placename meanings. The list contains names that occur frequently on maps, as well as throughout this guide. Some words that will be noticed on signs are also included. (Where some Spanish placenames are still lingering, these are shown in brackets.)

| Catalan | English |
|---|---|
| *Albufera* | lagoon |
| *Aljub* | small covered reservoir |
| *Alzina* | evergreen oak |
| *Aguila* | eagle |
| *Arena* | sand |
| *Avenc* | deep cleft |
| *Avinguda (Avenida)* | avenue |
| *Badia* | bay |
| *Baix* | low |
| *Bassa* | small pool |
| *Barranc* | ravine |
| *Bini* | house of (Arabic) |
| *Blanca* | white |
| *Bosc* | woodland |
| *Cala* | small bay or cove |
| *Caleta* | small bay |
| *Camí* | path |
| *Camp* | field |
| *Can/Ca'n* | house of |
| *Canaleta* | open canal |

| Catalan | English |
|---------|---------|
| Cap | rocky point |
| Capella | chapel |
| Carboner | charcoal burner |
| Carrer (Calle) | street |
| Càrritx | a tall pampas-like grass, Ampelodesmus mauritanica |
| Cas/Casa | house |
| Caseta | small house/hut |
| Castell | castle |
| Cavall | horse |
| Cingle | cliff |
| Clot | hollow/depression |
| Cocó/cocons | very small rock pool/s |
| Coll | mountain pass |
| Coma | valley |
| Comellar | small valley |
| Comuna | communal land |
| Corral | animal pen |
| Costa | coast |
| Cova/Coves | cave/caves |
| Des/d'es | of the |
| Embassament | reservoir |
| Ermita | hermitage |
| Es | the |
| Església | church |
| Finca | farm or country estate |
| Font | spring/fountain |
| Forn de calç | limekiln |
| Gorg | a pool in a gorge |
| Gran | big |
| Illa/Illes | island/s |
| Jardí | garden |
| Llarga | long |
| Lluc | Luke (personal name) |
| Major | main/big |
| Mar | sea |

| Catalan | English |
|---|---|
| *Marge* | drystone walled buttress |
| *Migdia* | midday |
| *Mirador* | viewpoint |
| *Mola* | tooth |
| *Moleta* | mill |
| *Monestir* | monastery |
| *Moro* | Moor (Arab) |
| *Morro* | snout |
| *Museu* | museum |
| *Neu* | snow |
| *Palau* | palace |
| *Parc* | park |
| *Pas* | a rocky scramble |
| *Penya/penyal* | steep-sided mountain |
| *Pic* | peak |
| *Pla* | plain/flat land |
| *Plaça (Plaza)* | square |
| *Platja (Playa)* | beach |
| *Pont* | bridge |
| *Port (Puerto)* | port or harbour |
| *Porta* | door |
| *Porxo* | shelter |
| *Puig* | hill or mountain |
| *Punta* | rocky point |
| *Racó* | hidden corner |
| *Rafal* | small farm attached to finca |
| *Rei* | king |
| *Roca* | rock |
| *Roig* | red |
| *Rota* | marginal farm |
| *Salt d'aigua* | waterfall |
| *Santuari* | sanctuary |
| *Sant/Santa* | saint (male/female) |
| *Serra* | mountain range |
| *Serreta* | a small serra |
| *Sitja/sitges* | charcoal-burning site/s |

| Catalan | English |
| --- | --- |
| *Talaia* | watch tower |
| *Torre* | tower |
| *Torrent* | river |
| *Vall* | valley |
| *Vell* | old |
| *Vent* | wind |
| *Verd* | green |
| *Verger* | fertile area |
| *Vinyes* | vineyard |

# APPENDIX B
*Public transport*

Transport de les Illes Balears (TIB) is the main transport portal for Mallorca. Bus and train timetables and route maps are available online at www.tib.org or tel 971 177777. Bus timetables are posted at bus stops throughout Mallorca, and train timetables are posted at railway stations. Printed timetables are not always easy to find, but for a few cents, photocopies are provided at the Estació Intermodal in Palma. This is a combined underground bus and railway station that also incorporates bicycle hire. While many of the walks in this guidebook can be reached by bus, a few of can't, but even those ones could be reached by taxi.

## Bus services
The following list illustrates which bus services can be used to access which walks. Always check the most up-to-date timetables, and always check exactly where the bus stops are located. Most bus services fan outwards from Palma, but some don't. Anyone considering regular use of public transport should enquire about using a 'Targeta Intermodal', which is an electronic card offering substantial discounts. Bear in mind that some services only operate in the summer. Some transport links on the following list are trains or ferries. Services marked * pass start or finish points, but these are not recognised stops and the bus driver might not stop there.

| Walk | Bus to start | Bus from finish | Bus in middle |
|------|-------------|-----------------|---------------|
| Walk 1 | 100/102/Ferry | Ferry/102/100 | None |
| Walk 2 | 100 | 102 | None |
| Walk 3 | 102 | 102 | None |
| Walk 4 | None | None | None |
| Walk 5 | 111 | 111 | None |
| Walk 6 | None | None | None |
| Walk 7 | None | None | None |
| Walk 8 | 140 | 140 | None |
| Walk 9 | 111 | 111 | None |
| Walk 10 | 140 | 111 | None |
| Walk 11 | 140 | 140 | None |
| Walk 12 | 200 | 200 | None |

| Walk | Bus to start | Bus from finish | Bus in middle |
|------|--------------|-----------------|---------------|
| Walk 13 | 200 | 200 | 200 |
| Walk 14 | 200 | 210 | None |
| Walk 15 | 210 | 210 | None |
| Walk 16 | 210 | 210 | None |
| Walk 17 | 210 | 210 | None |
| Walk 18 | 210 | 210 | 210 |
| Walk 19 | 210/211 | 210/211 | None |
| Walk 20 | 210/211 | 210/211 | 212 |
| Walk 21 | 354 | Ferry | None |
| Walk 22 | 210/211 | 210/211 | None |
| Walk 23 | 210/211 | 210/211 | None |
| Walk 24 | 212 | 212 | 354* |
| Walk 25 | 354* | 354* | None |
| Walk 26 | 211/220/Train | 211/220/Train | None |
| Walk 27 | 211/220/Train | 211/220/Train | None |
| Walk 28 | 221 | Train | None |
| Walk 29 | Train/320 | 320/Train | 221 |
| Walk 30 | 221 | 221 | None |
| Walk 31 | 354 | 354 | None |
| Walk 32 | 354 | 354 | None |
| Walk 33 | 354 | 354 | None |
| Walk 34 | 354 | 320/Train | None |
| Walk 35 | 354 | 354 | 330 |
| Walk 36 | 354/355 | 355/Ferry | None |
| Walk 37 | 330 | 330 | None |
| Walk 38 | 330/354/355 | 330/354/355 | 330 |
| Walk 39 | 330 | 330 | None |
| Walk 40 | 330 | 330 | 330 |
| Walk 41 | 330/354/355 | 330/354/355 | None |

| Walk | Bus to start | Bus from finish | Bus in middle |
|---|---|---|---|
| Walk 42 | None | 330/354/355 | None |
| Walk 43 | 330/354/355 | 330/354/355 | None |
| Walk 44 | 330/354/355 | 340/345/354/355 | 355* |
| Walk 45 | 355* | 355* | None |
| Walk 46 | 340/345/354/355 | 340/345/354/355 | None |
| Walk 47 | 340/345/352/353/354/355 | 340/345/352/353/354/355 | None |
| Walk 48 | 353 | 353 | None |
| Walk 49 | None | None | None |
| Walk 50 | None | None | None |

### Serveis Ferroviaris de Mallorca

SFM trains serve only the finish of Walk 28, but might also be used with linking buses to reach Walks 29, 34, 37, 38, 39, 40, 41, 42 and 43. Trains run frequently to and from Palma, but there are two levels of service – one that stops at all the stations, and a faster service that misses some of the stations, shown on timetables as *sense aturades* and/ or *sin paradas*.

### Ferrocarril de Sóller

The Ferrocarril de Sóller is a vintage electric train between Palma and Sóller that links with a vintage tram service that provides a bone-shaking service between Sóller and Port de Sóller. Both services are expensive, but should be sampled at least once or twice. They serve Walks 20, 22, 23, 26 and 27. For timetables, tel 971 752051 or 971 752028, www.trendesoller.com.

# APPENDIX C
*Useful contacts*

### Consell de Mallorca

The Consell de Mallorca administers the whole of Mallorca and their website contains an immense amount of useful information. When accessing the site, a complex Catalan version loads, but by choosing 'English' as the language, a simple set of links appears. These allow rapid access to information about walking routes and refuges, history and heritage information, as well as tourist information: www.conselldemallorca.net

### Getting to Mallorca

Most visitors fly to Mallorca from airports as far apart as Iceland and Israel, from all over Europe, including over two dozen British airports. The choice of routes and airlines is bewildering, but there are plenty of budget operators and deals for those willing to search online. It is worth accessing the Palma de Mallorca airport website to discover just how many routes and operators are available: www.aena.es (English-language option available; select 'choose airport')

For ferries to Palma from Barcelona and Valencia, check schedules with Trasmediterranea: www.trasmediterranea, and Balearia: www.balearia.com.

### Serra de Tramuntana

The Paratge Natural de la Serra de Tramuntana, or Nature Area of the Serra de Tramuntana, covers an area of approximately 625 square kilometres (240 square miles). It is administered from an office in Valldemossa, tel 971 612876, and maintains a visitor centre at Lluc, tel 971 517070, www.serradetramuntana.net

### Maps

The maps in this guidebook are extracted from the popular Editorial Alpina 1:25,000-scale maps of Mallorca. The Tramuntana Sud, Central and Nord maps cover the entire Serra de Tramuntana, while the Mallorca Nord map covers the Formentor and Alcúdia peninsulas. It is worth considering the 1:25,000-scale Editorial Alpina Serra de Tramuntana map pack, which contains two double-sided waterproof maps, Sud I, Sud II, Nord I and Nord II. These cover the entire Serra de Tramuntana as well as the Formentor and Alcúdia peninsulas. A useful general touring map is the waterproof 1:100,000-scale Editorial Alpina Bike Mallorca. While designed for cyclists, it serves as an excellent and detailed road map. For details see www.editorialalpina.com, and note that the maps are widely available around Mallorca and are kept fully up-to-date.

In the UK, maps are available from Stanfords (12–14 Long Acre, London WC2E 9BR, tel 020 7836 1321, www.stanfords.co.uk) or The Map Shop (15 High Street, Upton-upon-Severn WR8 0HJ, tel 01684 593146, www.themapshop.co.uk).

## Camins de Mallorca

The Alpina maps are kept up-to-date by Jaume Tort, who provided assistance and expertise while this guidebook was being researched. Jaume maintains the Camins de Mallorca website in four languages, which contains details of walking opportunities, route changes, new developments and guided walking services: www.camins-mallorca.info.

Jaume has always given enthusiastic assistance to the author while working on Cicerone guidebooks.

## Tourist information

Tourist information websites abound in Mallorca, but many of the private sites are geared to supporting particular commercial ventures. For impartial information, use the 'official' tourist information website, which is available in four languages: www.infomallorca.net

## Public transport

Transport de les Illes Balears (TIB) is the main transport portal for Mallorca: www.tib.org. Bus and train timetables are available online, or tel 971 177777. See also Appendix B for details of specific buses and trains running to and from the walks in this guidebook.

## Emergencies

The standard European emergency number 112 can be used to call the police, ambulance, fire service or mountain rescue.

If specifically requiring the police, there are three separate forces and three telephone numbers. The Policía Local, tel 092, are attached to local municipalities and wear blue uniforms. The Polícia Nacional, tel 091, are the national force and wear brown uniforms. The Guardia Civil, tel 062, wear green uniforms and are fully equipped to provide mountain rescue cover. If only wishing to report a crime, tel 902 102112.

If specifically requiring an ambulance (*ambulancia*), tel 061.

If specifically requiring the fire service (*bombers*), tel 080.

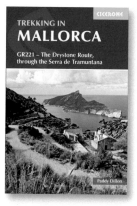
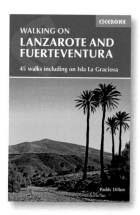
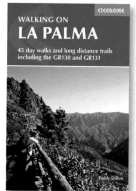
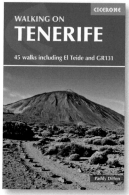

# LIST OF EUROPEAN CICERONE GUIDES

**AUSTRIA**
The Adlerweg
Trekking in Austria's Hohe Tauern
Trekking in the Stubai Alps
Trekking in the Zillertal Alps
Walking in Austria

**SWITZERLAND**
Cycle Touring in Switzerland
The Swiss Alpine Pass Route – Via
    Alpina Route 1
The Swiss Alps
Tour of the Jungfrau Region
Walking in the Bernese Oberland
Walking in the Valais
Walks in the Engadine – Switzerland

**FRANCE AND BELGIUM**
Chamonix Mountain Adventures
Cycle Touring in France
Cycling London to Paris
Cycling the Canal du Midi
Écrins National Park
Mont Blanc Walks
Mountain Adventures in the
    Maurienne
The GR20 Corsica
The GR5 Trail
The GR5 Trail – Vosges and Jura
The Grand Traverse of the Massif
    Central
The Loire Cycle Route
The Moselle Cycle Route
The River Rhone Cycle Route
The Robert Louis Stevenson Trail
The Way of St James
Tour of the Oisans: The GR54
Tour of the Queyras
Tour of the Vanoise
Vanoise Ski Touring
Via Ferratas of the French Alps
Walking in Corsica
Walking in Provence – East
Walking in Provence – West
Walking in the Auvergne
Walking in the Briançonnais
Walking in the Cevennes
Walking in the Dordogne
Walking in the Haute Savoie: North
Walking in the Haute Savoie: South
Walks in the Cathar Region
Walking in the Ardennes

**GERMANY**
Hiking and Biking in the Black Forest

The Danube Cycleway Volume 1
The Rhine Cycle Route
The Westweg
Walking in the Bavarian Alps

**ICELAND AND GREENLAND**
Trekking in Greenland
Walking and Trekking in Iceland

**IRELAND**
The Irish Coast to Coast Walk
The Mountains of Ireland
The Wild Atlantic Way and Western
    Ireland

**ITALY**
Italy's Sibillini National Park
Shorter Walks in the Dolomites
Ski Touring and Snowshoeing in the
    Dolomites
The Way of St Francis
Through the Italian Alps
Trekking in the Apennines
Trekking in the Dolomites
Via Ferratas of the Italian Dolomites
    Volume 1
Via Ferratas of the Italian Dolomites:
    Vol 2
Walking and Trekking in the Gran
    Paradiso
Walking in Abruzzo
Walking in Italy's Stelvio National
    Park
Walking in Sardinia
Walking in Sicily
Walking in the Dolomites
Walking in Tuscany
Walking in Umbria
Walking on the Amalfi Coast
Walking the Italian Lakes
Walks and Treks in the Maritime
    Alps

**SCANDINAVIA: NORWAY,
SWEDEN, FINLAND**
Walking in Norway

**EASTERN EUROPE AND THE
BALKANS**
The Danube Cycleway Volume 2
The High Tatras
The Mountains of Romania
Walking in Bulgaria's National Parks
Walking in Hungary
Mountain Biking in Slovenia
The Islands of Croatia

The Julian Alps of Slovenia
The Mountains of Montenegro
The Peaks of the Balkans Trail
Trekking in Slovenia
Walking in Croatia
Walking in Slovenia: The Karavanke

**SPAIN**
Coastal Walks in Andalucia
Cycle Touring in Spain
Mountain Walking in Mallorca
Mountain Walking in Southern
    Catalunya
Spain's Sendero Histórico: The GR1
The Andalucian Coast to Coast Walk
The Mountains of Nerja
The Mountains of Ronda and
    Grazalema
The Northern Caminos
The Sierras of Extremadura
The Way of St James Cyclist Guide
Trekking in Mallorca
Walking and Trekking in the Sierra
    Nevada
Walking in Andalucia
Walking in Menorca
Walking in the Cordillera Cantabrica
Walking on Gran Canaria
Walking on La Gomera and El Hierro
Walking on La Palma
Walking on Lanzarote and
    Fuerteventura
Walking on Tenerife
Walking on the Costa Blanca

**PORTUGAL**
The Camino Portugués
Walking in Portugal
Walking in the Algarve

**GREECE, CYPRUS AND MALTA**
The High Mountains of Crete
Trekking in Greece
Walking and Trekking on Corfu
Walking in Cyprus
Walking on Malta

For full information on all our
guides, books and eBooks,
visit our website:
**www.cicerone.co.uk**

# Walking – Trekking – Mountaineering – Climbing – Cycling

**Over 40 years, Cicerone have built up an outstanding collection of over 300 guides, inspiring all sorts of amazing adventures.**

Every guide comes from extensive exploration and research by our expert authors, all with a passion for their subjects. They are frequently praised, endorsed and used by clubs, instructors and outdoor organisations.

All our titles can now be bought as **e-books**, **ePubs** and **Kindle** files and we also have an online magazine – **Cicerone Extra** – with features to help cyclists, climbers, walkers and trekkers choose their next adventure, at home or abroad.

Our website shows any **new information** we've had in since a book was published. Please do let us know if you find anything has changed, so that we can publish the latest details. On our **website** you'll also find great ideas and lots of detailed information about what's inside every guide and you can buy **individual routes** from many of them online.

It's easy to keep in touch with what's going on at Cicerone by getting our monthly **free e-newsletter**, which is full of offers, competitions, up-to-date information and topical articles. You can subscribe on our home page and also follow us on **Facebook** and **Twitter** or dip into our **blog**.

**Cicerone – the very best guides for exploring the world.**

# CICERONE

Juniper House, Murley Moss, Oxenholme Road, Kendal, Cumbria  LA9 7RL
Tel: 015395 62069  info@cicerone.co.uk
**www.cicerone.co.uk**